7

CHALLENGES
PASTORS FACE

7 CHALLENGES
PASTORS FACE

Overcome Common Struggles and Thrive in Ministry

DAVID HORNER

BakerBooks

a division of Baker Publishing Group
Grand Rapids, Michigan

© 2008 by David Horner

Published by Baker Books
a division of Baker Publishing Group
PO Box 6287, Grand Rapids, MI 49516-6287
www.bakerbooks.com

Repackaged edition published 2019
ISBN 978-0-8010-9475-0

Previously published under the title *A Practical Guide for Life and Ministry*

Printed in the United States of America

The Library of Congress has cataloged the original edition as follows:
Horner, David, 1952–
    A practical guide for life and ministry : overcoming seven challenges pastors face / David Horner.
      p.   cm.
    Includes bibliographical references and index.
    ISBN 978-0-8010-9195-7 (pbk. : alk. paper)
    1. Pastoral theology. I. Title.
    BV4011.3.H67 2008
    253'.2—dc22   2007038370

19 20 21 22 23 24 25   7 6 5 4 3 2 1

To my wife, Cathy,
for her support and prayers
during the years of ministry God has given us together
and her part in making this work possible.

And a word of thanks
for the diligent labors of
Diana Mattix and Jennifer Sharpe
in preparing and editing the manuscript.

CONTENTS

PREFACE

Back in the summer of 1998, I began working on this book. Little did I know then that the first draft would not be completed for another six years! Although I didn't realize it at the time, the Lord used the prolonged period of composition to give me plenty of up-to-date examples and illustrations of the principles and observations included in the text.

During those years, our family has grown up, and Cathy and I have now celebrated thirty years of marriage. The church I pastor, Providence Baptist Church in Raleigh, North Carolina, has undergone radical transitions. We have continued to grow both in numbers and in the character of the lives of folks throughout the congregation who have been changed by the grace of Christ. Two major anniversaries of the church, the twentieth and the twenty-fifth years, marked wonderful milestones of God's faithfulness. We planted a new church as the book was under construction, and a healthy congregation of more than three hundred members was sent out from our congregation.

God has poured out incredibly good things upon me, my family, and our church. But all has not been easy. The two years after I wrote the outline for this book were the hardest years of my life as a pastor. When I returned from a three-month sabbatical, I found myself embroiled in several ministry crises that stretched me in ways I never thought possible. Those days were tough, and the nights were filled with questions and doubts about my ability to carry on. I wondered whether I was capable of being a pastor.

All of this was motivation to continue working on a book about how to develop and maintain a balanced spiritual life in the midst of challenging ministry situations. Learning to lead by leaning more on Christ forced me to depend on him to show me what he had in store for me. The principles and observations in this book did not emerge from studies in a library or a classroom. They are the product of years of personal learning experiences and long periods of reflection and prayer. After more than twenty-nine years as a pastor, I have discovered things through trial and error that no amount of classical research could have shown me.

The focus of this book is sharing wisdom gleaned from years of working through what it means to serve Christ well in all aspects of life. While I've made no attempt to offer the last word on any one of the subjects or to give definitive answers to the problems discussed, I have attempted to cover a wide range of issues that are important to pastors.

My prayer is that a passion for Christ and his glory shines through in what you find here. I love the calling he has granted to me. I cannot conceive of doing anything I love more than being a pastor, equipping the saints for ministry through the ministry of the Word of God! That love then extends to others who have been called to do the same and makes me want to help them avoid the traps into which I have fallen.

How to Read This Book

Some sections of this book may strike you as more vital to your current circumstances than others. I have made no prevailing effort to build each section on information gleaned from previous ones, so you can jump around as you like. I hope and pray that you will be encouraged—encouraged not to settle, not to back off, not to stay down when you have lost your balance and hit the dirt. I pray that you will be motivated—motivated to think, to ponder, to evaluate, and to analyze how the eternal truths of God's Word have shaped and are shaping your concept of what it means to serve Christ with all you have and all you are! I pray that God will equip you to better shepherd his flock as you consider what has taken me so long to learn—and even longer to write down for my benefit and yours.

Paul said it best when he wrote, "I thank Christ Jesus our Lord, who has given me strength, that He considered me faithful, appointing me to His service" (1 Tim. 1:12). When Christ appointed you, surely he did everything necessary to keep you faithful so that you can be in his service in all things—and not lose your balance in the process!

INTRODUCTION

SERVING WITHOUT A SAFETY NET

As he sat in his study staring at his books, the young pastor knew he'd better get busy with his sermon preparation, but his mind was still spinning from the phone call he had just finished. What happened to the dream he had of following God's calling to be a simple shepherd of a local congregation? All he ever wanted was to find God's will and do it. Pastoring this church had seemed like the perfect fit for his passions and ministry gifts eight years ago. Now everything he did seemed to make somebody unhappy, frustrated, or angry.

He could understand if he had become lazy, compromised doctrinally, failed morally, or acted arrogantly in his leadership. But even his most vocal critics would be the first to say that none of those problems were true. Why then was this so hard? He'd heard all the warnings in seminary and taken careful notes at conferences about the dangers pastors inevitably face when they assume the role of lead shepherd in a church. Yet nothing could have prepared him for the desperation he faced at this point in his ministry.

This latest phone call had been just one more in a series of confrontations with yet another member who did not appreciate the contributions he was making in the life of the church. A couple of his elders seemed intent on throwing barriers in

13

front of every initiative he suggested. Some of his deacons were making the rounds drumming up support for their accusation that his preaching was not as biblical as it should be. Some of his friends in ministry who had been confidantes and encouragers over the years had become so busy that sometimes they did not return his phone calls or emails for weeks at a time, if they ever got around to it at all.

He knew he was partially to blame. Even though he'd taken seminars on setting goals and gone to a conference on time management, the best he'd been able to do was keep the notes on the top of his desk with the hope that someday soon he would actually implement some of those great ideas. For all his talks, plans, and schemes, from where he sat now, he had lost more ground over the past couple of years than he had gained.

On top of that, he'd taken quite a scolding from his wife at breakfast for choosing the missions committee meeting over his daughter's piano recital the night before. He'd already missed dinner three times that week because of late afternoon meetings that he couldn't bring to a close. His son's cool attitude since he'd forgotten about their annual camping trip was just one more nail in his coffin. Every time he was about to get one area of his life under control, it seemed like three more fell apart.

"When is it going to let up? When is my ministry going to become more manageable?" All morning, these and many other thoughts left him wondering if it was worth it. "Why should I bother if no one cares about the price I am paying to serve the Lord? The Lord himself doesn't seem to notice the high cost of doing this kind of ministry. I feel like a circus performer on a high wire trying to keep my balance. People keep tossing me anvils and scolding me when I lose my balance! Is it even possible to keep my balance when my life is committed to ministry?"

So there he sat staring at the books, wondering if he'd made a mistake when he chose to pursue this calling to be a pastor. "What if everyone who is challenging everything I do is right? What if I don't have what it takes to keep my life and ministry in balance? What if this is the way it's always going to be for the next forty years! How can I find a way to be faithful to all that

God has called me to do and be? I need to figure out how to get some balance in my life and ministry! Is that even possible?"

—∞—

This young pastor is not alone. Most of us have struggled to the point of desperation trying to figure out how things could have gotten so out of control, how our plans and dreams could have been tipped so easily. The more we zero in on some aspects of our calling, the more we seem to fall behind in others. When we finally feel good about the level of our obedience in some particulars, we seem to have done so at the expense of others.

Living Out God's Will with Integrity

God's will for our lives does not demand that we abandon our faithfulness to him in some areas in order to be extraordinarily faithful in others. He calls us to wholeness, to lives of integrity, where our faith in him extends to all areas of our lives. The problem we face is that we are better at living with integrity when we can break life and ministry down into neat little compartments. That way we can choose which categories will be our specialties and which will have to suffer from neglect. After all, we rationalize, no one can be expected to be great at everything. We will do the best we can and hope everyone will understand when our unbalanced lives adversely affect them. And then we hope that we can live with ourselves for giving up on ever regaining our equilibrium.

Part of the problem we have as pastors and ministry leaders is that we have few role models of what a balanced life and ministry looks like. In fact, to hear some of the most successful leaders in ministry tell it, balance is the enemy of passionate and effective service for Christ. They oppose the whole concept of balance as if it were nothing more than a compromise with mediocrity and ask, "How can we expect to make a significant difference and have a powerful impact in our church or ministry if we do not make major sacrifices along the way?" It's not a

15

bad question, assuming that the sacrifices do not include those things which do not belong to us, but that belong to the Lord: placing our families at risk for the sake of advancing our careers, neglecting our personal relationship with Christ in order to focus on personal ambitions, compromising our integrity and taking ethical shortcuts to accomplish our agendas, or using people to get our way instead of loving them.

We cannot separate God's calling to our ministry from his calling to our character. In other words, the end we have in mind—effective ministry—cannot be achieved by ungodly and disobedient means. It cannot be achieved by misplaced priorities and misguided values. We cannot bring glory to the same God who established both the means and the ends if we pursue either one by neglecting his expectations and ignoring his provisions. Many of our heroes in ministry look great on the platform, sound great in the seminars, and achieve great things in their respective fields of service. But if the truth were known and they could be honest with you, a lot of them have made choices they regret to get where they are. They have sacrificed to do what they do so well, but not always with the godly wisdom needed to make sure they were not giving up the wrong things. Instead of acknowledging the areas of their failures and imbalances, they gloss over them and hide them behind their public successes and accomplishments. When that kind of unbalanced model is elevated to a position of prominence and lauded as the way to go, it is no wonder that both the poor young pastor and the members of his congregation are led to believe that a balanced Christian life is not expected of those who will have the greatest impact for the kingdom.

Being out of balance does not necessarily mean that you are perpetuating a life of sin, but it does mean that you are missing the opportunity to see the sufficiency of Christ at work in making you complete in him. The concept of living fulfilled, satisfying, balanced lives is quite foreign to many contemporary models of ministry, but in reality, it offers the closest version of a biblical perspective on what it means to serve Christ. Far too many of us have simply given up on the notion that we will ever get it right and are even now settling for lives and ministries woefully short of what Christ intends.

On the other hand, sometimes the absence of balance does involve sin that needs to be confessed and we need to repent for what we have done. When we ignore one aspect of God's will in order to focus more effort on another, we sabotage the intricacy of his plans for us. Instead of finding his sufficiency in all things when we do what he says, we get caught trying to make up for our failures in some areas by being very successful in others. We see people do that all the time: the executive who is a hero at the office but only a passive and disinterested bystander at home; the pastor who is patient and kind with people at church but is grumpy and abrupt with his or her family; the effective public speaker who is energized by the crowds but drained by the effort it takes to speak to individuals; and the chairperson who is a stickler for starting and ending meetings on time but never makes it home in time for dinner.

The Solutions We Seek

How then do you recognize potential challenges to your spiritual balance? What can you do to identify the factors that could bring about devastating losses of balance in your role as a pastor or Christian leader?

I hope that the issue of finding and maintaining biblical balance in your life is a passionate pursuit for you and not a passing whim. Having invested nearly thirty years as a pastor, I have watched the damage done in my own life and in the lives of my colleagues who have been careless and allowed imbalance to become the norm.

Although you may be able to survive for the short term in an unbalanced condition, in the long haul, the impact will be disastrous. You will not be able to sustain a vibrant life in Christ if you have settled for a life that refuses to seek the kind of biblical balance I am convinced God has prepared for those who follow him.

Several questions surface whenever I talk with others in vocational ministry. Answering these questions and addressing the attending issues and threats to biblical balance will help you find your way back into balance for the sake of Christ, for the church you serve, for your family and friends, and for your own spiritual health. Therefore, this book is broken down into seven sections, each of which relates to one of those questions, and each offering insights I have found profitable in my own life and ministry.

1. How do I make sure my calling is really from the Lord?

In the section "Juggling the Demands of Your Calling," I hope to help you address the insecurities and vulnerability issues that inevitably threaten to throw us out of balance when people and circumstances challenge what we believe to be our calling. The solution I hope to offer is that you may become *confident* of your calling.

2. With so many visions for ministry out there, which one does God intend for me?

Without a godly vision, pastors can become confused and anxious about where they should be leading the church, scattered in their thinking, and never sure about what to do next or what is really important. A clear vision answers many questions you need resolved if you are to remain balanced in your leadership, so you can take the people where the Lord wants them to go. The purpose of the section "Sharpening the Focus of Your Vision" is to help you become more *focused* by becoming more certain that your vision is from the Lord.

3. How can I be expected to do all that ministry demands of me?

Fighting loneliness and being overwhelmed by the sheer magnitude of the work to be done has driven many pastors out of the ministry. Either they have given up and pursued a less stressful career, or the stresses have made them more susceptible to career-ending moral or ethical failures. God provides a healthy balance to offset the problems of heavy labor and loneliness. He has designed his work to be done in teams of believers who labor together *reinforced* in a community of faithful servants of Christ. The "Gaining Balance by Building Teams" section will help you discover the biblical model for team ministry.

4. As a servant of Christ, how can I avoid a selfish attitude and proud spirit?

In the section "Cultivating Genuine Humility," I hope you will become as alarmed as I am by the subtle ways that pride can overtake those of us in ministry and throw us completely out of balance in the way we are supposed to view ourselves as servants of Christ. The antidote to such imbalance is first to humble ourselves before God and then maintain that attitude with others. One of the best ways to maintain a balanced perspective about our lives and ministries is to allow the Lord and the circumstances of our lives to keep us *humble*.

5. How am I supposed to deal with the troubles that always seem to come with ministry?

You will not be in ministry very long before you face the hardships and pain of significant troubles. The general observation for people in ministry is that you are either in troubled times, coming out of them, or getting ready to go into more of them. If ever a life can be thrown out of balance, it is one that refuses God's hand in the hard times. He will prune you occasionally, but if you can see that pruning as part of God's design for your growth, you can begin to gain his perspective. As you read "Learning to Grow Through Your Troubles," my hope is you will recognize his gracious touch even in the refiner's fire as you are *purified* as a vessel fit for his service.

6. Why is it so hard to get people to be willing to change?

When you figure out what God wants you to do, how he wants it done, and where he expects you to lead his flock, the natural assumption is that the hard part is over and the fruit of your labors is before you. All that remains is for you to share your vision, enlist the support needed, and move ahead to fulfill the calling of the Lord. But people resist change. Without a steady balance to your gait, you will find the footing unstable as you try to negotiate the pathways of change. Mishandling the change process can result in stormy times in your own life, and depending on how you handle it, with the congregation. It can also bring about some profound divisions within the body of Christ. The solutions I want you to consider in the section, "Facing the Inevitability of Change," will contribute to your effectiveness in leading change so that it can become a fruitful time. Instead of being stymied by all the resistance to change, you can lead through the change process in a way that leaves you *satisfied* with the results.

7. How am I supposed to provide spiritual leadership for others when I am so dry myself?

At one time or another, all of us find ourselves drifting out into the "dry and weary land where there is no water."[1] Even though you stand before your people weekly and pour out for them what they need to help them quench their spiritual thirst, the truth is that your own soul "cleaves to the dust"[2] and you are not sure what to do. Frankly, such periods of dryness in the souls of pastors are not rare. Yet we not only suffer from the dry conditions, we compound the situation by feeling guilty because we think spiritual leaders are supposed to be immune to that kind of thing. If we are not prepared to restore our balance during such times, we can slip into a sense of desperation and hopelessness. We are tempted to give up the idea that

1. Psalm 63:1.
2. Psalm 119:25.

20

we can ever recapture the sweet fellowship we once had with Christ. I hope that as you read the "Combating Spiritual Dryness" section, you will learn how to regain your balance sooner. If we understand how dry spells can happen, perhaps we can recognize the symptoms before they get too far along and put in place a plan so we can be *revitalized* and enjoy the fullness of Christ's love for us.

——— ∞ ———

If you feel like the young pastor at the beginning of this introduction, the good news of God's promises to us in Christ is that we do not have to give up when the difficulties of ministry knock us out of balance. We have to realize that overemphasizing some aspects of our life in ministry and neglecting others does not honor the commitment of our lives to Christ. We can drift out of balance more quickly than we can imagine if we do not practice the whole counsel of God in the way we walk with Christ. Take the word of someone who has been knocked from the saddle more than once: you can get back on the horse again! You can regain your stability in the saddle and get your equilibrium back if you allow the Lord to show you his ways.

What I share in the pages that follow, I would love to share with you in person, perhaps over a cup of coffee. It would be great to compare notes on how the Lord has taught us his faithfulness even in the middle of our most unbalanced days! Since we cannot sit down together, take this book and read it as one co-laborer passing on some things to another, things I have only just begun to learn. May the Lord give you greater and deeper insights while you are reading what I offer for your consideration. I hope that what I have to tell you is helpful; I know that what he will show you as you seek his wisdom will build Christ-centered, biblical balance in your life.

A life out of balance needs help! As you read my attempt to answer the seven questions I have confronted in my ministry, look for ways you can become confident, focused, reinforced, humble, purified, satisfied, and revitalized. God uses folks just like you and me, and he wants to keep us steady as we go; balanced and able to handle whatever comes our way.

PART 1

JUGGLING THE DEMANDS OF YOUR CALLING

=1=

ARE YOU DRIVEN
OR CALLED?

When God called you, what do you think he had in mind? If you have sampled some of the material written on what it means to be called into the ministry, you have probably been disappointed. Most people in ministry want more than broad, generic answers to questions about their calling. Although some may have doubts about what it actually means to be called to ministry, far more are dealing with very specific questions related to the circumstances of their particular place of ministry. Generalizations about the overall nature of God's calling do have value, but many of us want to address the particular issues with which we wrestle every day.

- Is the calling to be a pastor irrevocable, or can God have one sort of ministry for you now and another later in your life?
- If you become a pastor, does that mean
  . . . you never get a day off?

25

. . . you have to be an expository preacher? a topical preacher? an evangelistic preacher?

. . . you have to visit all your church members in their homes at least once a year?

. . . you should be prepared to drop everything the instant you hear of someone in the hospital and rush immediately to his or her side?

. . . you have to be on call to give counsel to anyone and everyone who knows your phone number?

. . . your family has to take a backseat to your ministry?

. . . you have to maintain the same standard of living as your congregation on a third to a half as much money?

. . . your wife has to be all things to all people (pianist, nursery worker, missions champion, Bible study teacher, modest but not dowdy, a model of motherly effectiveness with the children, and always at your side supporting you)?

. . . you have to be ready to move to a new location every few years?

- Can God really use someone to pastor a church who is not an evangelist and not even a particularly effective witness?
- What if you can preach but are not very good with administrative details? What if you are a great people-person but are lousy with planning and strategy development? What if you seem to be very effective in helping hurting, confused people one-on-one but are just average before a group?

Answers to these and hundreds of questions like them represent an extremely wide range of thoughts and concepts of what a pastor's calling ought to be. Many pastors find themselves flooded with confusion and doubt as they try to either measure up to or avoid the examples of pastors they have known in the past. The good news is that God never intended for pastors to try to satisfy the demands of every model for ministry ever developed. He did not call you to crush you!

God calls you to engage in a lifetime of effective, satisfying ministry in which he maximizes your spiritual gifts, considers *your* calling (not someone else's), recognizes your strengths and weaknesses, and commits to shaping you into a godly individual who grows more mature every day in your walk with Jesus Christ.

Your Calling Is from God

As difficult as it is for some to understand, our calling is from God. He can and will use the collective wisdom of others to help mold our comprehension of what that calling should look like, but essentially, he wants our personal calling to be measured by one standard: the Word of God. His will for your life may share similarities with his will for others, but in his perfect wisdom, he has tailored a purpose and a plan uniquely suited to each of us. Our individual calling to ministry will certainly reflect that distinctive design. In 1 Corinthians, the apostle Paul expresses it this way:

> For consider your calling, brethren, that there were not many wise according to the flesh, not many mighty, not many noble; but God has chosen the foolish things of the world to shame the wise, and God has chosen the weak things of the world to shame the things which are strong, and the base things of the world and the despised God has chosen, the things that are not, so that He may nullify the things that are, so that no man may boast before God.
>
> 1 Corinthians 1:26–29

Although some pastors stand out in our minds as "superstars" who give every appearance of having been blessed with more than their share of gifts, Paul assures us that there are "not many" like that. Our calling is not measured by the plethora of gifts we have received but according to the purposes God has for the unique gifts he has entrusted to each of us. In fact, Paul also says that we have been "called according to His purpose" (Rom.

27

8:28). Our responsibility in meeting the demands of ministry consists of being and doing all that fulfills God's purpose in our lives. To that end, we are called "to walk in a manner worthy of the calling with which you have been called" by honoring the special purposes God has established for us (Eph. 4:1).

Therefore, our calling will often be misunderstood, challenged, and even attacked by those who see pastoral calling as a one-size-fits-all issue. The churches we serve will have stated and unstated expectations about the particular calling they envision for their pastor. Individuals within those churches will further complicate matters by adding their own expectations to the mix and keep us, as pastors, off balance by their constant questions about why we do not do what "pastors should do." If that is not exasperating enough, deep down inside we wonder if perhaps they are right and we are not cutting it as a pastor. Talk about adding guilt on top of confusion! No wonder pastors have a hard time keeping their equilibrium!

You may ask, "Since my calling is from God, should I be unconcerned about the expectations people have?" No, that is unrealistic. You cannot simply ignore them, but you do not have to satisfy them.

I struggled with this for years. I was blessed to have been exposed to the successful ministries of several effective pastors, but to my dismay, I was not like any of them. I spent years trying to become like them, essentially living like David in Saul's armor, knowing that the fit was awful but sensing that it was not "okay" to come to the battle with my own sling and stones. Eventually I discovered what every pastor must learn: my calling is from God, and my equipping is from him as well.

How has he equipped you? Discovering this will answer many questions about your calling, because the clue to what he wants you to do is found in what he has equipped you to do.

Your Calling Is to a Balanced Ministry

Without debate, it is certain that if you have been busy trying to succeed in a style of ministry to which God never called you, you have been way out of balance in your life and have suffered untold misery. Juggling the demands of your calling as well as the demands of someone else's calling has caused the downfall of many pastors. The weight of responsibility simply overcame them and threw them over the edge.

Once you have learned to be content with the calling God has given you, you will find that you have quite enough to keep you occupied within the context of your own concerns. Within the ministry calling God has designed for you, there is still plenty of room for the perils of overload and imbalance. How you handle them will determine how well you stay in balance. In your ministry, you will find there are various factors that seem to compete against one another and make you feel pulled in all directions. The challenge is to recognize the difference between competing demands and balancing counterweights.

Should you spend more time in prayer or more time handling the dispute between two of your deacons? Should you be out visiting more or staying in the office to be available in case someone with a pressing need phones or stops by? Should you be spending more time cultivating a relationship with your unbelieving neighbor or knocking on the doors of people you would never meet otherwise? Which is it going to be this week—more time for counseling or more time for sermon preparation?

Life in ministry, even within the specific area of your calling, presents so many issues that compete for time that you can easily go to bed each night feeling like a complete failure because you never got it worked out in the right proportions. There is always something you think needs to be done but has to be slighted in order to do something else. Demands upon your time and energy will force you to make choices you would rather not make. How you make those choices and then how you feel about your decision afterward will largely be determined by the way you see yourself—as someone God has *called* or as someone who has become inexplicably *driven*.

Gordon MacDonald, in his book *Ordering Your Private World*, explains what it is like to be a person who is driven.

In an exploration of the inner sphere of the person, one has to begin somewhere, and I have chosen to begin where Christ appears to have begun—with the distinction between the *called* and the *driven*. Somehow He separated people out on the basis of their tendency to be driven or their willingness to be called. He dealt with their motives, the basis of their spiritual energy, and the sorts of gratification in which they were interested.[1]

MacDonald outlines the symptoms of a driven person, which I summarize here. As you read, ask yourself if some of your struggles in handling the demands of your calling might not be related to your tendency to be motivated by a driving force within you rather than a zealous calling to follow Christ.

Symptoms of Driven People

1. A driven person is most often gratified only by accomplishment.
2. A driven person is preoccupied with the symbols of accomplishment.
3. A driven person is usually caught in the uncontrolled pursuit of expansion.
4. Driven people tend to have a limited regard for integrity.
5. Driven people often possess limited or undeveloped people skills.
6. Driven people tend to be highly competitive.
7. A driven person often possesses a volcanic force of anger, which can erupt any time he or she senses opposition or disloyalty.
8. Driven people are usually abnormally busy.[2]

MacDonald continues, "This then is the driven person—not an entirely attractive picture. What often disturbs me as I look at this picture is the fact that much of our world is run by driven people. We have created a system that rides on their backs. And where that is true in businesses, in churches, and in homes,

1. Gordon MacDonald. *Ordering Your Private World* (New York: Oliver Nelson, 1985), 29.
2. Ibid., 31–36.

the growth of people is often sacrificed for accomplishment and accumulation."[3]

When driven people confront the competing demands on their time, they view them as counterproductive assaults against their agenda, their mandate to get things done. Competing demands confuse and delay their carefully conceived plans and leave them feeling frustrated by their inability to solve the riddle, to find a way to get rid of the distractions that impede the progress of their singular focus.

Obviously, I believe that pastors are supposed to be called, not driven! Certainly our calling will result in an undeniable drive to fulfill all that God intends for us, but we will not be controlled or consumed by ungodly motives measured in terms of achievement and accomplishment. Our greatest satisfaction arises from being faithful to Christ, first in the character of our hearts, and then in the conduct of our lives and ministries.

3. Ibid., 36.

2

DISCOVERING COUNTERBALANCES IN MINISTRY

God has a way of enforcing balance in our lives to keep us from spinning out of control into eccentric obsessions. Without the presence of competing demands, we would devote ourselves exclusively to those things we like to do and avoid those things we really should do but do not want to do. I believe that the Lord has provided competing demands to serve as a series of weights and counterweights to enable us to achieve and maintain equilibrium in our lives and ministries.

Counterweights Stabilize Called People

Life is full of examples of balance. The face of a clock is perfectly balanced. Each hour has its direct opposite, a counterpart exactly six hours away. A circle cannot have fewer than

360 degrees and still be perfectly round. Each point of the circle has a counterpoint exactly 180 degrees away. Every auto mechanic knows that for a tire's roll to be true, all four tires need to be in balance so the car's weight is distributed equally. With precision, a mechanic will place balancing weights at strategic points all around the tire's rim to correct any imbalance.

So it is with the demands that accompany our calling to ministry. Like so many points around the face of a clock, ministry conflicts pull at us every day and surround us with decisions about how to spend our time and energy. We feel like each choice we make threatens the delicate balance and symmetry of our ministry.

But what if what you think of as the delicate balance and symmetry of your ministry is, in fact, already imbalanced? Conflicting demands, or weights and counterweights, create much of the difficulty in maintaining the balance of our calling, but God intends them for our good. We often resent them and resist having to endure the tedious precision of God's hand when he works on perfecting and "rounding out" our ministry. The truth is that God will provide all we need to stay in balance and fulfill the demands of our calling, but sometimes he needs to correct our imbalances with weights and counterweights.

Driven people consider this process to be unnecessary, nothing more than a frustrating delay in their agenda to get the job done. Called people, on the other hand, recognize that God had more in mind when he called them to ministry than just accomplishing an agenda. For the Lord, the destination does not always matter as much as the way you make the journey.

When God calls a person to be a shepherd of his flock, God sees the entire picture through the balanced lens of his eternal perspective. We cannot ignore any part of his purposes along the way and consider it to be a successful trip. Therefore, he will remind us of the need to attend to all aspects of the calling. Like the wheels of a car on a cross-country trip, the "tires" of our ministry will eventually become deformed and misshapen when they hit potholes, deflate with the hot and cold climates of the seasons, and sometimes either wear out or get punctured. It is not the tire's fault that it encounters potholes, temperature shifts, or nails in the road. It is, however, the driver's job to pay attention to how his or her tires are responding to those demands. The Lord provides all the assistance we will ever need to keep ourselves in balance for the entire journey if we will be patient and trust him when he calls us aside to place the proper weight at the appropriate points to keep going.

In my own life and ministry, I have tried to determine where my balance is most threatened and which demands generate the greatest struggles. By looking back over the years and noting the points where the Lord applied additional weights and counterweights, I have been able to see consistent "wear patterns" that indicate where I am most likely to get out of balance. Although there are many others, I will detail six categories that I have found are common to pastors. Each category consists of two pressure points that compete for our time and attention, each generating a strong pull in the opposite direction. As long as the pull remains equal, balance is preserved. But when the strength of the pull, or the weight of the demands, shifts one way or the other, the Lord allow us to undergo a bumpy ride until we allow him to restore our equilibrium.

An Uncompromising Vision	vs.	A Teachable Spirit
Fixed Priorities	vs.	Flexibility to Respond
Spiritual Vitality	vs.	Administrative Duties
Servant-Minded Ministry	vs.	Delegated Ministry
Knowing Self	vs.	Knowing Others
Discernment and Sensitivity	vs.	Logic and Reason

As you can see from the diagram on p. 35, every area has a counterweight or an opposite responsibility of ministry. Attending to each point with care enables me to enjoy the kind of balanced ministry the Lord desires for me. In each case, I have a preferred point of emphasis, a natural bent. You, too, will likely be able to identify your natural bents and inclinations at a glance. Left to my own inclinations, I would persist in devoting myself to bulking up the strength of my preferences and neglect the building up of my weaknesses. A commitment to balance in ministry will not allow such negligence.

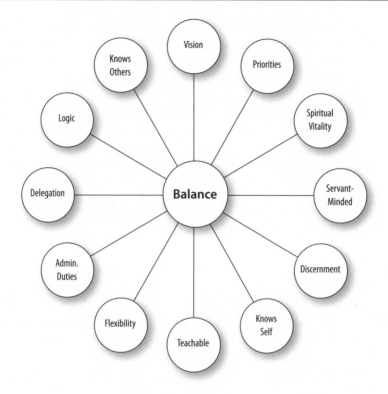

An Uncompromising Vision Balanced by a Teachable Spirit

Defining your vision can produce all kinds of stress. In presenting your ideas about what you believe the Lord has in store for you and your congregation, you are in constant danger of going overboard or slipping off the high wire. If not communicated sensitively and carefully, the way we share our vision can sound like a scheme to embellish our own careers and cater to our own egos. Therefore, as we begin to understand God's vision for our ministries, we must allow some time to clarify our thinking so that when we share the vision with others, they will hear God's heart in it and not personal ambition.

If you have never spent much time coming to terms with a clear vision of what the Lord wants to do in your life, I cannot emphasize enough how critical that investment can be. If you are not clear on where you believe the Lord is leading you, you will always feel insecure about your role as a pastor and a leader.

Does the Lord drop visions straight from heaven to every pastor? To hear some pastors tell it, you might think so! More than likely though, a godly vision develops over time as we listen to and learn from others, and as we demonstrate that we are willing to grow in our thinking with a teachable spirit. If you drew firm conclusions about your vision early in your ministry, you will probably struggle when the time comes to expand it. The Lord wants his shepherds to have a firm grasp on a clear vision, but he wants them to balance that firmness with a teachable spirit that always seeks to know more.

Resources abound if we are willing to listen. Other pastors, church members, books, tapes, seminars, and many sources of dream-building materials exist to enable us to grow our vision beyond our own limited perspectives. Don't be afraid to admit that you do not have all the answers. Even the most clearly defined visions can stand refinement if we are willing to ask good questions and listen with openness and a teachable spirit to the responses.

Fixed Priorities Balanced by Flexibility to Respond

"Isn't the problem of balance solved if you just figure out your priorities and then live by them? Pastors whose lives get out of line obviously never defined their priorities."

Have you ever heard anyone say something like that? Unfortunately, stating our priorities seldom takes into account all the possible scenarios we will face on any given day. No matter how well we have defined our priorities, issues arise that do not fit our carefully defined categories. I know that when I review my schedule and make the necessary adjustments to get my life back in line with my stated priorities, no sooner do I get the schedule written down, than something comes along that makes it all but impossible to keep!

It is true that you cannot expect to accomplish much toward your life dreams and vision if you do not set forth some working

priorities. Some things just have to be viewed as more important than others and treated that way in the amount of time
and attention we give them. Lives without priorities cannot
maintain any balance whatsoever and only succeed in generating a sense of futility because we never seem to get anywhere
we are trying to go.

With that said, have you ever met anyone who impressed you
with their methodical, disciplined set of priorities but lacked
spiritual vitality? Perhaps they succeeded in ordering their priorities but forgot that living for Christ is walking by the Spirit,
not checking off today's list of things to do.

The counterweight to fixed priorities has to be flexibility.
The Lord may have something more in mind for us today than
maintaining a rigid schedule of accomplishing important tasks.
Sometimes the Lord drops some unplanned events into our
routines just to see if we are willing to adjust our own agenda
to be flexible enough for his.

Along the way to do what God has given us, other opportunities often arise. This forces us to decide between what we were
planning and what might be a better choice. In the parable of
the good Samaritan, Jesus commends the one who delayed his
own journey long enough to respond to the wounded traveler.
Two others, a priest and a Levite, chose to ignore the unplanned
interruption and kept moving toward their destination. All three
had set out to make a journey along the same road, but only
one was willing to lay aside his original plan to respond to a
more immediate need. Jesus praised his actions as the good
and right way. Sometimes in our lives as pastors, unexpected
crises arise and we have to determine if they are from the Lord
or simply a distraction. Inflexibility, even when justified by lofty
priorities, can get in the way of the unique moments of special
blessing that come with "divine interruptions."

How flexible are you? Granted, some people are so flexible
that they throw out their priorities at the first sign of something
that appears to be more promising or more urgent. Others are
so determined not to be distracted from their plans that they
would not recognize the voice of the Lord if he shouted to them
in a closed room.

Our priorities are only valuable as the Lord assigns value to them. When he has something else in mind, we need to be flexible enough to pay attention. The form of his redirection may be a permanent change in our priorities or just a momentary response to an immediate need. It could be a gentle nudge as he impresses us to take action, or it could be a major calamity that crashes broadside into our lives.

How can we tell the difference between a temptation to compromise our priorities and a calling to respond to a sovereignly appointed ministry opportunity? There is no grid of questions to ask, no priority discernment test to take, and worse, no rulebook or policy manual that offers a definitive answer. The key is a balanced walk with Christ in the power of the Holy Spirit. A heart that has learned to listen to the quiet stirrings of the Lord has a desire to hold plans loosely with an open hand so that the Lord can replace our agenda with his at any given moment.

This may sound like overly spiritualized mysticism, but, in fact, it reflects the biblical teaching of "walking in the Spirit." As the apostle Paul wrote, "If we live by the Spirit, let us also walk by the Spirit" (Gal. 5:25). Godly priorities come from the Lord as he orders our days. Consequently, they can and should be adjusted by the Lord, which helps keep priorities and flexibility in proper balance.

Spiritual Vitality Balanced by Administrative Duties

Many churches frustrate themselves and their pastors by creating a false division between "ministry" and "running the church." With the best of intentions, different church members through the years have actually told me, "Pastor, you take care of the ministry part, and we'll run the church. Just because you've been to seminary and know about theology and the Bible doesn't qualify you to be involved in the administration of the church." While that may be true, behind such thinking lies an assumption that practical matters such as budgets and buildings are not addressed in the spiritual realm. It is also misguided to assume that administration and ministry are best kept separate for the sake of efficiency.

38

There are two common responses to the ministry versus administration dilemma. One is to say, "Amen!" to the parishioner above, and concern yourself only minimally in the running of the church. But to maintain balance, we need to develop good administrative skills. On the other hand, if our primary calling is to shepherd the flock of God as a pastor, we should not jump into the administrative arena with more gusto than good sense, assuming we will be a frontrunner for the "CEO of the Year" award.

No matter which side of the dilemma we fall toward, if we are not careful, our week will be consumed by everything but the main ministry the Lord called us to. Between the management of the church and the ministry of the Word, the struggle for balance never lets up. Few can honestly say they have mastered it.

The nagging fear that we are out of balance in this area is compounded by the number of conference speakers and authors who tell us how much time they require to prepare their biblically challenging and spiritually vital messages. We hear great preachers either say or imply that unless we spend twenty or more hours a week in sermon preparation and spiritual nourishment and growth, we cannot expect God's hand to work in our ministry. Sometimes the message is subtler than that, but not always. Would you not give just about anything to have one week in your entire ministry when you had that much time?

I used to think that I lacked large blocks of uninterrupted time for study and prayer because of poor planning and imbalanced priorities. You may already have reached the same conclusion about yourself. More recently, I have concluded that God has given each of us the kinds of ministries that are suited to our gifts. Even if it were available, I am not sure I would know what to do with twenty or more hours a week to study. Sure, I would love to have that problem, but that is not the kind of ministry the Lord has given me. After nearly thirty years as a pastor, I can say with confidence that I no longer feel guilty about that.

So what should we do about keeping our ministry in a proper balance between administration and organization and the spiritual dynamics of soul and sermon preparation? Set your priorities as the Lord leads. Then determine to maintain Spirit-led flexibility in carrying them out. In broad strokes, give your best time and energy to that which lasts forever, investing in both the souls of people and the Word of God. Look to reduce the amount of time spent in organizational and administrative duties by working smarter rather than harder.

Keeping these two competing time crunchers in balance will always present one of the greatest challenges of your life. Don't give up! Once in a while when everything falls in place and you hit the balance, you will understand why the struggle is worthwhile.

Servant-Minded Ministry Balanced by Delegated Ministry

Picture this scene. At a church leaders' meeting, a member of your board listens carefully to all that you have reported and all that has kept you busy putting out fires during the preceding month (many of which were created by the board itself!). Then with genuine concern a board member says, "Pastor, you need to delegate more, or you're going to run yourself ragged trying to do everything!"

While you are still processing this exhortation from your board member, you get a phone call on Monday morning after a church-wide workday on Saturday. The head of the grounds committee complains that you did not show up to help mow and cut back the weeds around the parking lot. "Pastor, when you pass off work to others, frankly, some of us are beginning to wonder if maybe you think you are too good to do any of the dirty work around here. You seem to expect the rest of us to be servants. Are you sure you haven't lost your spirit of servanthood?"

How do you handle the delicate balance between wise delegation and sensitive servanthood? Several factors complicate the situation. Not only are we forced to struggle with our own understanding of what is appropriate and right before the Lord, but we also have to deal with other issues, such as personal guilt, expectations of the board, perceptions of the members, availability of volunteers to whom work can be delegated, competing events on our calendars, and a host of other variables we may not be able to control.

To gain any equilibrium in our thinking and action, the starting point has to be an honest assessment of our own hearts. Leaders in the body of Christ are first and foremost called to be servant-leaders. Those who have not learned to be servants can expect only limited effectiveness in providing spiritual leadership to any group of believers.

Our attitudes about ministry tasks are shaped by our understanding of the role of a servant. The prevailing attitude of servant-minded leaders should reflect a willingness to do any task, to perform any function, and to engage in any duty with a cooperative and humble spirit. No job should fall beneath the dignity of those who see themselves as true servants. Status and personal dignity should have nothing to do with our willingness to perform any task, no matter how lowly and routine or how exalted and special. As servants, leaders must have willing hearts.

With that said, you might think that delegation has been effectively ruled out as a legitimate option. Not so! Just because we are *willing* to do anything does not mean that we *should* do everything. Balancing our role as a servant and our responsibility to be a good steward of our ministry gifts requires a clear grasp of our priorities and a profound sense of what is important in moving toward accomplishing the purposes of our ministry.

Although we must be willing to fold the bulletins on Thursday mornings, for the spiritual nurture of the sheep we are responsible for feeding on Sunday, would it not be better to have unfolded bulletins than an unprepared sermon? Even though we must be willing to change diapers in the nursery on a Sunday morning, your presence in the pulpit may be the best use of your ministry gifts at that time. Granted, we can mow the church lawn with the best of them, but if someone else could do that, should we not invest time in doing what that person may not be called or qualified to do?

41

At the heart of the matter of servant-minded ministry and delegated ministry is our attitude. When we face challenges from the head of grounds committee, or others who question our choices, rather than argue the point, perhaps a gentle answer would accomplish more than a lecture on godly priorities: "You know, you may be right. Maybe I should have been there on Saturday, but I struggle with what is best sometimes. Perhaps you could pray for me and the elders as we try to figure out how I can make good choices and wise decisions on things like that. By the way, you guys did a fantastic job." Who knows? Maybe all he needs is to know that you think what he is doing matters, and you can affirm him in other ways besides showing up!

There will always be detractors and critical people ready to second guess every choice we make. We will never be able to settle the issue of what others think. We cannot make them embrace our priorities. What then is the primary concern in keeping balance in this area? Attitude.

> Have this attitude in yourselves which was also in Christ Jesus, who, although He existed in the form of God, did not regard equality with God a thing to be grasped, but emptied Himself, taking the form of a bondservant, and being made in the likeness of men.
>
> Philippians 2:5–7

With a conscious effort to monitor the attitude of our hearts, we can move toward a proper balance between servant-mindedness and wise delegation. The greater our sphere of influence in ministry and the weightier our responsibilities for ministry oversight, the more difficult we will find the task of maintaining our balance as a servant-leader. Do not allow yourself to listen to those who would sway your thinking into biblical imbalance, but train your ear to hear the voice of the Spirit. If we are following Christ, both in the direction we choose to go and in the attitude we demonstrate, we will keep in step with the Spirit and keep our lives and ministries in balance.

If you continue to have concerns, strive to maintain a diligent check on your attitude in this area. Set up a regular plan to evaluate your progress. With the help of trusted friends who know you well, ask the hard questions about the way you are handling your workload.

- Am I passing off duties because I simply don't want to do them?
- Do I ever take into consideration my desire to project a certain image in my position before I decide whether to get involved? Do I see myself as above any task?
- Is this choice of action based upon a sound application of my priorities or an effort to avoid an unsavory task?
- Am I developing a pattern of always doing just what I want to do rather than what I ought to do?
- When did I last function in a purely servant role simply because I recognized a need and responded? Was my initial reaction to try to find someone else to do it instead of me?

The following questions may help you get some clear, helpful answers.

Knowledge of Yourself Balanced by Knowledge of Others

How well do you know yourself? Before you get nervous, this is not just a "touchy feely" question. I'm not talking about self-knowledge for its own sake or as some self-improvement scheme. If we do not take the necessary steps to gain some basic knowledge of who we are and what we are like, we cannot hope to provide any consistent leadership to others. Before we can lead others and give them pastoral direction, we also need to develop our ability to understand what makes people tick. That skill begins with learning how to understand ourselves first and gain a sane estimation of our own hearts and minds.

We do not have to reduce everything to psychological terms to pursue a reasonable understanding of ourselves and others. The proliferation of self-help books and pop-psychology theories among Christians has almost obliterated the biblical instruction that Paul gives for the body of Christ to function with a clear understanding of ourselves: "For through the grace given to me I say to everyone among you not to think more highly of himself than he ought to think; but to think so as to have sound judgment, as God has allotted to each a measure of faith" (Rom. 12:3). We cannot expect to capitalize on resources we do not realize we have, or to compensate for deficits we do not realize we have. If we want to work effectively in a balanced ministry with others, we need to have sound judgment about ourselves.

The problem with not knowing ourselves is that we cannot monitor and correct our responses if we are not aware of our own patterns of behavior, emotional responses, and thought processes. At one crisis point in the first ten years of my ministry, I could not figure out why I was running into so many roadblocks in my efforts to get things done. Frequently, I found myself in conflict with other leaders in the church and could sense that they were as frustrated as I was. After one exhausting and exasperating meeting, one of my friends pointed out what he thought was the problem. As he saw it, something in my leadership style, or maybe just my personality, rubbed him and some of the others the wrong way. The result was an occasional effort on their part to thwart my efforts, to put me in my place, and to keep me off balance.

He told me what his perception was of me—I was ambitious and always pressed hard to get what I wanted, regardless of how long it took and how many people or processes I had to go over or around. Now remember, this was a guy I considered a friend! I was appalled to think that anyone could see me in that light! The next day at lunch with a couple of other friends from the church, I asked if they thought the same thing. As they stared at their meals, silently considering how to answer my question without hurting my feelings, it dawned on me that I had a problem. Obviously, I did not know myself as well as I thought. When they finally answered, they agreed. I realized then that I needed to become a better student of my own nature if I ever hoped to provide sound and balanced leadership to the ministry team around me. Together with those friends, we determined

44

to work on the problem now that it was identified. On my own, I decided to learn as much as I could about myself and what I am really like so that I could be a more effective servant-leader to the body of Christ. Asking honest questions helps.

- What are your spiritual gifts and natural abilities?
- Are you motivated to excel in any area? What is the area that motivates you?
- What are your personal goals and aspirations?
- What frustrates you as you seek those goals and fences you in as you pursue your aspirations?
- Are there influences and circumstances within your family life that impact you either positively or negatively? Are some of those due to the season of life in which you find yourself, or are they part of your normal patterns and conditions of your life?
- Have you discovered what means of communication works best for you when someone assigns you a task? When you need a word of criticism? Affirmation? Appreciation? Love? What is the best way for you to communicate those things to others?

Even if the answers prove to be embarrassing, we need to ask them. If we don't someone else eventually will!

Learning about yourself is seldom a pleasant experience, but you have to make a commitment to do so if you expect to grow as an individual and as a leader. Yet knowing yourself is not enough. You have to work just as diligently to know the others you work with in ministry. Knowing them will make it easier to understand why they do what they do and communicate to them that you care enough to find out who they really are.

The balance required to know ourselves and others mandates a diligent spirit and genuine interest in the growth of the individual toward maturity in Christ. If we do not know ourselves, we will continue to blunder along the same lines as long as we are in ministry, finding it necessary to change ministries periodically rather than face the inevitable need for personal growth and self-discovery that long-term relationships bring. If we do not know others, we will risk an inefficient utilization of available resources or we will offend and abuse a valuable ally and co-laborer in the work of the kingdom through our insensitivity. Seeking balance in the knowledge of yourself and others will always pay practical, relational dividends in your life and ministry.

Discernment and Sensitivity Balanced by Logic and Reason

Logic and reason cannot provide the answers for everything. Leaders who try to reduce every issue to its least common denominator and apply deductive reasoning processes to make all their decisions soon find that their neat, tight, logical conclusions inexplicably become unraveled.

Discernment and sensitivity cannot provide solutions for all circumstances either, much to the dismay of those who seek to lead and make decisions based primarily on intuition. In many cases, choices based exclusively upon subjective criteria will not address the multitude of issues facing ministry leaders.

Sound reasoning and the ability to think logically will give us a rational foundation for decision making. If we have not learned how to think carefully and thoroughly, plans and decisions that may at first appear to be wise will often fail due to some flaw in our thinking. Many great ideas never materialized because someone did not take the time to think through all of the factors involved and thereby omitted crucial steps. Be careful not to allow your leadership to suffer because you were not prepared to follow a logical and reasonable course of action.

If you know that you are not strong in this area, find ways to improve by enlisting the aid of those who are gifted thinkers, problem solvers, process developers, and planners. Read and study materials that open your eyes to new ways of planning,[1]

1. Books like Bobb Biehl, *Master-Planning: The Complete Guide for Building a Strategic Plan for Your Business, Church, or Organization* (Nashville: Broadman & Holman, 1997), or Stephen Douglass, *Managing Yourself* (San Bernardino, CA: Here's Life Publishing, 1978).

tried-and-tested procedures for decision-making, and other means of following a path of consistently applied logic with attention to details. Whatever tasks we face, we will be greatly served to develop the ability to think with greater care.

Some ministry leaders excuse their deficits on this point and make no effort to improve, calling on their people to follow them by faith. All that is needed to undermine the effectiveness of our leadership is to take off on some project without a rational foundation of thoughtful planning, without careful management in assembling and presenting all the facts. We lose credibility quickly when it becomes apparent that we did not do our homework and did not apply the basic principles of logic before enlisting the support of those we lead.

Yet once we have done our homework to build a rational foundation based on the practical application of objective biblical truth and logical thinking, there will still be areas that force us to rely on a more subjective approach. Not everything can be reduced to a carefully reasoned and objectively outlined argument. Also, some issues will arise in ministry that defy a "chapter and verse" answer from Scripture. That is when it becomes necessary to learn how to develop a dependence upon the Holy Spirit to give us understanding of biblical principles and direct our steps when we can find no specific command or instruction to guide us as we lead the way.

There is a subjective side to leadership. Circumstances will arise that demand a decision for which you can find no direct answer from Scripture or a logical answer from careful reasoning. Therefore, in the realm of the subjective, God gives us what Proverbs calls "discernment" and "insight" for those times when we need godly wisdom in our decision-making beyond the objective standards we normally rely on. "Make your ear attentive to wisdom, incline your heart to understanding; for if you cry for discernment, lift your voice for understanding; if you seek her as silver and search for her as for hidden treasures; then you will discern the fear of the LORD and discover the knowledge of God" (Prov. 2:2–5).

For example, when someone asks me why we do not sing certain styles of music in our corporate worship services, I can offer objective reasons related to the demographic composition of our congregation, the changing nature of Christian music, or other somewhat objective realities. But the real issue has to do with subjective matters like taste and preference. For reasons that are largely subjective we choose what we believe best fits our congregation. Try to explain that using reason alone! For every logical explanation you come up with, people with different tastes counter with equally substantial reasons for their preferences. Someone needs to make the call, and that call requires a profound sensitivity to the leading of the Holy Spirit and the presence of godly discernment in the hearts and minds of the leaders.

Leaders have to make many choices that are more subjective than objective by nature. We cannot always rely on a carefully outlined and logical course of action, nor can we count on finding a Bible verse to support every decision we make. Therefore, we need to balance our logical, rational side with a discerning, "sensitive to the Spirit" side. Both should be biblically informed and motivated. However, there will be occasions when we must discern which way offers the best application of biblical wisdom when reason alone is an insufficient guide. Discernment as a subjective means of making choices must still rely on the Scriptures as much as reason does, but in the absence of a specific command or instruction, we often must exercise godly discernment in knowing how to make application of biblical principles that lead us to choose wisely.

We do this all the time in the course of our lives but seldom distinguish between reason and discernment because we hope to keep them in balance so that one constantly informs and assists the other. We have certain reasonable applications of biblical teaching in selecting a spouse: most obviously, they must be believers. But we also count on the Lord to give us that subjective sense of connection we desire when we get ready to devote our lives to a relationship with a husband or wife. Many single adults have sat in my office and said how grateful they would be if they could just find a verse telling them the right one to marry! Reason clearly helps but has to be aided by a healthy dose of godly discernment!

48

The key to maintaining healthy balance between reason and discernment is to keep both well within the context of the Scriptures, not allowing reason to lead us to the extreme of basing everything on logic alone, nor allowing discernment to lead us to the other extreme of decision-making based entirely on feelings and preferences. Without biblical presuppositions, logic can lead us astray from God's will. At the same time, without biblical principles and teaching holding a firm rein, those who rely entirely on personal impressions and uninformed discernment run the risk of justifying all kinds of aberrant behavior that runs contrary to God's revealed will.

Balance between godly discernment and sound reasoning can only be maintained as both yield to the final authority of God's Word.

One final observation on this point needs to be made. My natural tendency is to try to offer rational points of support for what I do even when those points did not actually influence the choice I made. On such occasions, I made my decision subjectively but tried to explain it objectively. Gaining a healthy balance between the two allows me to be more transparent and trustworthy in the eyes of those I lead.

Your Own Weights and Counterweights

If we try to keep ourselves in balance without making sure that we give proper attention to all the demands of our calling, our negligence will cost us. Juggling the demands of God's calling requires great care to balance all that he calls upon us to carry.

Like the spokes of the wheel, the tools of a balanced life in ministry must be of equal weight, all in proper balance. How often does that happen? I am not sure it ever does, at least not to perfection. But the goal is to persist, to continue to work toward equilibrium.

Since the categories I have explored in some detail may not cover the exact problems you are facing, a blank version of the wheel is provided in the appendix so that you can fill in your own areas of concern. Take some time to make a list of the competing demands you face. This may enable you to see more clearly how to begin putting things into balance with each other. When I did this, I realized why I kept getting more frustrated than fulfilled in trying to do what I knew the Lord had called me to do. As I saw the weights and counterweights of each demand upon me, I was able to recognize where I had been struggling. You will be able to see where you have been trying to balance feathers against anvils, devoting too much attention to one thing and not enough to another. Granted, simply identifying the problem does not solve it, but until we know and understand what we are up against, our efforts to find a solution will fail.

Thankfully, we can trust God to make his way clear for us to keep each aspect of our calling in balance. Even when we seem to lose it for a while, we can be confident that the Lord will keep us through to the end. "For I am confident of this very thing, that He who began a good work in you will perfect it until the day of Christ Jesus" (Phil. 1:6).

PART 2

SHARPENING THE FOCUS OF YOUR VISION

3

RUNNING WITH YOUR EYES CLOSED

MINISTRY WITHOUT A GODLY VISION

One night when I was seventeen years old, I was at a basketball tournament and decided to leave early. The weather was rainy, and in my haste to reach the refuge of my car, I did not notice that the crowded parking lot had me completely blocked in. After two unsuccessful attempts to exit the way I came in, it occurred to me that I had two choices: wait for the last game of the night to end or find an inventive way to get out. The combination of my impatience and the adventure involved in the challenge of discovery made the choice a simple one. Immediate action was best.

In hindsight, one major factor should have been considered. The defroster on my 1965 Ford Mustang had not worked since I'd owned the car. Little did I realize at the beginning of this adventure how important it would be to see where I was going. Within a matter of minutes, the windshield was completely fogged over. Rather than taking a moment to collect my thoughts and sort out the reasonable options available to me, I continued. Not for a moment did I think that the absence of vision would impede my progress. With my head half in and half out of the side window, water dripping into my eyes, I thought I saw a new way out.

Through the blur of the steamy front window and the sting of the driving rain in my eyes, a gravel road invited exploration out the back side of the parking lot, leading toward the new college dormitories a couple of hundred yards away. As a matter of fact, although I could barely make them out, a pair of headlights seemed to be coming toward the gymnasium from the direction of those dorms. Without delay, off I went down the narrow gravel road, which to my dismay quickly narrowed to a width not much wider than my car. Undaunted, I pressed on. A few more feet and the gravel road had become a footpath . . . and then . . . a sidewalk! *But what about the headlights I saw through the haze?* I thought, as panic struck me and the axle of my car bottomed out in the mud beside the walk. The "headlights" turned out to be the lights on either side of the dormitory doors at the end of the sidewalk! All hope of escaping with any dignity was lost. To make a long story short, the field surrounding the sidewalk was so muddy that a tow truck couldn't reach my car without tearing up the newly sown grass for two or three days.

As a pastor, have you ever rushed ahead before you had a clear vision of where you were going and how you were to proceed? Pastors have always known that they are supposed to do something, so we sometimes ignore the clouds surrounding us and try to bluff our way along, hoping that our complete disorientation does not sink us in the mire before we find our way to someplace respectable.

Since none of us is born with a fully formed vision for ministry, the Lord does not expect us to know what it is as soon as we answer his call to serve him as pastors. I know I didn't. My early years as a young pastor brought enough insecurity without my having to know all the ins and outs of God's long-term vision for my life and the life of the church he would have me pastor. Recently someone asked me if the church I pastor matches the vision the Lord gave me before we started it. When I realized that he was serious, I regained my composure (I laughed at the question, assuming that he was joking!) and assured him that in no way had I envisioned what God was going to do in our congregation. There may be some young pastors who are mature enough to handle the big picture of a wholly developed vision for a lifetime of ministry, but I was certainly not one of them!

Vision develops and matures as the biblical principles of ministry begin to reveal not only the unique person you are, but also what is unique about the place and people God has called you to serve. Just as there are advocates of a "purpose-driven church,"[1] I classify myself as an advocate of a "principle-based church." A principle-based church allows the vision to arise from the principles at work in your life and the lives of the people who are growing in Christ around you.

Sometime between your earliest days as a pastor and the clarification of what God's unique vision is for you, you will experience many days of insecurity while you try to figure out where you fit in his scheme of things for the church. If that is where you still are, take heart and keep working on understanding as much as you can about the biblical principles for the church, for the maturing of the men and women of God. Sure, you can try to figure it all out from the beginning, before you really know who you are in ministry or what God intends your special contribution to his work to be. But it makes a lot more sense to define your dream as you make progress in your ministry.[2]

The Need for a Clear Vision

Although many childhood games include playing blindfolded or closing your eyes, you would never seriously consider

1. There is great value to this approach, as Rick Warren's book *The Purpose-Driven Church* (Grand Rapids: Zondervan, 2002) demonstrates. For that purpose to drive the church toward a Christ-centered, God-honoring ministry, it must, of course, be anchored on biblical principles.

2. See Bobb Biehl, *Dream Energy: Making a More Significant Difference in Fulfilling Your Life Dream* (Orlando: Quick Wisdom Publishing, 2001). The exercise of ten questions to clarify your dream in Appendix C is especially helpful.

running any distance with your eyes closed, would you? Besides the danger of running into things, you need your eyes open to maintain your balance. Living without any compelling vision is much like running with your eyes closed. We need to see the value of what we are doing and sense that our lives are invested substantively, not wasted foolishly.

There is deep significance attached to lives invested in the pursuit of a noble vision. Do you have such a vision, a dream of your life as you would hope it would be someday? On August 28, 1963, a young preacher named Martin Luther King Jr. spoke on the steps of the Lincoln Memorial in Washington, D.C., about his dream and his vision, a dream that stirs me every time I hear it. The passion of his words comes through with vivid images of life the way he longed for it to be one day. Try to remember the fervor and moving cadence in his voice as you read a portion of what he said that day.[3]

I say to you today, my friends, so even though we face the difficulties of today and tomorrow, I still have a dream. It is a dream deeply rooted in the American dream.

I have a dream that one day this nation will rise up and live out the true meaning of its creed: "We hold these truths to be self-evident, that all men are created equal."

I have a dream that one day on the red hills of Georgia, the sons of former slaves and the sons of former slave owners will be able to sit down together at the table of brotherhood.

I have a dream that one day even the state of Mississippi, a state sweltering with the heat of injustice, sweltering with the heat of oppression, will be transformed into an oasis of freedom and justice.

I have a dream that my four little children will one day live in a nation where they will not be judged by the color of their skin but by the content of their character.

I have a dream today.

3. Dr. Martin Luther King Jr., "I Have a Dream" (address delivered at the March on Washington for Jobs and Freedom, Washington, D.C., August 28, 1963), http://www .stanford.edu/group/King//publications/speeches/address_at_march_on_washington .pdf. Accessed June 19, 2006.

I have a dream that one day, down in Alabama, with its vicious racists, with its governor having his lips dripping with the words of "interposition" and "nullification," one day right there in Alabama little black boys and black girls will be able to join hands with little white boys and white girls as sisters and brothers.

I have a dream today.

I have a dream that one day "every valley shall be exalted, and every hill and mountain shall be made low; the rough places will be made plain, and the crooked places will be made straight; and the glory of the Lord shall be revealed, and all flesh shall see it together."

This is our hope . . .

Let there be no doubt about it. A passionate vision can be a powerful, motivating force for good. When God is the author of that vision, how much more should our passions be ignited to seeing his vision for us become a living reality. God has plans for us. The Lord wants to reveal them to us and expand our vision, to enable us to dream dreams that see his perspective, to see what could be if we allowed him to work freely in and through his people. Every believer should be able to say with conviction and passion, "I have a dream!"

A passage in the book of Proverbs makes a bold statement about the need for a vision. The most memorable translation of Proverbs 29:18 is from the King James Version—"Where there is no vision, the people perish." The New American Standard Bible and the New International Version render the verse somewhat differently but no less powerfully: "Where there is no vision, the people are unrestrained" (NASB); "Where there is no revelation, the people cast off restraint" (NIV).

Four issues suggested by this verse address the importance of having a clear vision.

1. *People without a vision invite their own destruction.* If you see nothing but desperation in the future, no way to improve on current circumstances, a cloud settles over your heart. You lose your sense of purpose and ultimately conclude that life is meaningless. Why not cast off all

restraint and do whatever pleases you if you have no vision, no hope of life ever being any different than it is now?

2. *People without a vision have no measure for spiritual progress, making goals inconsequential, God's purposes irrelevant, and personal worth indiscernible.* How can you know you are making any progress if you have no way of seeing the goal or whether there is a goal? Goals become just busywork to occupy our time on earth if they do not advance the cause of a meaningful vision. Even our personal sense of worth gets lost without a vision, because we can justify nothing in our minds that explains to our satisfaction why we even exist.

3. *People without a vision see growth, change, and development as arbitrary and unintentional rather than an unfolding of a sovereign design.* Having no vision takes away our sense of direction, so any movement may just as well be backward as forward, since no reference points exist. All change becomes capricious, not connected to anything God might be doing.

4. *People without a vision see God's will as an enigma with no practical manifestations to reveal his plans and unveil his intentions.* Whether God has a will or not does not matter to a people without a vision. The mystery of what it might be loses its power to make us curious if we have no dream of ever living according to it when we discover it. The impact of this little verse can be devastating . . . if, in fact, there is no vision.

As the shepherd of the flock charged with leading your congregation, you have been placed by God in a position of strategic importance. Without leadership, the status quo becomes the vision.[4] Therefore, developing a vision falls to the pastor and his or her leadership team in order for the church to make progress in its calling to be made complete in Christ (Col. 1:28).

4. Allan Acker, Providence Equipping Center for Church Development, Advanced Leadership Training Curriculum, September 2002.

58

Many people talk about their dreams for their lives, while others have visions of what they think would be the ideal life, so it is important to have a frame of reference for determining whether our dreams and visions are from the Lord. What are the characteristics of a vision that the Lord has given versus a vision of our own imaginations?

The prophet Jeremiah had to answer this question when he confronted the false prophets who were leading the people to pursue false hopes and ungodly visions.

> Thus says the LORD of hosts, "Do not listen to the words of the prophets who are prophesying to you. They are leading you into futility; They speak a *vision of their own imagination*, not from the mouth of the LORD."
>
> Jeremiah 23:16, emphasis mine

In this chapter and the next, I outline some of the characteristics of visions that are from the Lord and visions that obviously are not. What a difference this will make in how you invest your life, whether you pursue God's vision or one of your own imagination!

How can you tell when your vision is not from the Lord? Following are several characteristics that apply. If you can place your vision alongside these characteristics and find frequent matches, you need to come out of the darkness of an ungodly vision and discover what the Lord has in store for you. As you work through this list, I pray that the Lord will either confirm your direction or confront it as he has done on many occasions in my own life and ministry.

A Vision *Not* from the Lord Will Be . . .

Full of Selfish Ambition

Even Christian leaders are susceptible to the temptation to pursue a course of action for less than noble and honorable purposes. Many churches have been begun, ministries established, and careers chosen based on purely ambitious motives.

I have seen churches started for the wrong reasons and others perpetuated for the wrong reasons. Some have started churches out of anger, after an escape from another church, because running was easier than reconciling. Some have started churches out of convenience, just to make it easier on the family by having a church closer to home. Others have started churches to be the biggest, the best, the fastest growing, and so forth. Some older congregations have no higher vision than to perpetuate a place where a few families remain in control in order to maintain a place for marrying, burying, and building a monument as a memorial to their family's benevolent heritage.

Likewise, I have seen pastors go to churches intent on building a reputation, establishing a track record, and then using their position as a "stepping stone" to satisfy their own personal ambitions to "move up" in ministry. A lot of ego can get involved. If pastors are not careful, they can do the right things for the wrong reasons and gain nothing of eternal significance in the process.

Several years ago, as Providence was experiencing some growing pains, I was reading through Revelation and came upon the following words: "To the angel of the church in Sardis write: These are the words of him who holds the seven spirits of God and the seven stars. I know your deeds; you have *a reputation of being alive, but you are dead*" (Rev. 3:1 NIV, emphasis mine).

I was struck at once by the ease with which we can fall into the trap of pursuing personal reputation or church reputation while missing the reality of living for Christ alone. You can become so consumed with preserving a reputation and building a following that nothing of the life of the Spirit empowers the dream anymore. Guard against building a dream and cultivating a vision filled with selfish ambition. It can happen to anyone, so be careful to guard your heart and walk humbly before the Lord as you seek his vision—not your own.

Futile in Its Direction

When you subject your dreams to careful scrutiny, you may find that you are spending massive amounts of time, energy, and resources on tangential directions that lead nowhere. It is easy to veer off course when we take our eyes off Christ, even for a moment. The scenery along the detours becomes so compelling that the entire journey gets diverted to a different destination. Instead of finding your dream, the one given to you by the Lord, you end up nowhere close to where you intended. What is worse, you do not even remember where or when your passion became just an interest, and your interest gave way to less strenuous pursuits, until finally you lost sight of what you originally envisioned as your dream.

The utter futility of a journey that strayed off course leaves many, in their later years, to ask themselves what they have to show for their lives. Fresh, enthusiastic leaders launch every year to begin dynamic, significant ministries, their eyes filled with the promises of a life well lived. Somewhere along the way, however, the wheels get knocked off, the cart goes in the ditch, and they never get back on the road again. Lots of road-side stands have been erected on side streets because once-passionate dreamers and visionaries found the main road to their dreams too tough and decided to settle for the place they landed when they last fell.

Don't settle for a "settled for" vision! No matter how long you've been traveling or how many years you think you have left, why not do whatever it takes to get it going again? Can you think of anything that would charge your batteries more than pulling your old vision out of mothballs and realizing that the Lord never revoked it, that it had no expiration date stamped on its side? What is the best use of your time over the remaining years of your life? If you have just gotten started, just think what you can accomplish by the grace of Christ in the power of the Spirit over the next forty-plus years! The middle years of ministry still offer significant potential for great and glorious things if your vision is God's vision. Even in your later years, it is never too late to crank it up a notch and get moving again. Don't think about how little energy you have left; think about how much time you've spent resting to get ready for the last leg of the race!

Look honestly at what is consuming you and ask yourself if this is what the Lord has equipped and called you to do. *Do* you have a dream, or *did* you have a dream? God wants his people to keep their vision fresh and current, not spin their wheels in futile efforts that go nowhere.

Compromising and Unprincipled

Many visions that appear to be noble and righteous prove to be empty shells because of the means chosen to reach their end. These visions get hollowed out: the cancer of expediency eats away the integrity of the vision by violating its very character. Can the end really justify the means? In the minds of many, the conclusion is yes. But when you dare to dream God's dream and see God's vision, the journey is as important as the destination. How you travel matters just as much as where you are going. The end cannot justify the means for those who seek to follow Christ.

Dishonest business dealings, fraudulent financial schemes, violent acts of murder, libelous and slanderous trashing of political opponents, deceptive words, misleading practices, venomous verbal attacks and unrestrained bitterness—all of these things have made the headlines during the past decade, describing the actions of those who profess to follow Christ. Excusing their ungodly behavior by pointing to the end they seek to achieve, imbalanced men and women have done much harm to the name and cause of Christ. Bombed federal buildings by right-wing groups, an abortionist murdered by a self-appointed executioner, public scams by "televangelists" on cable television, election-year mudslinging by Christian candidates who boldly lie about and misrepresent their opponents' records, tense battles in church board and business meetings where winning the vote becomes more important than yielding to Christ—have you not seen it happen?

When we choose to reach the goal by compromising the principles and the character of the one whom we claim to serve, the vision cannot be from the Lord. From beginning to end, God's vision includes a godly end as well as a godly means of moving forward.

Fueled by Competition and Result in Division

When a vision is not from the Lord, it is filled with competition and proves to be terribly divisive. The roots of competition will never yield the fruit of unity in the Spirit and glory for the Lord Jesus.

Something in the nature of American culture gives rise to the tendency to turn everything into a competition. Whether racing down the freeway, jockeying for position in the fast lane, promoting one child over another for a place in the best private schools, or trying to be the pastor of the biggest, best, or fastest-growing church, being number one dominates the vision in too many lives. For believers, this competitiveness tends to separate us and damage our testimony as the people of God.

When Cathy and I sensed the Lord's calling to begin a church several years ago, we were excited about what God was doing and assumed others who loved him would be just as excited. As I began to talk with people from leadership positions in established churches in our city about this newly formed congregation, I will never forget the vastly different responses of two pastors with whom I talked.

One rejoiced with me, saying, "If you and this new congregation can minister to even half of the new people in our area who are visiting our church and never coming back, you can build in our parking lot!" That pastor had a refreshing vision of what the church is all about and how important we are to one another in the body of Christ. However, it was with tears in my eyes and a lump in my throat that I sat across from another pastor who, with unrestrained anger in his voice and eyes, told me in no uncertain terms that no new church was needed in *his* area. He told me that all we would ever succeed in doing would be to steal people away from his church, people who were needed to pay for his new building. "This congregation brought me here to build a sanctuary, and every member who joins your church will be one less for us to bring in here to help pay for this new building." You may think that I am exaggerating to make a point, but that is actually what he said.

What a difference between one pastor who had a vision for building the kingdom of heaven and another who had a vision for paying for a church building! To one, we were reinforcements, to the other, we were competitors.

How do you see your vision? Is it going to complement the ministries that currently exist, or establish a spirit of competition with other churches and ministries? If you are already comparing yourself to others and measuring your vision and its anticipated successes against the work of others who labor in the same vineyard, something is amiss. The Lord wants to find clear motives and a pure vision in the hearts of his people. He does not want to see them working against one another in a divisive manner.

Established on Unstable Presuppositions

Any vision that begins with faulty assumptions cannot progress successfully. Like the parable Jesus told about the house built on the sand, unless the foundations of your vision are stable, there can be no stability in what you build. Ministry visions and dreams are particularly susceptible to this kind of problem. If the foundations are not biblically sound, neither can the vision nor the resulting ministry be.

We often rush ahead in pursuit of our dream without taking the time to evaluate the basic trustworthiness of our presuppositions—our foundation. This is especially true if we have heard them repeated with enough frequency that we accept them without question. When pastors and churches begin with the assumption that numerical growth is the only validation of effective ministry, for example, that presupposition can lead to compromise on important issues in order to attract people. Theological assumptions will give way to more practical and popular ones.

Some visions for ministry assume that by keeping a church small they can preserve the fellowship better than if the congregation expands. With that assumption in the back of the minds of their members, many pastors and leaders have been frustrated by efforts to thwart any attempt to reach new people. I remember one occasion when a member raised a question during a budget discussion for the coming church year. Why, it was asked, was there money in the budget for advertising when more people were coming than we wanted right now? The assumption behind the question was that smaller is better because comfort is better than sacrifice.

Between the assumptions of pastors who want to build mega-churches and members who want to keep churches small and comfortable, there is a balanced perspective on visions for ministry from the Lord. The balance builds on eternal principles rather than insubstantial presuppositions.

Prayerless and Self-Reliant

Does your dream depend upon prayer for its fulfillment? The Lord has given no vision, nor has he inspired any dream that can be realized without prayer. Never settle for any dream you can plot out and plan from beginning to end without any aspect of mystery. Dreams that require no walking by faith may be achievable, but they are unlikely to be expansive enough for the glory of the Lord to be made known through them.

Our natural tendency is to be pragmatic, to assess the potential for any dream's success on the basis of apparent resources. If you are in the habit of always counting the costs before taking action, a practice lauded by the Lord Jesus in one of his parables, you will likely find it difficult to launch out in pursuit of a dream that demands more faith than sight. There is nothing wrong with careful thinking and planning, as long as you do not resist when the Lord directs your steps in a way you cannot measure, calculate, or determine in advance.

The visions God blesses cannot be fulfilled apart from total dependency upon Christ. That dependency results in fervent, sometimes even desperate, prayer for the Lord to move on our behalf. Lofty dreams that inflame the heart are born out of prayer and grow to maturity in prayer. May the Lord increase our dependency on him and show us to our knees as we dream his dreams.

Pushing You Toward Unbalanced Spiritual Living

Last of all, when our dream or vision goes beyond what the Lord asks of us, our lives can get completely out of balance. When your dreams require you to forsake the necessary attention you should give to your daily walk with Christ, to your family responsibilities, to your physical well-being, you need to reevaluate what you are doing and why. God would not call you to commit yourself to pursue a life dream that cannot be realized without violating the basic responsibilities and commitments you have to make to follow Christ in all things. Pastors cannot forge an identity as a pastor without first making sure they are living up to their identity as a Christian.

Which of us has not been through this to some extent or another? We are so busy working for the Lord that we do not have any time to talk with him, to sit quietly and listen patiently for his voice. We are so wrapped up in meeting the next deadline that we neglect the most immediate field of ministry to which God has called us: our families. We are so consumed in helping the church reach some arbitrary goals that we do not engage in any significant interaction with our unbelieving neighbors, co-workers, and classmates. We are living out of balance when we are shooting for dreams that demand we forsake the fundamental issues involved in walking by the Spirit.

Opening Our Eyes

Having a dream does not enable you to reach your maximum potential unless that dream is from the Lord. Small ideas, petty pursuits, and ungodly endeavors stand in the way of God's best. You can never afford to run with your eyes closed to what he wants. Open your eyes and see what he has placed before you.

What confidence do you have that your life vision will come true? Without a sound foundation and the undergirding stability that a vision is from God, those who dream up exciting possibilities have no confidence that the Lord is committed to their dreams. Their steps become labored and uneven as they struggle with their balance, stumbling over the uncertain footing of an unstable course. They do nothing more than build castles on clouds, imaginary playhouses of the mind filled with "what ifs." Confidence and certain success come only with dreams and visions that have God as their designer.

How can you know the vision that has captured your heart and mind is from the Lord?

> "For I know the plans that I have for you," declares the LORD, "plans for welfare and not for calamity to give you a future and a hope. Then you will call upon Me and come and pray to Me, and I will listen to you. You will seek Me and find Me when you search for Me with all your heart."
>
> Jeremiah 29:11–13

When the Lord opens our eyes to his vision for our lives, this vision will always be consistent with the character of Jesus Christ. That is what you will find in your dreams when you search for him with your whole heart.

═══ 4 ═══

DEVELOPING A BALANCED VISION

WHEN GOD SHOWS THE WAY

In the previous chapter, I identified several characteristics of visions that are *not* from the Lord. Visions *from* the Lord have a number of traits in common as well.

A Vision *from* the Lord . . .

Is Consumed with Christ

Perhaps the surest and quickest test of the godly validity of your vision is to consider how sharply focused it is on Christ and how deeply rooted it is in his Word. Naturally, a vision that looks only occasionally to Christ and can take or leave what those passing glances reveal about him and his will may be consumed with a lot of things, but Jesus Christ is not one of them. When God authors the vision, central to every aspect of it will be the express image of the Father and his Son. Nothing else matters more than to know that where we are going, Christ is, that what we are doing, Christ honors, and that how we are doing it, Christ applauds. Simply put, Christ Jesus is our vision and must remain so even as the rest of the details unfold before us. Although the specifics will differ from person to person, this characteristic will always be the same in every vision God bestows.

How does the dream you want to see realized feed your passion for the knowledge of Christ? Since you've experienced the "surpassing value of knowing Christ," should not the vision for your life provide a variety of ways to make sure that you are growing in the knowledge and grace of the Lord (Phil. 3:8)? It should be one of your highest priorities to make sure the vision provides this. No passion should ever displace your passion for knowing more of Christ. A vision from the Lord will not give top billing to any other purpose.

Have you listened lately to all the competing visions being promoted for what the church ought to be doing? This week alone, I have heard it said that nothing is more important in our day than for the church to speak out against abortion and fight for legislation to outlaw it. Another voice declared that every church should enlist every member in voter registration efforts because the most important role is to promote righteous standards through elected officials, chosen through the vigorous labors of church members. Still another cried out for a greater passion for lost souls because the church exists solely for winning lost people to Jesus. How about one more? Churches should stay out of politics and legislating morality and get back to doing what they are supposed to be doing in the first place—feeding the hungry, caring for the needy, housing the homeless, clothing the naked, and ministering to the poor, oppressed, and victims of injustice.

Do you see what I mean? Is there anything wrong with any of these ideas about what the church should be engaged in doing? Hardly, for each of them arises from a diligent pursuit of its chief end: to glorify the Lord God and forsake all else that we might know Christ in all of his glory. The problem comes when these take the place of and supplant the consuming passion we must have to know Christ. Any vision that gains dominance over knowing Christ needs either to be forsaken or rearranged until first things are first. Until we actually "seek first His kingdom and His righteousness," all the other things that seem so significant at the time will prove to be our undoing (Matt. 6:33).

Integrates Personal Belief with Practical Living

When what we do contradicts what we say we believe, we are caught in a vice of our own creation. Visions given by the Lord are always fleshed out on the cutting edge of life by practical application. What you genuinely believe will determine what you do, and what you do will demonstrate what you believe. Your rhetoric may protest, the principles you espouse may argue the point, but in reality, if what you say you believe is not integrated into your life, you become a living contradiction.

Godly visions unfold with integrity throughout our lives. The connection between the words *integrity* and *integrate* should not be missed. Both are derived from Latin words that speak of "wholeness," or that which is intact and undivided.[1] An integrated life demonstrates wholeness and completeness as faith and practice link cohesively together, forming an undivided unit.

This kind of vision integrates biblical principles and demonstrates Christlikeness. Any time you find it necessary to lay aside biblical principles or do something contrary to the character of Christ to advance your cause, you compromise the validity and integrity of your vision. If, in the course of moving forward with your vision, you find that you entertain thoughts of unethical behavior, morally questionable actions, or the kinds of deeds described in the Scriptures as fleshly,[2] you need to ask

1. *Integrate*, the verb, is from the Latin *integrare*, meaning "to make whole, to renew." *Integrity*, the noun, is from the Latin *integritas*, meaning "whole."
2. "Now the deeds of the flesh are evident, which are: immorality, impurity, sensuality, idolatry, sorcery, enmities, strife, jealousy, outbursts of anger, disputes, dissensions, factions, envying, drunkenness, carousing, and things like these" (Gal. 5:19–21).

yourself, "Can the realization of this dream be so important that I have to act in a manner unworthy of Christ?"

Some years ago I attended a pastors' conference with a number of noted speakers. Since the conference was statewide, a large auditorium was rented for the occasion. The seating arrangements were more than adequate, but the rented sound system left much to be desired and proved to be quite a challenge for the person running the soundboard. As each speaker came to the platform, the soundman had to adjust for the differences in volume in their voices to avoid feedback through the system. As one of the speakers was several minutes into his message from the Scriptures, he turned in the middle of his comments and looked directly at the person working the soundboard and railed at him in front of the entire audience for bothering the sound levels while he was speaking. The humiliation the man must have felt at the cold, harsh treatment from the speaker was shared by everyone who witnessed the intimidating confrontation. I could not listen to anything else the speaker had to say. He had totally nullified his credibility as a spokesman for the Lord.

In my own ministry I have experienced the same thing because of careless, unkind, and thoughtless actions I have taken toward others. One evening I received a phone call from a good friend and church member. She asked me if I knew her neighbor and told me her name. The name was not familiar to me. She said that she had recently invited her friend to a special outreach event at church. In response to the invitation, she asked, "Is that the church where David Horner is pastor?" My friend said, "Oh yes, do you know him?" Her sobering reply came quickly. "No, and I will never go anywhere near any church he is a part of."

What could possibly have prompted such a violent reaction in this neighbor of my friend? We discovered that years ago, when we had put our house up for sale, this woman, a Realtor, had called me about the possibility of listing it. Although I could not remember talking with her, evidently she had called right about dinnertime when I had reached the end of my patience in dealing with callers with grace. In my hurry to dispatch her and return to my meal, I obviously was curt and rude in dismissing her call.

I never thought another thing about it. She never forgot it. I did not know who she was. She knew exactly who I was. What she could not bring together as a whole in her mind was how a man could represent the love of Christ in the pulpit on Sunday mornings and then treat someone with such disdain during the week. In me, this poor woman had seen a blatant lack of integrity, a flagrant violation of everything I said I believed, and an inexcusable failure to integrate my words with my actions.

Immediately after hanging up with my friend, I called her neighbor and apologized profusely for what I had done. The Realtor was gracious and somewhat embarrassed, and she thanked me for calling. But I knew that the damage had been done because I had not lived out what I said I believed. Think of how easily that can happen to you in incidents that pass by without so much as a thought or a care. If our vision for living as wholly devoted disciples of Jesus Christ has come from him, we will develop a growing sensitivity to the ways he wants to see his character shine through us as we walk his way.

Is Clear of Ungodly Influences

To keep the vision clear of obstruction, we need to be certain we have removed any barriers that stand in the way. Circumstances beyond our control that arise as we go cannot be helped. However, when we know that areas of sin in our own lives are impeding our progress, we proceed at our own risk if we do not stop and deal with them. Only by confessing our sin and laying aside all unworthy goals, dreams, and motives can we hope to clear the way for God's vision to come true in our lives.

When a vision for ministry originates in division or broken relationships, it cannot succeed in bringing glory to God. The American landscape is dotted with churches started out of anger and unforgiveness. The mathematical principle behind these groups supports the idea that the best way to multiply is to divide, but where is the passion to see Jesus Christ exalted? Is your vision in reaction to something or someone other than the calling of God? If it is, until it has been purified and cleansed of those ungodly influences, your vision cannot enjoy the favor of the Lord. When conflict is unresolved and relationships are unreconciled, you can change churches as often as you like, but you will never be free to pursue God's best for your life until you go and try to be restored to your enemy. Too many pastors get mad and then get out, leaving in their wake a path of pain and a trail of bitterness that follow and disable them wherever they go until they are ready to take Christ at his word: "Leave your offering there before the altar, and go; first be reconciled to your brother, and then come and present your offering" (Matt. 5:24).

Do not hesitate to do whatever the Lord shows you to do to make sure that your vision is free and clear of all obstructions and remnants of ungodliness. Only then will you clearly see all that he has placed before you.

What happens when you make allowances for personal failures and irresponsibility within the scope of your dream? You will settle for an unworthy vision. When that happens, your aspirations will be shaped by what you expect to be the realistic outcome of your efforts. You will in all likelihood continue to tolerate low standards of holiness, limited levels of spiritual authority and power, and a *laissez-faire* approach to life. Why spend your life on an unworthy vision? Make no allowances for anything less than God's best so that the holiness suitable for his house will also mark your vision as suited for his glory.

Advances the Gospel

Many churches are dying today because they are pursuing a vision that neglects proclaiming Christ. Unless there is a persistent effort to proclaim Christ that involves the entire body of believers, a church cannot and will not fulfill God's vision. His vision for our lives always includes our commission to be his witnesses—nothing less will do!

Granted, many in the church have bought into a one-dimensional approach to evangelism that sees only the full presentation of the gospel outline to someone as *real* witnessing.

73

God's approach is much broader, much more inclusive. When Christ told his disciples, "You will receive power when the Holy Spirit has come upon you; and you shall be My witnesses,"[3] he included not only his immediate audience but all of us who belong to him (Acts 1:8). His intentions are in no way unclear. He wants all of us to share in the process of presenting Christ, integrating our witness into the entire fabric of our lives as opposed to something that we periodically go out and do. God's vision for the church and for those who lead it will always include the ministry of evangelism.

What is there about your vision for ministry that incorporates this mandate for evangelism? It may not be a central feature or play a dominant role, but if your vision has come from the Lord of the harvest, it will include something that expresses his heart for people who still do not know him. My own vision for ministry primarily has to do with equipping, not evangelizing. Yet if I am to understand my vision in full balance as God wants it to be, part of my commitment to equipping will always include training and preparing and teaching other believers how they can be actively involved in being witnesses for Jesus Christ. Anything less than that throws my vision out of balance and out of line with what the Lord has committed himself to do through his people.

Bears Godly Fruit

When the Lord gives the vision, he is responsible for bearing the fruit if we pursue his vision in faithfulness. God's best fruit is not always visible to the human eye because it is not easily quantifiable by large numbers or big successes. He wants to produce in us and through us the character of Jesus Christ and to reproduce in us the blessed fruit of the Spirit. Our success in the achievement of our goals, in the realization of dreams, and the fulfillment of visions will always be measured according to heaven's standards, not earth's.

3. Since the Holy Spirit comes upon and dwells in every believer, the conclusion that he addresses all believers when he says we shall be his witnesses is fully supported by this and many other texts.

One missionary I met years ago had labored in a Muslim country for fifteen to twenty years with very little outward success to show for his efforts. Because of the lack of apparent success, some would question whether his vision to remain in that land for so long could have been from the Lord. No such question concerned this godly man who had seen the powerful hand of the Lord building bridges and opening eyes and ears to the gospel through his steadfast love for the people and his unwavering devotion to his Savior, both in proclamation and personal devotion. The fruit God was bearing through this faithful witness was not visible to human eyes. Nevertheless, God honored the steadfast labors of this trooper for Christ.

To this day, when I think of godliness, Christlike character, and what it means to be a man of prayer, I think of this humble missionary who learned Christ in the crucible of what many would call an "unfruitful" place of service. I believe that the Lord would testify to the abundance of his fruit, demonstrated in the life of this dear brother!

However, although the fruit may not be immediately visible, whatever fruit God produces is always genuine. Knowing that bearing fruit authenticates a God-given vision as nothing else can, the temptation to "manufacture fruit" is sometimes too great to resist. As difficult as it might be to believe, some pastors have sold out their integrity to justify what they are doing in their ministries. Over the years, I have heard reports of, and actually heard with my own ears, highly inflated testimonies of the effectiveness of certain ministries. Unfortunately, numbers can be manufactured or manipulated to tell different kinds of stories. Whether the numbers have to do with attendance figures, budgets, numbers of converts, size and capacity of buildings, or something else, some pastors are inclined to lie in order to build popular support for the notion that their vision is obviously ordained by the Lord. Pride and ego, competition and comparison, compel people to do strange things! But since the evidence of numerical fruit seems to be "an industry standard" for checking the validity of a vision, abuse is inevitable in a fallen world. Pastors can fall victim to their own ambition and need for approval and success, and these things really do happen.

All of that is to say, be forewarned. You can be tempted, both to believe some of the stories you hear and to invent some of your own to make your vision look better in the eyes of others. Let the Lord bear the fruit and then give him the glory. It really is that simple. When he is the author of the vision, he knows what kind of fruit he wants to bear, and he alone is responsible for producing it. You are only called to be faithful in doing what he wants you to do. Guard your heart against desiring anything else but abiding in him and bearing much fruit as he works within you. God's vision is validated and authenticated when fruit is born in his name and for his glory.

Draws Widespread Support

When a vision has the fingerprints of the Lord on it, it will be a vision that is much larger than any one of us can hope to fulfill. God's visions for his people are profound enough and expansive enough that they attract numbers of people to work together, cooperating in the power of the Holy Spirit to see his plan accomplished.

Of course, there are exceptions to that premise. Some dreams may seem small but from God's perspective they capture a particular passion on his heart. He gives some a vision and a desire to labor anonymously among unreached people groups that cannot even be named for fear of jeopardizing the work. Others have been called to less visible places than others and do not find widespread support, or even notice, for what they are doing. I firmly believe that some of God's choice saints will never enjoy recognition and acknowledgement for their labors. The only widespread support their godly dreams will draw may come from unexpected sources. Behind the scenes, there will be unknown prayer warriors, discreet financial underwriters, and others whose part we would not understand even if their roles were revealed. God alone knows the size and shape of the team needed to accomplish the visions he gives. So do not be afraid to share your dreams, whatever the scope. That way the Lord can surprise you with what he can do to get others involved in seeing a godly vision realized.

Dreams from the Lord can demand strong people with a capacity to share, to delegate, to enlist, and to broadcast the vision far and wide. The Lord can even give you a vision for how you can support a broad vision articulated by someone else. When Bill Bright founded Campus Crusade with a vision for what he thought the Lord wanted done, he spread the news and had no problems asking for the best and brightest to join him in the pursuit. James Dobson's vision for godly families has enjoyed enormous response, as many are drawn together to pursue a common dream. Billy Graham's crusade ministry has succeeded in bringing diverse and powerful people together in the common pursuit of proclaiming the gospel.

Churches like the ones you and I pastor all over the world are declaring that we are in pursuit of God's will and long to do what pleases him in all things. In our congregation, we have announced his vision unashamedly to glorify Christ through the means of worship, evangelism, and edification, and many have joined with us in that awesome task.[4] God's vision will always be broad and profound in the depth of its appeal to people who want to be associated with what the Lord is doing.[5]

Extends Beyond Human Limitations

Frankly speaking, if your vision can be laid out like a business plan with carefully devised steps to be followed and all the variables explained and accounted for, there is probably not much use trying to attribute such a plan to the Lord. Any vision that can be outlined and defined in human terms and achieved through human effort takes no faith and therefore leaves God out entirely. I realize how that might sound, and no, I am not

4. For further discussion on the principles of how Providence was founded, see David Horner, *Firmly Rooted, Faithfully Growing* (Raleigh, NC: Providence Communications, 2003).

5. The strong appeal of Henry Blackaby's book *Experiencing God* seems to be found in one of its basic principles—that we are to find out where God is at work and then get in on it: "He is presently at work in our world. Because of His love He wants us to have the privilege of working with Him as His ambassadors." Henry Blackaby, *Experiencing God: How to Live the Full Adventure of Knowing and Doing the Will of God* (Nashville: Broadman, 1994), 42.

saying you should not plan and do all that you can to prepare and execute a reasonable strategy. But if that is all there is . . . let me tell you, there is so much more to a vision that has been authored by God!

Not everything God calls on us to do requires seas to part down the middle and stones to roll away, but anything we can do without having to trust him for its ultimate success does not sound much like a vision he would give. A vision with God as its author will always extend us beyond our capacities and throw us into absolute dependence upon the sufficiency of the Lord.

When God gives a vision, it will always be proportionate to the majesty of God. The heat from a fire is often directly related to the size of the flame and the nature of its fuel. The brightness of the light from a bulb is proportional to its wattage. The height of a person most often is related to the size of his or her parents. So it should be easy to understand that if a vision has little of the majestic splendor of the Lord in it, if it does not aspire to holy and glorious purposes, if it is not anchored in eternal truth—then its divine origin is suspect.

If our vision as pastors is only to be a *little* more spiritually minded and a *little* less sinful than the world around us and a *little* less ambitious than the pagan junior executive, we may well succeed, and in so doing prove to know nothing of a vision from the Lord. If our vision is to keep from becoming fanatical about walking with Christ, careful not to become too concerned about being distinguished as holy unto the Lord, once again we may progress toward such shallow dreams but never know the glory of living in his way.

If a sprinter was content with a thirteen-second one-hundred-yard dash, a baseball player with a batting average of .125, a basketball player with a 25 percent free-throw percentage, we'd be unimpressed with their vision, their drive, their desire to do their best. If that was the very best they could do in proportion to their talent, then so be it. But if they were gifted athletes with unusual ability, such goals would be a tragic waste of ability! When we settle for spiritual dreams and visions disproportional

78

to the majesty and glory and power of the God who called us, we can be sure that our vision is not from the Lord.

When a vision is from the Lord, no amount of planning and pleading and plotting will substitute for well-invested hours in prayer. A vision promoted through the most sophisticated media can never equal tireless intercession before the throne of God. When we have God's vision, we will also have a firm conviction that nothing but prayer will do in seeing that vision become a reality.

In the nineteenth century, George Müller operated with the distinctive conviction that in his ministry to orphans in Bristol, England, he would tell no one of the needs of that ministry except the Lord, and then only in private prayer.[6] God heard and answered those prayers! Others combine faithful prayer with humble communication of needs, and God honors that as well. Many ministries send out prayer letters faithfully to inform their prayer support teams of specific needs. In our own church, we have an intercessory prayer ministry committed to praying for the multitude of requests that come in every week, and we rejoice together when the Lord answers those prayers. We also have a senior pastor prayer team praying for me every day so that the Lord will work in my life to see his vision accomplished in and through me. One sure characteristic of a godly vision is that it will always be promoted through a posture of persistent prayer.

A Closing Comment

A clear vision of where you are going significantly improves your chances of getting there. Foggy windows and clouded sight do not make for substantial progress in anything that matters. But with the end in mind, and perhaps even in sight in some cases, the steps you need to take to get where you are going become clearer much more quickly.

6. See the chapter entitled "Learning to Live by Faith" in George Müller, *The Autobiography of George Müller* (New Kensington, PA: Whitaker House, 1985).

Just a few months ago, I had temporarily lost my balance because the focus of my vision from the Lord had lost some of its sharpness. Tasks that had nothing to do with the vision were consuming vast amounts of my time and energy for no good reason. Instead of recognizing the source of the problem, taking my eyes off of the vision God had given, I was busy trying to correct the symptoms—adjusting my schedule, trying to find more efficient ways to accomplish mundane duties, looking for jobs to delegate to others, and so on. What I really needed was to lift up my eyes, see once again what God wants me to do with my life, and then watch in amazement as the balance came back, the steps toward the fulfillment of the vision became apparent, and what I needed to do suddenly made sense. A balanced vision allows you to weed out the trivial and the time-consuming matters that clutter your life and throw you out of balance. It is so refreshing to have that kind of clarity from the Lord. When I have it I'm able to say no without guilt to a multitude of things that could be my undoing.

When the dream you have matches the dream God has, you have the assurance of his companionship along the way. You also have his resources to equip you in reaching the vision of his own creation, uniquely suited for you and especially honoring to him. Define your dream. Clarify your vision.[7] Then you

---

7. Sometimes the vision God gives you seems to stall. You know it is from him, but obstacles arise at every point, preventing the fulfillment of your vision. It does not make sense to you that the Lord would let you see such a wonderful vision of what he wants and then apparently hold you back from enjoying its fulfillment. Selwyn Hughes, a pastor in and around London for many years, made this astute observation that might help you see that the Lord is up to something far greater than just the achievement of a vision.

Usually, the next step after catching a vision is to see it die. There is a special reason for this: our vision often contains a combination of godly concerns and human perspectives, so God has to engineer a way whereby the godly concerns remain and the human perspectives are changed to divine perspectives. His way of doing this is to cause the vision to die. . . .

Why, we ask, does God bring a vision to birth and then allow it to die? For this reason: the waiting time in which we find ourselves during the death of a vision is God's classroom for the development of godly character in us. It is in the waiting time, as the vision "dies," that such qualities as patience, persistence,

will enjoy the freedom and the stability of ministry as never before—balanced, focused, effective ministry for the glory of Christ!

---

perseverance and self-control are built into us. Has God given you in the past a vision of something that you knew was definitely from Him—but now the vision has died? Then don't be discouraged. This is the way God works. He is using the waiting time to change your ideas to His ideas and your perspectives to His perspectives. . . .

An important thing to remember is that Satan is extremely operative at this time, for his purpose is to get you to fulfill the vision by your own human effort. And whenever you do this, you will finish up in conflict.

What happens when God causes our vision to "die" and His purpose of building into us the characteristics of Christ have been achieved? This: He then resurrects the vision and brings it to joyous fulfillment. His purpose in doing this is not just to fulfill the vision, but to do so in a way that points to His supernatural intervention. In that way no onlooker can be in any doubt as to whose power lies behind the success of the ministry—everyone will recognize it to be God. (Selwyn Hughes, *Every Day Light* [Nashville: Broadman & Holman, 1997], 277–79.)

PART 3

GAINING BALANCE
BY BUILDING TEAMS

5

MORE SHOULDERS, LIGHTER LOADS

GOD'S DESIGN FOR TEAM MINISTRY

There is strength in numbers. When we are joined by like-minded people, we find much-needed strength when others put their backs to the load, much-needed encouragement when we fall down, and much-needed security when threatened by outside forces. These passages in Ecclesiastes and Proverbs are representative of many others:

> Furthermore, if two lie down together they keep warm, but how can one be warm *alone?* And if one can overpower him who is alone, two can resist him. A cord of three *strands* is not quickly torn apart.
>
> Ecclesiastes 4:11–12

> Without consultation, plans are frustrated, but with many counselors they succeed.
>
> Proverbs 15:22

Having help brings strength to any aspect of the ministry God has given you. God calls you to accept his co-workers with a grateful heart, knowing that he has prepared them for the work of ministry just as surely as he has prepared you. Team ministry means you never have to be alone in the work of the Lord.

A Biblical Example

Exodus 18 records a fascinating account of a life-changing conversation Moses had with his father-in-law, Jethro, when he came for a visit. Jethro was delighted with all the Lord had done for Israel and saw the blessings firsthand as he wandered around the camp and talked to the people. The next day, Moses got up and went to work. All day long he listened to the complaints and disputes of the people. After watching this tedious, draining process unfold, Jethro approached Moses. The advice he gave Moses can change any pastor's life:

> Now when Moses' father-in-law saw all that he was doing for the people, he said, "What is this thing that you are doing for the people? Why do you alone sit *as judge* and all the people stand about you from morning until evening?" Moses said to his father-in-law, "Because the people come to me to inquire of God. When they have a dispute, it comes to me, and I judge between a man and his neighbor and make known the statutes of God and His laws." Moses' father-in-law said to him, "The thing that you are doing is not good. You will surely wear out, both yourself and these people who are with you, for the task is too heavy for you; you cannot do it alone. Now listen to me: I will give you counsel, and God be with you. You be the people's representative before God, and you bring the disputes to God, then teach them the statutes and the laws, and make known to them the way in which they are to walk and the work they are to do. Furthermore, you shall select out of all the people able men who fear God, men of truth, those who hate dishonest gain; and you shall place *these* over them *as* leaders of thousands, of hundreds, of fifties and of tens. Let them judge the people at all times; and let it be that every major dispute they will bring to you, but every minor dispute they themselves will judge. So it will be easier for you, and

they will bear *the burden* with you. If you do this thing and God *so* commands you, then you will be able to endure, and all these people also will go to their place in peace." So Moses listened to his father-in-law and did all that he had said.

Exodus 18:14–24

From this incident alone, you find two clear consequences of a solo approach to ministry: it wears the people out and it wears you out. A third consequence also becomes obvious as you think about the impact this approach would have on any expansive vision of what God would have you pursue. A solo approach actually restricts the growth of the ministry, limiting it to only those things that can pass through you.

Going It Alone Wears the People Out

In my first few years as a pastor, carrying a pocket calendar filled with appointments made me feel important, needed, and in a strange way like I was a "real pastor." The heady experience of pulling out my weekly schedule and checking for the availability of openings in my schedule made me feel perversely impressive to those who'd come after worship services to see when they could get together with me. The thrill of that didn't last long before it was replaced by a growing sense of frustration, on my part as well as theirs, when the times available were no longer in just a few days, but in a few weeks. I could imagine them thinking, "What kind of pastor are you if you are not around when I need you?" as they walked away disappointed. That does not have to happen too many times before you send the wrong message to the folks you are called to serve. They get worn out waiting for you and will seek alternatives that can meet their needs.

But what if there were team members prepared to step up and assume responsibility for meeting with many of the people who do not really need *you* at all? Jethro suggested a plan that made so much sense that Moses must have felt foolish for not coming up with it himself. The best option for the Israelites was certainly not standing in line all day waiting for their turn with Moses. God had in mind something far better—training and delegating the work of ministry to many others who could effectively accomplish more than was ever possible if Moses had remained stuck bearing the burden alone.

Wearing people out is no good for their spiritual health. Waiting forever for one shot at the "head guy" seems to appeal to some people, so I am sure that Moses and the elders of Israel faced significant opposition when the plan was initially put in place. I can hear the protests now, "I don't want to talk to his assistant. I have to see Moses; it is him or nobody! What do you mean he can't see me today? This is an emergency. He is the only one who can help me."

I'm sure you've heard similar comments, suffered the same kind of guilt, endured the same kind of manipulation, and worried about how indispensable you are to the survival of the kingdom of God. Take it from one who's been there—you cannot possibly meet with every person, accommodate every schedule, offer workable solutions, or render acceptable judgments to all who demand that you do.

Going It Alone Wears You Out

Can you picture Moses looking to see if there was a break in the line somewhere, a moment of relief from the steady stream of hurting, troubled people appealing to him for his best wisdom and judgment? Jethro understood: "You are going to wear yourself out if you don't get some help around here! This is absurd and profitable for no one." How much easier the load would have been had Moses had that counsel from Jethro before the daylong sessions were consuming him! I want to be your Jethro, if no one else has taken that role. If you are trying to do it all by yourself, "what you are doing is not good."

God's plans work when we trust him and put them into practice. So form a team and share the load, just as Moses did.

Going It Alone Restricts Growth

Bottlenecks always slow things down. If you require that everything be channeled through you, you will personally impede

88

the flow of the Spirit in your congregation. Any vision for a church that can be effectively accomplished by only what you can do is not likely to be a vision worthy of the body of Christ. The church needs a vision that utilizes all of its members exercising all of their gifts. If your vision can be accomplished without a functioning team, something is not right. God wants unrestricted freedom to grow his church by using all the resources he has made available.

Why go it alone when God has surely called you to something far greater?

New Testament Leadership

In the New Testament, perhaps the most specific passage outlining the practical significance of team ministry is found in Ephesians 4.

> But speaking the truth in love, we are to grow up in all *aspects* into Him who is the head, *even* Christ, from whom the whole body, being fitted and held together by what *every joint supplies*, according to the proper working of *each individual part*, causes the growth of the body for the building up of itself in love.
>
> Ephesians 4:15–16, emphasis mine

There was no doubt in Paul's mind as he wrote these words that ministry was intended to be shared by everyone in the entire congregation. There was to be a place of ministry for every person.

In the churches of the New Testament, there were usually two offices represented, deacons and elders. Elders (*presbuteroi*) are also called bishops or overseers (*episkopoi*) and are occasionally referred to in their shepherding function as pastors (*poimaines*). All three names are used with reference to the leaders of the church at Ephesus: "From Miletus he sent to Ephesus and called to him the elders of the church . . . be on guard for yourselves and for all the flock, among which the Holy Spirit has made you overseers, to shepherd the church of God which He purchased with His own blood" (Acts 20:17, 28). In addition, within those two offices, more than one person was selected to serve in the appointments and selections described in the Scriptures.

In an era when many churches have a single leader, a pastor, it is refreshing to note that the New Testament model always had multiple leaders. The word "elders" always appears in its plural form when referring to their appointment in the various churches in the book of Acts. That there was more than one elder in each church suggests that the concept of team ministry is hardly a modern innovation.

Not all of the elders had to be equal. As a matter of fact, Paul specified that those who ruled and those who worked hard at preaching and teaching were to be considered worthy of double honor (1 Tim. 5:17). But within the group of elders, their plurality guarded against a single ruler or an autocratic type of leadership taking over a congregation. Multiple leaders serve as a check and balance to avoid what Peter warns against, an abuse of the authority granted to the elders. He exhorts the elders by saying,

> Shepherd the flock of God among you, exercising oversight not under compulsion, but voluntarily, according to the will of God; and not for sordid gain, but with eagerness; nor yet as lording it over those allotted to your charge, but proving to be examples to the flock.
>
> 1 Peter 5:2–3

Unfortunately, the practice of "lording it over" the flock is so often a part of the corrupting influence of having authority that Peter felt he had to issue this special challenge. But to protect the body further, the Lord established a plurality of godly leaders who hold each other accountable to be servant leaders.

When a church, or any other ministry, builds its work on one person, it cannot ultimately succeed because it is human-centered, rather than Christ-centered. Shared ministry protects both the church and its leaders, and as its pastor, you should welcome the opportunity to work together with a team of godly leaders.

A Present-Day Realization

Looking back, I can see how Moses, Paul, and the leaders in the early church profited from the practice of shared ministry and team leadership. The members of the team got to make contributions in keeping with their abilities and gifts.

Do you recognize what you do well? You probably have a good idea of your ministry strengths. It is equally important to recognize what you do not do very well.

Crisis ministry for me is always a double crisis, one for the people directly impacted by the crisis and one for me personally, since I do not handle such situations very well. The church I pastor began with very young families twenty-nine years ago, meaning that hospital visitation and regular funerals did not characterize my ministry at all. Seldom did I even go to the hospital with the exception of those happy occasions of welcoming new babies into the world.

As the church grew, so did the needs of the congregation. Not only were older families becoming members, but all of us younger families were starting to get older too. As the number of people increased, the number of crises rose proportionally, often leaving me bewildered and completely helpless to know what to do. I remember some cases when I was certain that I needed more help dealing with my grief than the family members did.

Did I need to find another place of ministry, where presumably people did not have needs, where folks never got sick and died, never had car accidents and were killed, never suffered the loss of small children to rare diseases? You can see how ludicrous that question is. The issue was not whether I needed to get out of there, but whether God had not foreseen the need and already provided the solution. I soon realized that there were gifted people already in the congregation who not only were excellent caregivers, but who loved doing it.

If we will let him, the Lord wants to raise up a team of people in our congregations to complete the work of the ministry. Granted, there are some multi-gifted pastors who can do it all, but even they need to share the joys of ministry with others God

91

has called to help fulfill the vision of that particular church. As the years have gone by, I have grown more convinced than ever that this is the way God intends ministry to be done. I came to this conclusion not by more study or the discovery of more supportive scriptural evidence, but by watching gifted members doing things I never thought possible and enjoying the fruits of their labors firsthand.

Reasons Pastors Go It Alone

After years of seeing the biblical basis for team ministry work, my question for many pastors is just this: "God has given you so much help, and the tasks are so insurmountable by yourself. Why would you ever want to go it alone?"

There are several reasons why we pastors sometimes try to go it alone.

1. *Limited vision.* If a pastor's vision is so limited it needs only one person to reach it, then that pastor actually may not need anyone to come alongside to be a part of the team. Pastors with this limited vision need to lift their sights and see a broader, more excellent way to spend their days than just doing something they can do by themselves.

2. *Insecurity.* Pastors are certainly not alone in their insecurities; most people are insecure in one way or another. But when that insecurity impacts their willingness to share ministry with others, pastors have a problem! Usually the source of the insecurity is the fear that someone will do the tasks of ministry better than him or her or that others will realize that he or she might not be as irreplaceable as he or she may have wanted them to think. But is that not just a self-fulfilling prophecy, to not allow anyone else to do anything and then complain that all will fall apart without you? Believe me, God has a better way!

3. *Impatience.* The trend among pastors these days is to approach ministry in blitzkrieg fashion, zooming into a local church, dropping their bombs (ministry ideas, programs, sermon package, etc.), and then getting out of there before the flak starts. We are masters at putting a spiritual spin on that

scenario, never admitting that moving on can be just an excuse to avoid long-term commitments to team ministry. If you knew you wouldn't be at a church for very long, would you take the time to invest in the kinds of relationships needed for building a team?

Those who are looking for immediate results will find that the process of working with a few people initially, establishing a vision, cultivating trust, and observing gifts and levels of faithfulness takes too much effort with too little to show for it. Making a big splash with high-impact programs does not require as much patience, and it seals your reputation as a growth-oriented pastor capable of producing the much-sought-after numbers.

Pastors who ignore biblical principles and adopt the "blitz-krieg approach" leave people out who are essential to the construction of a team that will last over the long haul. One pastor friend of mine even recommends taking the first couple of years and investing nearly all of your time (outside the teaching and preaching ministry) in building a group of leaders. For pastors intent on staying only for two to three years, of course, this does not compute. Impatience will not allow it; therefore, the team never gets established and the Lone Ranger rides again!

4. People problems. Teams bring people together. If there are people problems in your church, the thought of intentionally choosing to build a team sounds like borrowing trouble! The problem may reside in the pastor who may be, how shall we say it, "relationally challenged"? If the pastor does not relate very well to others, the idea of being a part of, much less leading, a team has no appeal whatsoever. Poor communication skills, an inability to trust others, resistance to ideas that do not originate with them, extreme introversion, a controlling personality—all of these will cause solo pastors to do whatever they can to keep out of prolonged association with people they have to count on if they get into team ministry.

5. Priorities. Ironically, pastors often work solo simply because they cannot get their priorities in order. They never get around to putting the solution in place because they are so busy handling the urgent daily demands on their time. They think about building their team all the time but never do anything about it because of misplaced priorities. The last thing they want is to go it alone. But they cannot break the pattern that has trapped them, so their frustration continues.

6. *Ignorance*. Ignorance can be remedied. Choosing to remain ignorant once you recognize your problem cannot be excused. If you do not know how to develop a team, or what one looks like in a church context, you might be surprised to learn that there are folks in your church who have been fairly successful in team building in the business world, or with sports, or even under your nose in one of the ministries right there in your own town. Most of them would be honored if you asked for their help.

7. *Past failures*. "I tried that 'team thing' in one of my first pastorates, and it bombed. I vowed never to make that mistake again!" What can I say but the obvious? So it failed—try again. If team ministry is God's idea, and I believe it is, then you simply cannot give up on it. For some reason, people in ministry do not think the old adage applies to them: "If at first you don't succeed, try, try again."

Every Member Is a Minister

When the church is described as a body in Romans 12 and 1 Corinthians 12, it is one body consisting of many parts, each necessary for the proper function of the whole. None can be viewed as unimportant or inconsequential, because the parts are inseparably linked together through their connection to the head of the body, Christ himself (see Eph. 1:22; 4:15). Each part is equipped to function so that the church accomplishes the purposes for which the Lord has set it apart. No one can legitimately abdicate and shift responsibility to others without damaging the overall effectiveness of the ministry of the body.

When a small percentage of the body labors to do a large percentage of the ministry, the plan and purpose of Christ for his body is compromised. In subtle ways, the church has historically encouraged the idea that there are some who hold special claim to the title "minister." But the New Testament teaches that *every member is a minister.* The term should never be limited to one particular group of ministers who are perhaps more appropriately called pastors.

It follows that if every member is a minister, every member has a ministry. The body of Christ will never know how great its potential ministry effectiveness can be until all its members are functioning in their own areas of ministry.

Pastor as Equipper

What about your role as pastor? Two significant verses have shaped my understanding of that role, each having to do with equipping. If all the members are expected to be involved in active ministry with me so we function as a team, my calling is to make sure they are equipped to do what God has called them to do. The Holy Spirit gives them gifts and calls them to areas of ministry suited to the exercise of those gifts. As a pastor, you must make it your constant duty to see that all are prepared for the work of their ministry.

The following verses describe with clarity both what a pastor is to do and how he or she is to do it. As a pastor/teacher (according to Eph. 4:11), you are called with a particular responsibility: "for the *equipping* of the saints for the work of service, to the building up of the body of Christ" (Eph. 4:12, emphasis mine). The companion verse that specifies how that is to be done is found in 2 Timothy: "All Scripture is inspired by God and profitable for teaching, for reproof, for correction, for training in righteousness; so that the man of God may be adequate, *equipped* for every good work" (2 Tim. 3:16–17, emphasis mine). The pastor's priority of equipping his or her flock relies upon the sufficiency of Christ through his Word.

In his challenge to Timothy, Paul wrote, "The things which you have heard from me in the presence of many witnesses, entrust these to faithful men who will be able to teach others also" (2 Tim. 2:2). The legacy a pastor should leave behind is a band of men and women who have been trained and equipped to embrace opportunities to carry on the ministry from generation to generation.

The vision for rebuilding the walls of Jerusalem came to Nehemiah along with a commission from the Lord to trust him and take the job. Many leadership books have been written using Nehemiah's strategy as an example of how to mobilize people for ministry. He knew how to divide the tasks, select good leaders under him, and motivate and engage large numbers of people for the work, and together they accomplished the goal of rebuilding the walls of the neglected city of Jerusalem. He said to the people of the city, "You see the bad situation we are in, that Jerusalem is desolate and its gates burned by fire. Come, let us rebuild the wall of Jerusalem so that we will no longer be a reproach," to which the people replied, "Let us arise and build" (Neh. 2:17–18). Nehemiah never attempted to do the job himself but actively took on the task, trusting God to provide all the resources, both the physical materials needed and the human laborers required. Getting others involved in doing the work was the key to his eventual success. Throughout the Scriptures, God shows us a consistent pattern of leadership that provides a place for everyone to contribute to get the job done.

The Qualities of Godly Leaders

Godly leaders should reflect the character of Christ. In 1 Timothy and Titus, an impressive list of character traits (though in neither place does it appear to be exhaustive) makes it clear that the Lord wants the integrity of his name upheld by those who accept his call to lead his people. When you find leaders whose lives demonstrate the character of Christ, ministering with them can be a great joy.

Selecting leaders of this caliber always presents a challenge. Inevitably, you will find that some of the leaders suggested or approved by others fall far short of what you believe to be in the best interests of the church. The process by which leaders are selected remains one of the biggest points of contention in many churches. Teaching your congregation the importance of maintaining biblical standards for leadership will pay tremendous dividends both for you and for those who come after you. One responsibility you cannot afford to yield is that of holding high standards for leadership positions. You must instill the importance of careful scrutiny of the candidates in those charged with the selection process.

In his instructions to Timothy on selecting elders and deacons, Paul said, "[Let them] first be tested; then let them serve as deacons if they are beyond reproach. . . . Do not lay hands upon anyone too hastily and thereby share responsibility for the sins of others" (1 Tim. 3:10; 5:22).

What criteria should you use for determining whether someone is ready to serve in leadership, and in which capacity of leadership? Certainly there are folks who can be plugged in immediately at less critical positions so you can watch for their servanthood and faithfulness and spiritual maturity. Others will be ready to assume more responsible positions. But for the offices of deacons and elders, the biblical standards cannot be ignored without great peril to the spiritual vitality of the church and the much-needed balance of your own life and ministry. You may want to develop your own list of nonnegotiable character traits for your teammates in ministry, but here are a few that warrant consideration:

- the character traits of 1 Timothy 3:1–13 and Titus 1:5–9
- evidence of a shared vision and common values for the ministry
- evidence of brokenness, humility, and the heart of a servant
- a teachable spirit and attitude
- faithful and trustworthy
- competent and spiritually gifted

Assessing the qualifications for those who will be your teammates in ministry protects you and the ministry from much controversy, divisiveness, and unrest. It is far better to weather the storms upfront, during the selection process, than face years of unresolved conflict if unqualified leaders take their place on the team. The standards of spiritual leadership cannot be compromised if you expect to enjoy fruitful years of ministry in a loving, growing community of like-minded teammates.

But what if the pool from which to choose is woefully understocked? Never allow the absence of spiritually qualified leaders to deter you from persistently working to build a team for ministry wherever you happen to pastor. The challenge for you is to refuse to be content with the level of spiritual maturity and vitality in the church you serve. Grow them up as you labor with them intently: disciple them, share your vision with them, mentor them, delegate ministry to them, and observe them. Find those who are faithful in little things and entrust them with greater things. With steadfast resolve, build a team of godly leaders who will do as Moses's leaders did, "so it will be easier for you, and they will bear the burden with you" (Exod. 18:22).

Team leadership is what God has prepared for you as you shepherd his flock. It is his plan to keep you in balance by surrounding you with a supportive cast to help you maintain your equilibrium.

$$=== 6 ===$$

THE CHARACTER
OF A BALANCED TEAM

KEYS FOR BUILDING AN EFFECTIVE TEAM

Since I was a child, athletics have been an important part of my life. As early as I can remember, I was part of some kind of team, playing baseball, basketball, or football. Every afternoon during the school year, and whenever we could get a game going in the summer months, you could find me with a bunch of guys, practicing or playing some kind of sport. Being part of those teams helped me understand how to contribute to the collective effort of the entire team. We needed each other. We depended on working together as a team to be competitive and to achieve success.

One of my sons was on a team that had a reasonable amount of talent among the players but could not seem to get it together consistently enough to win more than a game or two in a row. The problem was that the players did not understand the importance of playing as a team. Each one was trying to display his own talents. They did not seem to comprehend how destructive their individuality was to the building of a cohesive unit that could accomplish much more than a bunch of isolated "lone rangers." About halfway through the season, they finally came together and began to function as a team, but it was too bad that it took them so long into the season to figure it out.

What kinds of things are basic to building a team? Over the years, I have observed several keys that make real teamwork happen. Not every team will have all of these, but when most of these ten keys are present, the team will be stronger and more effective.

- Identity   • Integrity
- Unity   • Dignity
- Diversity   • Community
- Humility   • Chemistry
- Charity   • Longevity

Since human nature is essentially self-centered, the whole idea of "team" goes against the grain of anyone who has not experienced a transformation of heart by God's divine act of grace. Once in a while we can change our actions and occasionally even change our attitudes, but it takes a work of intervention by Jesus Christ to change our nature and give us the desire to forsake our own interests for the best interests of others.

Therefore, as we explore these ten keys to building a team, keep in mind that they only work properly when God is in full control. As we see how these keys work in the body of Christ, we must always be reminded that this is not some tricky formula for success. These keys are hallmarks of those who simply live out the life of Christ in the power of the Spirit.

1. Identity

When you walk into the lobby of the gym at Broughton High School in Raleigh, North Carolina, you immediately step back in time. The trophy case is filled with shelf after shelf of trophies dating back to the 1930s, with pictures of teams in funny-looking uniforms posing proudly with their prizes in hand. In the center of the case hangs an old basketball jersey with a number that has not been used on another Broughton uniform since it was retired many years ago. The uniform was worn by one of the greatest basketball players ever to step on the court. "Pistol Pete" Maravich played high school basketball at the same school where my sons were students.

As the team suits up to play each game, they know that they are taking part in a grand tradition, that they are carrying forth the identity of one of the great names in basketball history and the team on which he played. This gives each player a sense of identity and pride: he not only belongs to something special, but he is also responsible for upholding the heritage that has been passed on to him.

An effective team has a sense of identity. And when we are part of an effective team, we experience a prevailing sense of privilege that we have the honor of belonging to something great. We need to identify with our team!

God identifies himself with us and calls us to accept our new identity as a part of his team: "But you are a chosen race, a royal priesthood, a holy nation, a people for God's own possession" (1 Peter 2:9). "A great cloud of witnesses" preceded us along the same route and now cheer us on as we pursue the same goals they did (Heb. 12:1). They remind us that we are not the first to share the identity as God's people; together we are a mighty team gathered to run the race all the way through the finish line.

If we are to become more effective as a team, then we must grasp our identity, cling to our distinctive heritage, and live up to the standard of those who have gone on before us. What an amazing team has taken the field before we arrived on the scene! God's Word and the history of the church provide a rich pattern of excellence. No team can succeed if it does not have the ability to identify with its team members, both in their present and past forms.

As the church, we have an identity as the body of Christ, citizens of the kingdom of heaven, along with all who have gone before us in every age. But we also share a unique identity with the congregation of believers in our local church. This can be a blessing and less than a blessing when, due to today's highly mobile culture, pastors and church members who identify strongly with one congregation have to move to another. Because what they had worked so well in the prior church, they try to reproduce the same team identity in the new situation. More than likely, their new church has its own identity already, so these new people will be unfulfilled until they identify with the new body. Deal gently but firmly with them (or yourself if you are the one who's moved on) as they (or you) move through the inevitable "this is how we used to do it in our other church" phase.

What a great privilege to know that the Lord creates unique identities, not only for individuals but also for churches! The quicker we discover the identity of our team in our church or ministry, the quicker we will begin to function as a true team.

Have you discovered what sets your team apart as unique? What characteristics of your team's identity do you most want to preserve and pass on? As a pastor, you are the team leader, and one of the best things you can do for your team members is to find ways to remind them regularly of their identity.

2. Unity

At a recent sporting event, I heard two players on the same team putting each other down while bragging about their own accomplishments. This destructive display of "one-upmanship" was doing nothing for the unity of the team. Rather than looking for ways to encourage and spur on their team member to higher levels of performance, these two players were more interested in looking good at the expense of the other—to the detriment of the team effort.

To be effective, teams must find as many ways of building unity as possible. If a team member tends to be divisive and unsupportive of the team, without a doubt the consequences will be felt sooner or later. Professional sports offer numerous examples of this. When free agency became a common practice among professional athletes, the entire concept of team was threatened in every sport. Players who have special skills move around from team to team, sometimes contributing to the unity of the program, but often assuming a one-dimensional perspective about their value to the team's system. If players know that they will not be around very long, what reason do they have to worry about building team unity? Eventually, such an attitude builds resentment among other team members, and the unity of the team fragments.

The same thing can happen in ministries. I have seen churches roll out the red carpet for pastoral staff members who are especially gifted in their area of ministry. In at least one case, other staff members were released in order to make room in the budget for the high cost of attracting the "superstar" team member. The resulting disunity that came from these actions can never be measured accurately. Sacrificing unity for short-term gains will eventually destroy any team. The entire team needs to feel affirmed, appreciated, informed, and included. If a team is to function properly, it must function together, united in its purpose, clear on its objectives, and jointly focused on its goals.

Does everyone on your team understand the value of unity? Paul wrote that we should be "diligent to preserve the unity of the Spirit in the bond of peace" (Eph. 4:3). The teams we build must be committed to unity in Christ as we join together under his headship, willing to forsake any personal agenda for the sake of oneness. As spiritual leaders, we have a responsibility to set the tone by modeling a spirit of unity in the way we treat other team members, in the manner of our speech to and about other team members, and in the direct confrontation of behavior that presents a challenge to the unity of the team. We must be united in the biblical truth we believe, in the values we hold dear, in the goals we pursue, in the attitudes we maintain, in the love we demonstrate toward one another, and in the Savior we serve.

Having stressed the importance of unity, let me also say unity alone cannot be the ultimate goal, because once in a while an issue emerges that makes it necessary for there to be a parting of ways. The idea of maintaining unity at any cost has unfortunately led many different kinds of teams to fall apart. Still, unity is an important factor in team building, even if it should not be the ultimate priority.

3. Diversity

Does unity imply uniformity? Not at all! In Ephesians, Paul addresses the issue of God's genius for variety. Diversity plays a significant part in his plans for his body, the church, to fulfill its calling: "what every joint supplies, according to the proper working of each individual part, causes the growth of the body for the building up of itself in love" (Eph. 4:16). In both Romans 12 and 1 Corinthians 12, Paul goes into greater detail about the concept of diversity: each one brings something unique to the mix of each assembled body of believers. Diversity is the marvelous means by which the Lord accomplishes his purposes.

No single individual has sufficient ability to accomplish all that needs to be done by a team. Regardless of the skills possessed by any one member of a football team, the game cannot be won unless the players work together, each one carrying out his own responsibilities. So it is with all team sports: each one needs the others on the team for the team to succeed.

If we are not careful, we can fall into the trap of exalting some ministry positions and demeaning others. Whether such things happen by design or by default, any attitudes and actions that undermine the value of diversity must be rooted out lest they destroy one of the most basic reasons for having a team.

One of the most common mistakes churches make when they build a pastoral staff team is to insist on uniformity rather than diversity. Granted, diversity can be threatening, because anything that does not match up with our accepted methods can be perceived as a threat. Rather than thinking diversity is a threat to unity, wise team leaders take advantage of every opportunity to celebrate diversity and reinforce the value of team performance over individual performance.

Are you threatened by the diverse gifts practiced by your team members? Have you protected yourself from that threat by selecting team members who are either very similar to you or not as gifted in their area as you are? A frequent ploy of insecure team leaders is to choose staff and team members who pose no threat to their leadership. Because they themselves do not excel in any particular area, they do not want to have anyone else around who will outshine them. Therefore, they avoid strong team members, choosing instead those from whom they fear no competition.

One of the greatest threats to a healthy diversity among team members is a lack of respect for one another's differences. Nearly everyone can sense when they are being patronized instead of respected. Condescending attitudes and tones of voice communicate with remarkable clarity when team members do not respect the perspectives, methods, and decisions of one another. No team will ever benefit from its diverse members if great care is not taken to work together with mutual respect for those who are different from us.

4. Humility

Bringing humble people together in the formation of a team advances the possibility of success significantly. On the other hand, gathering a group of prima donnas who hold inflated views of their own importance almost guarantees disaster. What a pleasant relief it is to find humble team players who are not only willing to share the glory, but selflessly give up themselves so that others might shine!

Today we are bombarded with the idea that success depends on our ability to push ourselves into the limelight. Assertiveness training and constant appeals to elevate our self-esteem do wonders for the ego but dreadful things to the establishment of an effective team. No one seems willing to play a supportive role unless proven benefits are attached.

During a high school basketball game a few years ago, some of the starters were not doing too well. The coach took them out and put in some of the substitutes from his bench. Almost immediately, the fresh players turned the momentum of the game around and began to cut into the lead held by their opponents. Meanwhile, the starters on the bench moaned and complained about not getting the playing time they thought they deserved. With great patience, the coach ignored them and continued to direct his troops on the floor, watching as they made a heroic comeback. With several minutes left to go in the third quarter, two of the benched starters had had enough. These two brash young men grabbed their warm-ups and stormed off the bench toward the dressing room in protest against the coach's decision to replace them with others who were getting the job done. Because of their arrogant disregard for the team and their extremely high view of their own importance, both players found themselves removed from the team immediately.

If you rely on the stereotypes reported in the media, or on the occasional egomaniacs most of us have run across sometime in our lives, the picture can be bleak. Unfortunately, the words "humble" and "pastor" are not often mentioned in the same sentence. Yet any ministry that represents Jesus Christ must have a humble team leader.

The key to humility boils down to two main issues: what we think about ourselves and how we treat others. In each case, the Lord provides specific direction for those who want to follow Christ. "For through the grace given to me I say to everyone among you not to think more highly of himself than he ought to think; but to think so as to have sound judgment, as God has allotted to each a measure of faith" (Rom. 12:3). While others cry out that we all need to hold a higher opinion of ourselves than we do, Paul states just the opposite. He does not suggest that we opt for false humility, holding to a view of ourselves that is inferior, but that we make an accurate assessment based upon sound judgment. In other words, determine what to think of yourself based on what the Lord thinks, certainly no more or less.

How then do we treat people if we are humble? Once again Paul speaks to the matter at hand when he says, "Do nothing from selfishness or empty conceit, but with humility of mind regard one another as more important than yourselves; do not merely look out for your own personal interests, but also for the interests of others" (Phil. 2:3–4). If humility plays a role in the building of an effective team, it must shape the way we, as pastors, relate to others and the way we treat them.

5. Charity

In the King James Version, the word sometimes used for love is "charity." The English word *charity* actually has its roots from the Greek word *charis*, which means "grace." A good team cannot function without either.

Three aspects of charity deserve special mention in the context of building an effective team. The first act of charity is the way you communicate what you expect of one another on the team: the best. This not only means that you should communicate this to your team members, but also that you should feel that expectation from your team members. If you thought that the rest of your team fully expected you to mess things up, you could neither function freely nor live up to your potential.

The second aspect of charity relates directly to the first. Good teams express charity when they are kind to one another in times of failure. Kindness is the only true expression of charity when someone has just suffered a disappointment or has in other ways failed to meet their own expectations, much less those of the team around them. Although any communication is hard to bear when we have not succeeded, genuine, heart-felt encouragement will build solid team relationships. Caustic, critical, or even teasing comments will do the opposite. As one who has a tendency to tease too often, I have wounded too many people unnecessarily by careless words intended to be humorous. When others fail, they are especially vulnerable to what we say so we need to choose our words wisely and charitably. If you are a team leader, model this aspect of teambuilding yourself and never allow unkind words about team members to be spoken in your presence. Send a message that charity through kindness will build the team, and you will be well rewarded by the benefits to team morale and confidence. The way we respond when team members fail makes a tremendous difference.

The third aspect of charity that builds effective teams is forgiveness. Holding grudges and determining to get back at your attackers will stir dissension on the team. The old saying, "I don't get mad; I get even," is the ultimate expression of this kind of attitude. It will destroy your team!

What should you do when someone wrongs you? According to the Scriptures, you must forgive them. What should you do when you realize you have wronged someone else? You must ask for their forgiveness and assure them that you know that what you did was wrong and will not be repeated.

Grudges weigh too much to carry with us while trying to fulfill our roles on a ministry team. Looking over your shoulder all the time to make sure you are not going to be hit from the blind side only makes progress toward the goal in front of you more difficult. Those who say, "I'll forgive, but I won't forget, lest they do it to me again," find that until the issue is resolved with their teammate, the team can never function effectively.

The old saying "Charity begins at home" still applies. It begins with your home team. Expect the best from your team members. Be kind when they fail and forgiving when they wrong you, and you will soon grow together into the kind of relationship God can use to mold a team for his glory.

6. Integrity

Teammates need to have confidence in one another's integrity. Integrity is born out of a commitment to do all things with honesty and excellence. The standard is raised in Colossians 3:23: "Whatever you do, do your work heartily, as for the Lord rather than for men." All that we do must be consistent with the character of Christ.

When I am trying to determine whether someone would be a good fit for our team, I observe his or her integrity in four specific areas: healthy work ethic, playing by the rules, respecting confidentiality, and refusing to undermine his or her teammates.

Healthy work ethic. People of integrity have an excellent work ethic because they understand that they are not working for the approval of just another person, but they are laboring for the Lord. I have always found it hard to understand those who want to be generously compensated for their work but want to work the least amount possible. Each team member's work ethic impacts the rest of the team. That is why believers have a serious responsibility to give their best all the time, regardless of what others on the team are doing. It can certainly be discouraging to see others profit even though they are slothful, but our motivation comes from a higher source that compels us to be team members of integrity in our work ethic.

Playing by the rules. A serious threat to team unity emerges when one or more players on the team seem to play by a different set of rules than the rest of the team. When a team member is always looking for exceptions to the rules, always finding ways around established procedures, eventually that person sends a message to his teammates: "I am above the rules. They were made for everyone else, but I am different so I need special treatment."

Effective team members need to demonstrate a wholehearted, complete, fulfilled, and integrated manner of life if they are going to walk in a manner worthy of Jesus Christ. If a member of the team feels exempt from the standards of behavior, the rules of procedure, and the type of interaction accepted and practiced by everyone else, he or she effectively drives a wedge between himself or herself and the rest of the team.

Refusing to play by the rules of the team signals that problems may emerge in how a person plays by the rules in other areas of life. How is he or she operating in the area of personal fiscal responsibility? Will problems emerge in the area of sexual purity? Does he or she treat the "rules" of sexual propriety as if they apply only to others? Integrity fades quickly once we allow ourselves to indulge the privilege of playing by our own rules.

Respecting confidentiality. Integrity in one's ability to keep confidences enhances our trust in each other unlike anything else. If I know that I can share something with my teammates and it will be protected as a sacred trust, I can count on them in just about anything else. However, if I find that what I have shared in private becomes common knowledge, I feel violated and betrayed, and my confidence in the team is eroded.

Each member of the team should be able to trust the others with personal and private information, both about themselves and about others. Integrity means keeping confidences, even when we are not sworn to secrecy, but when the subject matter suggests discretion. I have seen too many teams crippled because one member could not handle privileged information and spoke when the better choice would have been silence. Busybodies will paralyze the effectiveness of a team, because they have an insatiable desire to know everything about everything and everyone. Their passion drives them, not for the sake of being a better team member, but for the sake of brokering their information for more control or power within the team. A team member who cannot be trusted with confidential matters will eventually weaken the entire team.

Never undermining a teammate. Getting stabbed in the back by a trusted ally has to be one of the most destructive things that can happen in our lives. Integrity demands that we never say or do anything to undermine a teammate. Gossip and libelous comments, slander and insinuations of wrongdoings or mixed motives—all are wicked tools sharp enough to pierce even the toughest skin when they are wielded by the hand of one in whom you have put your trust.

Integrity demands that we not allow our opinions to be shaped, nor attempt to shape them in others, without first checking the spirit of such a report when it is given. Is this going to help or harm the team? Is there some hidden motive behind what I am hearing that I should explore further? Before I say what I was going to say, have I examined my own heart to see why I would want to share something negative about my own teammate? Until we are prepared to stand against backstabbing and refuse to allow it, the integrity of the team and the individual members on it will be challenged.

These four areas—a healthy work ethic, cooperation (playing by the rules), confidentiality, and never undermining a teammate—shape the integrity of a team and its players. The importance of building an atmosphere of the highest integrity among the members of a team is paramount.

7. Dignity

A good team demonstrates dignity, both among themselves and to those outside the team. You cannot always determine whether you will succeed, but you can determine whether you will behave with dignity, acting in a manner that brings honor to the name of your team.

A team that can maintain its dignity regardless of the circumstances usually has a strong sense of its own identity. If the identity of a team is well defined, then the ability to maintain its dignity increases greatly.

Do not confuse dignity with indifference, class with arrogance, or self-containment with aloofness. A team does not need to deny its emotions, disregard its feelings, or disown its passions to maintain its dignity. Losing one's dignity simply means allowing emotions to control us rather than mastering them and keeping them under our control.

In the setting of the body of Christ, I have "lost it" too many times to recall, but I can remember a few occasions that called for immediate action on my part to make amends for the way I acted. At one particularly difficult deacons' meeting, I seemed to be at odds with a couple of the guys on just about every point discussed. I argued with them and attributed ungodly motives to them. After the meeting ended, I was compelled to call them and ask if I could meet with them. By this time, it was well past ten o'clock, but they kindly allowed me to come to one of their homes and apologize to them both for my atrocious behavior.

Those gracious men forgave me, and we agreed together to help each other any way we could to avoid any further confrontations

111

such as we had just endured. The dignity of their response, their charity in receiving me, and their integrity in the way they handled the entire matter has always served as a reminder to me of what God really desires. Today we have maintained a special relationship because the three of us trust each other and know that each will help the other keep a level of dignity in place—even when we disagree and things do not go our way. As painful as that evening was, I will never forget the lesson God taught me about the need to act with dignity at all times. After all, I am always on duty as an ambassador for Christ.

Dignity does not cost much, but it pays handsomely. All it costs us is the "right" to act inappropriately. Whatever the circumstances, we must not allow our team to suffer the indignity of our undignified behavior. The impact of presenting ourselves to one another and to all who see us as a team with dignity reflects favorably the glory of the one we represent.

8. Community

A recent article in a sports magazine told of a professional basketball team with an odd conglomeration of players, one of whom had made it clear to his teammates that he wanted nothing to do with them off the court. So firmly resolved was he in this eccentric condition for team membership that he let them know through an intermediate source that he did not intend even to speak to any of them when they were not practicing or playing a game. How long do you think such isolationism will last before the team either explodes or sends him packing? Teams that enjoy the most success over the long run must develop a sense of community.

God, by divine providence, created us as social creatures who function best in the context of gathered groups of fellow creatures. Whether that group is a family, a local body of believers, or a team of some sort, we operate best when we find our proper place among others, enjoying unity in the midst of our diversity. Take away our community and we suffer accordingly.

Although a team can certainly function without community, it does so without the depth of joy it could otherwise experience.

112

Players who have been on vacations together, cooked burgers on the deck together, stood up at each other's weddings, laughed at each other's jokes, kissed each other's babies, and in a thousand other ways shared life together when they were "off duty," will inevitably work better together when pressing on toward their common goals as a team. Community builds team loyalty and brings depth to everyone's commitment to support one another, come what may.

When we really belong to one another as a family, the privilege of working together becomes as significant as what we are looking to achieve. How far we have wandered from that perspective, even in the body of Christ! Over and over again in God's Word we find the message that relationships matter, people matter, and community matters.[1] A team cannot measure its effectiveness only in the tangible area of goals reached and problems solved. Affection, accountability, fellowship, stability, security, and affirmation—all these exist in a team that has learned the value of investing in building a sense of community among its members. God has called us to cherish one another and to relate to one another as family when we come together and accept our identity as members of his team.

9. Chemistry

Sometimes things blend together well and sometimes they just do not! Occasionally a team will bring into the mix a player who, for whatever reason, just doesn't fit. Once in a while that lack of chemistry appears immediately, and steps to correct the problem can be taken before too much damage is done. But more often, the chemistry problem doesn't show up until the mixture has had time to ferment, so resolving the problem can be much more difficult. For that reason, adding members to your team should be a careful and prayerful process. By the time we recognize our need for a new player on the team, we are so

1. Relationships matter: John 13:34–35; Galatians 5:13–14; Ephesians 4:32; 1 Thessalonians 2:7–8. People without Christ matter: Romans 9:3–4; 1 Corinthians 9:19–23. Community matters: Acts 2:42–47; 1 Corinthians 14:12.

overwhelmed by the need that we move too hastily to get anyone who meets the position description as soon as possible. Many painful partings have resulted from bringing someone onto the team who has the technical qualifications for doing what needs to be done but who does not match up with the team's chemistry. The tasks may get done, but the team suffers.

The addition of the wrong person to a team can change things dramatically by sending the team in the wrong direction—not immediately perhaps, but eventually. Within the past several months, I have seen the damage that this lack of chemistry can produce in a couple of wonderful ministry teams. Significant amounts of time, blood, sweat, tears, and other valuable resources were spent trying to resolve the difficulties created by the introduction of an "unblendable" staff member to an existing team. After all other avenues were blocked, the only solution was removal. Valuable time that could have been invested profitably was consumed by a situation that began because the chemistry wasn't right.

Great care and diligent selection of team members will not always prevent chemistry problems from emerging, but I am convinced that this intangible factor in team building must be given serious consideration. We cannot afford to give all our attention to the measurable qualities on a resumé and neglect the vital matter of whether or not a candidate will fit with the other team members. Pay attention to that nagging sensation in the pit of your stomach when everything looks good on paper. I have ignored it and regretted it, and paid attention to it and been thankful for it. Try to picture the person you are considering with the rest of the team and ask yourself before going any further if the fit is right. Team chemistry is too important to settle for a pragmatic answer based on skills alone. Go for a team-conscious answer that gives appropriate weight to team chemistry.

10. Longevity

When a good team comes together, keep it together. I am a strong advocate of longevity as a key toward building an effective team. Having served as pastor of only one church for my entire ministry thus far, I believe in getting together a team and keeping the team members as long as the Lord allows. We communicate right up front to each new member that we want to raise our children and grandchildren together. I cannot think of anything more wonderful than retiring together after long years of meaningful service, growing together in our love for Christ and his people.

The first few years are always the hardest. That is why I believe so many bail out during those critical years when the foundations are being poured. If you have ever been around any construction sites, the messiest time of the entire project occurs as the lot is being cleared of all the trees, rocks, and everything else in the way of the new building. Mud and dirt are everywhere. Then, as the footings are dug for the foundation to be poured, mounds of earth rise up all over the site and create an eyesore until that phase of the project is completed. What if the new owner saw the mess and couldn't envision the end result? Nothing would ever be built!

Teams that stay together over the long haul get better over time. When teams are committed to longevity, they allow themselves to take advantage of the opportunity to get used to each other. That in itself is no insignificant matter. Ask any husband or wife about those early years of getting used to all the little habits and ways of doing things that at first seem so odd but eventually blend into the background of who this special person really is and why he or she means so much to us. Their idiosyncrasies—which at first strike us as radical and severe impediments—can actually become endearing qualities over time. Similarly, as a ministry team gets used to each other, they find that they are grateful that they stuck together long enough to see through the initial impressions to discover the valued colleague and team member with whom they have shared treasured years of ministry.

Another benefit of longevity comes with the inevitable abrasions and bruises that occur when we allow others to rub off some of our rough edges and in turn are used to rub off some of theirs. This painful process can cause the fainthearted to run for the door, but the wise team member realizes this is an obvious and necessary part of growing and living up to our potential. The Lord speaks of the value of this: "Iron sharpens iron, so one man sharpens another" (Prov. 27:17).

If we stick with one another long enough, the Lord can use us to shape and mold each one in his own image. We see each other during good times and bad, during periods of great progress and periods of heavy duress. Facades eventually drop, and we discover that we are all real, vulnerable, needy people who need Christ and each other. Longevity allows for all the cycles to run their courses, for the ups and the downs of our lives to be observed by team members who see them and love us anyway! Longevity provides the opportunity for trust to grow. Our Lord calls us to a long walk in the same direction with others of kindred spirit as we follow Jesus Christ together.

——— ∞∞∞ ———

These ten keys to building an effective team will play an important part in how you spend your years of ministry. It is my firm conviction that the Lord has called us to serve him in the context of a team, of a group of believers who commit together to seek Christ and obey him.

There is something special and right about savoring good things with others. Even the secular world knows that. The Lord created us for fellowship with him and with each other. That is why I am so committed to the concept of team ministry and to the principles and keys that go into building an effective team. Not every team will have all ten of the keys as presented here, but the more of these ten keys they have, the stronger and more effective they will be in accomplishing what they set out to do.

PART 4

CULTIVATING GENUINE HUMILITY

= 7 =

THE INDISPENSABLE
QUALITY OF HUMILITY

Like many young pastors, early in my ministry I had somewhat naive ideas about what constituted greatness in a
pastor. At pastors' conferences and conventions, I would
watch and listen to the speakers and dream of one day joining
them on the platform. Occasionally I would encounter one of
my heroes off the platform; I found some of them to be genuinely humble servants of Christ whose demeanor reflected his
character. They treated people like me with warmth and care
and gave no appearance whatsoever that they were impressed
with their popularity. One year I attended a conference featuring several well-known pastors. In addition, I had recognized
some others in the hallways and exhibit areas and secretly
hoped that I might have an opportunity to rub shoulders with
the "big boys," or at least get a chance to meet some of these
role models.

As it happened, at the beginning of one of the sessions I was
heading back to my seat when I saw an acquaintance of mine

talking to a pastor whose church was held in high regard by nearly everyone I knew. I figured this would be a good opportunity to meet him, so I went over to speak to my friend, hoping for an introduction. As anticipated, when I greeted my friend he turned to introduce me.

Then it happened. You know the experience, I am sure. You are being introduced to someone, and even as you are shaking his hand, you notice that he is scanning the room over your shoulder for someone more interesting or more important to be the focus of his attention. Granted, I did not expect much more than a casual greeting, but I was not expecting to be dismissed by his impersonal and cool manner. Needless to say, I was disappointed. To give him the benefit of the doubt, I hoped that I caught him on a bad day. Well, I have met this same pastor several times over the years, only to find the same response on his part. He has made it clear that he does not pay much attention to the "little guy." After these encounters, I could not help but wonder, what happened to his shepherd's heart? How does he balance his calling as a servant of Christ with his lack of interest in the people who belong to Christ?

What Happened to Humility?

Where is the humility anymore? What happened to the picture of the pastor as a humble servant of the flock of God? Respect for pastors has degenerated so significantly over the years that pastors no longer stand for sacrifice, meekness, or humility in the minds of the general population. With egos running rampant, many pastors seem to have forgotten who they are and who they represent. They instead work hard to develop a carefully crafted image of one who knows what he wants and will not be deterred on his mission. When he wants what God wants, that can be a wonderful trait, but when his desires spring from selfish ambition and personal promotion, humility is lost.

Perhaps there is something about standing before a group of people every week who are willing to listen to what you have to say that swells the head and shrivels the heart. A humble pastor receives the thanks and praise of the people and turns it all over to the Lord, but how tragic to see those who are willing to give God the glory as long as they get the credit. Too many prima donnas take over the pulpits each Sunday, preside autocratically over the board meetings on Wednesdays, and whenever possible finagle invitations to clubs and finer restaurants with well-heeled members of their churches. I have watched with dismay as pastors have justified lavish and opulent lifestyles, loudly and rudely demanded clergy discounts from retailers because they are pastors, and even spoken openly about using congregations as "stepping stones" to get to bigger churches that will pay them the wages they believe they deserve! I hope you do not think I am exaggerating, because I have seen each of those things happen with my own eyes and heard them with my own ears. Each time, I was embarrassed, both for the people subjected to such a prideful display and for the strutting peacock posing as a humble shepherd of souls. The challenging part of all this is that no one is immune from drifting into the currents of pride. Unless the Lord guards my heart, I can be the next pastor to fall prey to this dreadful disease.

When did pride and egotism become fashionable for those called to be pastors of God's little flocks? Humility is an essential quality for every believer and can be found only in those who have put on Christ and put off their old nature with all of its corruption. But it is especially necessary in pastors if we are to lead our congregations toward maturity in Christ. By humbling himself, Christ became "obedient to the point of death, even death on a cross," and would not allow personal concerns to cloud his calling to do the Father's will (Phil. 2:8). In the same Philippians passage, Paul also addresses the essential nature of personal humility: "Do nothing from selfishness or empty conceit, but with humility of mind let each of you regard one another as more important than himself; do not merely look out for your own personal interests, but also for the interests of others" (2:3–4). I cannot help but believe that if pastors emblazoned those verses in their mind's eye to be reviewed and practiced daily, the state of our churches would be significantly different.

Humbled by Humility

Several years ago, my son Scott and I took a mission trip together and felt privileged to spend one evening sitting by a fire with some friends in a small Nepali village. We listened quietly as the tribal leader of the village explained in gentle tones the journey that had first led him to Christ and then led him to become the pastor of the only Christian church his village had ever known. The glow of the fire caught the moisture in his eyes as he spoke of what Christ had done in his family, in him, in the village, and beyond to several new churches planted by this gentle-spirited pastor. The humility of the Lord himself shone through him with a brightness that rivaled the flames from the fire before us. The likelihood that he will ever speak at a pastors' conference, chair a board, write a book, or put together an expansive global ministry is virtually nonexistent. Yet, as this dear brother labors in a tiny farm village in a small nation on the other side of the world, his very life and ministry bring me to my knees. His model compels me to confess my prideful attitudes and makes me long to be the kind of humble man of God that he is. He is Asman Tamang, and except for here you probably will never hear his name, never meet him, or visit his church in your search for the secrets to successful ministries, but he must surely be known in heaven as one who has impacted this world for the Savior because of his servant heart and his humble spirit. I am convinced that God wants more humble pastors than "successful" pastors.

Could you labor away in relative obscurity for twenty, thirty, or forty years if God asked you to? Could you find joy and contentment in that kind of calling? The question probably sounds too hypothetical to cause you to give it serious consideration. But if we are to discover the true disposition of our nature, to see if true humility can be found in our hearts, it is crucial for us pastors to know how to answer that question honestly.

A Command Not to Be Taken Lightly

Without humility before the Lord, it is impossible to keep your spiritual life in balance. Since the Lord has established that we must walk humbly in his presence, we lose his steadying hand when our pride and ego assert themselves. We have to remember that God does not suggest that we be humble. Instead, God commands us to take action and humble ourselves. Two passages in the New Testament issue this exhortation: "Humble yourselves under the mighty hand of God, that He may exalt you at the proper time," and "Humble yourselves in the presence of the Lord, and He will exalt you" (1 Peter 5:6; James 4:10).

In each of these New Testament verses, God leaves no room for misinterpretation or confusion. Each offers an unequivocal exhortation that compels a direct response of obedience on the part of every believer. Somehow pastors have managed to exempt themselves from certain points of application by convincing themselves that they need to make up for some of the humbling circumstances of their calling. Persecution complexes abound among pastors. Low salaries, long hours, and constant criticism from every quarter tend to make us, as a group, somewhat touchy about how much humility one person can take. With only slight sarcasm, it has been noted that this is the prayer of many church boards: "Lord, we'll keep the pastor poor, and all you have to do is keep him humble." Being kept both poor and humble, some pastors find it hard to resist occasional fits of ego gratification and allow themselves to forgo the discipline of heart and mind necessary to maintain a humble spirit. The examples of egocentricity I mentioned before bear witness to the easy slide into patterns of unhealthy behaviors and attitudes. Soon, what is obvious to everyone else remains undetected to ourselves. As pastors, we have to understand that the command to humble ourselves is a nonnegotiable essential. It is essential for us as servant leaders and shepherds of the flock of God.

With that unequivocal exhortation to humble yourself comes a divine guarantee, a promise from the Lord, that when you humble yourself, he will exalt you. There is no need for you to compensate for the humbling treatment you receive at the hands of others by trying to exalt yourself. God has committed himself to do that on your behalf. If you humble yourself, he will exalt you.

However, he seldom exalts us when we expect it or in the way we expect. The way he chooses to exalt us may not even appear to be exaltation from our perspective. Yet in his sovereign design for our lives, God will lift us up at the proper time and in the way best suited to our temperament, our circumstances, and our giftedness. He knows what we can handle without getting puffed up. Most of the time we have no idea what will puff us up, make us proud, cause our egos to inflate. A lot of what we desire in life would not be good for us, and God knows better than to give us what would be detrimental to our character. Consequently, our responsibility is very simple and does not include telling God what is best for us! His instruction for us tells us to humble ourselves and let him handle the rest.

An Attitude without Substitute

Without a firm grasp of God's grace, we will never sustain a humble heart. Periodic episodes of guilt may drive us to reconsider our lack of humility and force us to take a more realistic look at ourselves. But if we are convinced that we deserve special consideration and are entitled to all that comes our way (a common attitude to grow up with these days), grace will remain nothing more than a noble concept.

Anyone who has experienced the unmerited favor of God in Christ Jesus has also had to wrestle with the humbling impact of our total inability to accomplish anything of eternal value apart from his work of grace in our lives. Every vestige of pride, every tendency to boast, is stripped away when we come to grips with the fact that everything good about us can be ascribed to the grace of God at work in us. Consequently, there is no room for boasting or pride when there is nothing in us that God did not give to us. Paul wrote, "For who regards you as superior?

What do you have that you did not receive? And if you did receive it, why do you boast as if you had not received it?" (1 Cor. 4:7) We can claim no credit for our gifts and should, in fact, be quick to offer disclaimers to anyone who may not understand that God is responsible for any good in us.

Therefore, humility follows grace. Grace is the great leveler, because it removes all reason for pride. Once pride loses its power to dictate what our attitude will be, a genuine humility begins to grow. I have discovered that the more I learn to value the importance of God's grace and appreciate how desperately I need it, the less likely I am to become prideful, thereby losing the humility I must have to serve Christ faithfully.

Quite naturally, thanksgiving and expressions of gratitude follow closely behind a practical understanding of grace. All that I have and all that I am are the result of what Jesus has done for me and in me. What other attitude could I possibly have except one of thanksgiving? I owe everything to him, so I should not only be quick to offer him thanks with my words, but I should also live in such a way that gratitude permeates my attitudes toward all of life. Even as a pastor, my perspective on ministry must be shaped by a thankful heart. I want to be able to say what Paul said and mean it: "I thank Christ Jesus our Lord, who has strengthened me, because He considered me faithful, putting me into service" (1 Tim. 1:12). The privilege of living for Christ cannot be measured, but to be considered faithful and put into his service as my life's calling is too awesome for words! Realizing this generates within me a thankful heart, a heart that was shown mercy by the Lord Jesus.

Thankful hearts are humble hearts. Until I recognize how unworthy I am to receive all that I have, somewhere in the back of my mind, part of me will insist that I have the right to all that comes my way. When you accepted God's call to be a pastor, you stepped into a position that gave you every opportunity to demand to be treated differently. You will have to figure out how you will handle the attention your congregation gives you, the special favors people will shower upon you because you are their pastor, and the subtle temptation to tell yourself that you deserve all these things because of all that you "gave up" to follow the call of God into vocational ministry. You will realize how easy it is to fall into the trap of ingratitude when you begin to complain (at least in your heart) when special recognitions do not come your way.

When you have a humble heart, you will simply be grateful for who people are, rather than be hurt and disappointed when they do not feed your ego or play up to your pride. The threat posed to our spiritual equilibrium by pride is effectively nullified when we take the low place and allow ourselves to be pleasantly surprised at how gratifying it is to serve. That is the way it is with people who learn how to walk humbly with the Lord.

A Lesson in Humility

Perhaps balance is easier to gain in the area of humility than in some of the other areas discussed in this book, but it is also one of the most subtle and difficult to maintain. So many things in our lives humble us every day that it is not difficult to gain humility. But difficulties arise in those gray zones in which we mistake false humility for the genuine article. We play the part of the humble one but secretly wish for recognition. Saying the right words does not guarantee that they come from a pure heart.

One morning, I was having breakfast with a veteran pastor friend of mine. As we were talking after the meal, he asked why I thought God had blessed our church with the numerical growth it had enjoyed. Since I'd often thought about that question, I answered with what I thought were the three or four reasons that made the most sense to me. When I concluded, he looked at me across the table and inquired, "So you don't think it's because of your preaching?" No one had asked me that point-blank before, but I knew the answer: I am an adequate but not unusually talented preacher. Even as I was answering, "No," something inside of me was begging for a compliment from this man I loved and respected.

His response made me laugh . . . at his honesty and at the exposure of my own false humility. He said, matter-of-factly, "I am

126

glad you know that!" Well, I wanted him to say, "Oh no, David, surely you know that you are a great preacher and God has used that gift to build the church!" Although I never confessed it to him, I was embarrassed in my heart that my humility was not as genuine as I like to think. How easy to speak *of* a humble heart but how difficult to speak *from* a humble heart!

Yes, you must maintain the quality of humility in your life if Christ is to be glorified in your ministry. In fact, the broader the extent of your ministry, the deeper the base of your humility must descend as you build upon a foundation of total dependence upon Christ. There is no substitute for the indispensable character of a humble heart.

8

FIGHTING TO MAINTAIN A HUMBLE PERSPECTIVE

After a particularly exhilarating weekend of ministry, I was elated. Enduring hard times in the past had given me a deep appreciation for the good times we were experiencing in our church at that time. During the previous year, people made sure I knew about their complaints—somehow they felt great liberty in letting me know when I had done something that did not meet their approval or when the church tried something they did not like. But now it seemed we'd turned some kind of corner and attitudes were positive, comments were favorable, and all was right with my world!

As I gushed on and on to a friend about the nice things people had been saying about the church and even my preaching, she listened patiently. During the tough times, many of my friends watched me take the direct hits of harsh criticism. She appeared to be pleased that I could now enjoy this time of relief. When I finally gave her time to respond, she said something I have never forgotten. To this day I do not think it was a rebuke, or even a mild word of correction. She simply made an astute observation when she noted, "You know there will always be cellar voices in the church. For them, nothing you ever do will be good enough, nothing will ever be right. But then there will also always be balcony voices. They love everything . . . all the time . . . they take great pleasure in pumping you up. Still, the truth always tends to be on the main floor." What a great word to bring things back into perspective!

Let's face it, we must fight a conscious battle every day to keep our perspective and maintain our humility. The balance between listening to the cellar voices or to the balcony voices requires diligence and wisdom.

Three distinctive dangers threaten to destroy the balance provided by the presence of genuine humility in our lives: egocentric patterns of thinking, selfish perspectives in ministry, and personal prerogatives.

Egocentric Patterns of Thinking

I heard someone say that a person without habits wastes a lot of time. In almost every area of our lives, we develop habits that save us from having to make thousands of decisions each day. How we comb our hair, what we eat for breakfast, how we take our coffee, when we shower and shave, which route we take to work—these and a host of other habits keep us from having to think about each little thing we do. These habits represent patterns of behavior that benefit us in many ways.

Of course, we also know that habits can be negative as well as positive. Once we develop certain patterns in our lives, breaking them and replacing them with other kinds of patterns can produce significant stress. The familiar, even if it's unhealthy, brings a certain degree of security and makes us feel that we are in control, in balance. That is one of the reasons people find it so hard to change. Patterns that have provided stability in our lives do not yield easily.

129

In each of our lives, there are patterns to the way we think. We habitually process information in the same way, sift it through the same grids, and subject it to the library of assumptions we've cataloged in our minds. Again, that can be a good thing: for example, we don't have to review the alphabet each time we read a book. We know how to read because we've learned how to recognize the sounds represented by the letters in each word—it has been patterned in our brains. We are freed from having to think about some things so we can release our minds to consider others.

But patterns of thinking can imprison us as well as free us. Racial prejudice, for example, arises from learned patterns of thinking that determine how we think about people of a different race or nationality or ethnic heritage. However, the way we think can be changed as old habits give way to new ones. Old patterns of unhealthy and improper thinking can be transformed into the new patterns of a healthy mind.

As a new creature in Christ, Paul tells us that "the old things passed away; behold, new things have come" (2 Cor. 5:17). He also reminds us that we have a responsibility to give up the old patterns of thinking that have shaped our past and embrace the new mind we received when we came to Christ: "For who has known the mind of the Lord, that he will instruct Him? But we have the mind of Christ" (1 Cor. 2:16) and "Do not be conformed to this world, but be transformed by the renewing of your mind" (Rom. 12:2). God wants us to operate with a new mind in Christ Jesus. The transformation of that mind has a direct impact on how we view ourselves as individuals and, more to the point, how we view ourselves as pastors.

In the next verse in Romans 12, Paul goes on to say, "For through the grace given to me I say to everyone among you not to think more highly of himself than he ought to think; but to think so as to have sound judgment, as God has allot-ted to each a measure of faith" (Rom. 12:3). If we are to have sound judgment (or a "sane estimation"), we must recognize and forsake any patterns of thinking that lead us to think more highly of ourselves than we should. How many of your patterns of thinking are egocentric and selfish in nature? Consider with me a few patterns of thinking that threaten our balance in the development of humility.

Seeking the Approval of Others

From the earliest years of our lives, we are taught to value the opinions others have of us. Although few will ever state it outright, the unmixed message from cradle to grave is that you must live in such a way that others approve of you, accept you, and only then affirm you. In other words, if you earn someone's disapproval, they will not accept you and cannot affirm you. That is the way of a fallen world, and yet much of our behavior is geared to operate within that framework. Our thinking works through a process that considers what others will think of us to be a matter of great importance.

Living to please people instead of the Lord has brought many a pastor to a sorry end! Once we decide that what we say and do will be based on how others will respond, we may as well announce that our fragile egos are now calling the shots. We are no longer saying and doing only what pleases the Lord. Pleasing people is not always wrong, especially if we do so humbly, as a means of ministry to them: "just as I also please all men in all things, not seeking my own profit but the profit of the many, so that they may be saved" (1 Cor. 10:33). The key difference, of course, is that Paul is not intending to win the personal favor of others for his "own profit," but for their greater good and the good of the gospel in seeing them saved.

No, the danger is not just in doing what pleases others or what invites their approval. The danger is being motivated by a desire to have their approval for yourself as a boost to your own pride and a feather for your own cap. The world has seen enough pastors willing to water down or even sell out the message of eternal truth in order to curry the favor of their listeners. Paul reminded Timothy that the time will come when people pleasers will be the favorites of the crowds and their approval ratings will soar according to the acceptability of their message: "For the time will come when they will not

131

endure sound doctrine; but wanting to have their ears tickled, they will accumulate for themselves teachers in accordance to their own desires" (2 Tim. 4:3).

Rare indeed is the pastor who has not stood before his congregation to preach and had to fight back thoughts of how his message will be received. Many times I have approached the pulpit, struggling to control my mind so I am not swayed in what I am about to say by any thought of what others may think. After all, I am not there to be accepted or to win approval, but to preach the truth in love and with the power of the Holy Spirit. But those old patterns of thinking can be strong, and my ego can ascend quickly unless I allow Christ to give me a humble heart and mind like his.

Early in our married life, Cathy would accompany me to the small churches where I made my first attempts at preaching. On the way home, in the car, this insecure, young preacher dared to ask her what she thought of my sermon. Well, let me tell you, she had the audacity to answer . . . in detail! As a well-taught Christian and an English teacher to boot, she usually had no trouble offering quite a list of suggested improvements. Between my subjective involvement in what I had just preached and my longing for approval as validation of my personal worth, it all proved to be too much for me. I'd get defensive and argue with her about every point she made, legitimate or not, because I needed for my ego to be stroked, not for my preaching to improve. Why could she not understand that? How did we solve this problem? Simple, I stopped asking! And yes, eventually I started to grow up and put away my egocentric patterns of thinking and allowed my proud heart and mind to be humbled so I could learn and grow.

Until the people-pleasing stops and our need for the applause of others ceases to drive us, we will continue to be controlled by our desire to draw attention to ourselves instead of Christ. The first church I served in kept a small card inside the pulpit that simply read, "Sir, we would see Jesus."[1] I've never forgotten it, though the addition of two more words

1. John 12:21 (KJV).

132

would make its meaning more pointed: "Sir, we would see Jesus . . . *not you!*" Our attitude in preaching needs to match that of John the Baptist when he said, "He must increase, but I must decrease" (John 3:30). To break the pattern of egocentric thinking, you must see exalting Christ as a higher and a greater calling than exalting yourself. Humility cannot be had any other way.

Oversensitivity to Slights

If I am convinced that life is all about me, I will read myself into every situation and gauge what happened, for good or bad, on the basis of how it impacted me. That is the direction egocentric patterns of thinking lead us. Have you ever manufactured slights where none were intended? Have you imagined that comments you overheard were meant to be taken personally by you, then found out later they had nothing to do with you? When we filter life through an egocentric grid, we are bound to come out on the other side feeling abused and overlooked, unloved and unappreciated.

Pastors are supposed to have tender hearts but thick skins! If we do not have a transformed mind, we will be susceptible to all kinds of paranoia and we'll read things into situations that have nothing to do with us. The tendency to look for slights comes from the idea that we deserve certain considerations because of who we are (or think we are). Pastors can subtly convey the idea that we have sacrificed so much to do what we do that we deserve special treatment. The feeling of being overlooked may be related to the level of our compensation, or the lack of additional staff members to share the workload, or the absence of recognition on special occasions such as ministry anniversaries or times of extraordinary effort. When we begin to wear our feelings on our sleeves and start looking for the next point of evidence to support our case that we are not appreciated, we can be sure that our humility has been knocked out of balance by the demands of our egocentric thoughts and prideful attitudes.

Building Esteem Rather than "Mortifying" Sin[2]

Our desire to feel good about ourselves sometimes super-sedes our desire to die to ourselves so that Christ might live in us—which is God's call for us. Think about the issues that crowd the agendas at pastors' conferences. Compare how many sessions address the practical realities of our daily spiritual battles with the number aimed at making us more successful in producing and building larger, more efficient churches. Conversations among pastors more often deal with finding shortcuts to success and prosperity in church growth rather than with how to grow up to maturity as humble men and women of God. That is to our shame and can be blamed, in part, on mania created by the idea that our identity as pastors has more to do with how many people show up in our buildings on Sundays than on how much Christ is being formed in us.

The personal self-esteem of a pastor has become so inter-twined with the size of the church that I am not surprised at the number of young pastors who are ambitious, not for the sake of the gospel, but for the building of their own reputations and the boosting of their own self-esteem by all that they accomplish. Tragically, even when we do find an emphasis on the mortification of sin and the battle to keep sin from reigning in us, it often comes in the form of a special emphasis designed to attract more people, not always for the glory of Christ. Faulty patterns of thinking can quickly defeat us and throw our humility right out of balance if we do not keep our hearts and minds open to Christ's transforming work in us. When Christ is transforming us by the renewing of our minds, by making all things new, only then will the old ways of egocentric thinking be overcome and the new ways of Christ prevail. Only then can we walk humbly with the Lord.

2. Early Christian writers frequently refer to the biblical concept of dying to sin, or "putting sin to death in our mortal bodies" as the "mortification of sin." It is a useful phrase we would do well to preserve!

Selfish Perspectives in Ministry

Every pastor faces conflict when his perspective in ministry begins to appeal to the selfish rather than the humble nature. Without even being aware of it, a pastor can surrender ground by giving in to selfish ways of carrying out ministry.

Showing Partiality to People with Status

If we have a humble spirit and have been released from personal selfishness, we tend to take people as we find them. Our interaction will not depend on what they can do for us or whether we see any profit or value from talking with them. Easy words to write, but a difficult principle to put into practice.

Think about it. Have you ever passed up a conversation with someone you viewed as less important to pursue one you viewed as more important? As I've already recounted, I've been on the receiving end of that kind of treatment. A humble perspective about yourself is essential; otherwise, as soon as your guard is down, you will dismiss someone without even a courteous word, excusing yourself because your time is too valuable for them. Then in the next moment, you turn right around and make all the time in the world for someone you regard as a person of value. But can we, as pastors, value some people and not others? James nails that attitude for what it is.

> For if a man comes into your assembly with a gold ring and dressed in fine clothes, and there also comes in a poor man in dirty clothes, and you pay special attention to the one who is wearing the fine clothes, and say, "You sit here in a good place," and you say to the poor man, "You stand over there, or sit down by my footstool," have you not made distinctions among yourselves, and become judges with evil motives? . . . But if you show partiality, you are committing sin and are convicted by the law as transgressors.
>
> James 2:2–4, 9

I am ashamed to admit it, but I know of times when I turned down requests for appointments one minute because of my hectic schedule, only to accept another appointment the next. The shameful part is that I rejected the one and accepted the other for purely selfish reasons. Pleading temporary spiritual insanity will not justify such a wrong, only the admission of defeat in my battle to maintain the balance of a humble heart before God. Humility—and its absence—impacts the way I treat people. The same is true for you. Be on your guard. Showing partiality toward people can ruin your ministry, but more importantly, it must break God's heart when he sees us treat those he loves in a heartless way.

Ambitious for Self-Advancement

When humility retreats, selfish ambition advances. Pastors fall prey too easily to the pressure to "advance" in ministry, to develop schemes and plans to do what it takes to "produce results" that will be noticed. I will not dwell on this painful truth too long but feel compelled to call it to your attention. Once in a while, I have to take inventory of what I am doing and ask the probing question, "Why?" in an effort to search my heart for indications that I have succumbed to the temptation to strive to advance my own cause.

Lest you think this would be an easy culprit to arrest, let me assure you that it tests me to the deepest level of my motives. Decisions that seem to be reached with ease by others force me to examine my personal ambition before I can proceed. Perhaps you will understand better if I invite you into a current struggle, one I still have not resolved.

As a pastor, I am convinced that my greatest impact in life will be as one who equips "the saints for the work of service" through the ministry of the Word of God (Eph. 4:12). Each week of my adult life has been devoted to preparing biblically sound teaching, not only so that those who hear might grow to maturity, but also so that we in the body of Christ might present everyone complete in Christ (Col. 1:28). As a result of all those years of preparation, I have amassed untold hours of messages on audiotapes and thousands of pages of teaching and preaching notes.

Here is my dilemma. How do I make those resources available so that others might profit from them without becoming an ambitious self-promoter? Obviously there are practical considerations I need to take into account because of the cost associated with producing and distributing the materials, whether in audio or printed form. But should I personally profit from the sale of these resources? Am I more interested in self-promotion and self-advancement than I am in making the materials available? As I said, many others have resolved these issues, and to a certain extent and in specific categories, I have as well or else you would not be reading this book! But I cannot go into such an endeavor just because I see other pastors doing it. One day I hope to find a way to maintain the balance of personal humility and the desire to equip more of the saints in a broader audience. Until then, I will continue to resist the temptation to launch any project that might lead me down the path of ambitious self-advancement. Believe me, I have seen some of our colleagues in ministry neglect their personal humility on the way to the spotlight—and to the bank! May God protect us from such inclinations and keep us from anything that even remotely resembles self-promotion.

The Need to Win

Too many pastors end up confusing their calling as a shepherd who leads the sheep with a cowboy who drives the herd. The debate about pastoral authority continues to engage better minds than mine. The tension between being a "church boss" who has to have all the answers and being a "co-laborer" among other biblical leaders who share responsibility in a team environment does not appear to me to be a tension at all. But then again, my prejudice toward the latter model is apparent throughout this book. But in either situation, the pastor can become obsessed with his or her role as the one who must assert confident leadership through bold initiatives and courageous stands. Taking the reins of leadership in a church does not make us immune to weaknesses and failures that show up regularly in other areas of our lives.

If we do not walk humbly before the Lord, our spiritual leadership degenerates quickly into carnal arrogance and haughty attitudes. If you mistake strong leadership with a compulsive need to be right all the time, it will lead you straight out into stormy waters. I cannot even recount all the times I was foolish enough to argue my point long after I knew I was on the wrong side. God did not give me the gift of infallible discernment on every issue, so I have to allow for that fact when engaging in discussions with those who disagree with me. Prevailing in the end does not always turn out for the best, either for you personally, for the ministry team with whom you serve, or for the good of the church. Only an inflated ego without any balancing influence of godly humility has to win all the time.

Moreover, be careful not to drop the trump card of pastoral authority into controversial discussions unless you are absolutely convinced you have exhausted all other options. When you are tempted to do so, ask yourself the following questions. Have you given the principal parties time to reflect and pray about the issue? Have you explored alternative points of view? Have you demonstrated that you are not trying to railroad the decision just to get your way? Appealing to their blind loyalty to support their pastor without reservation may be the right approach on a rare occasion, but it will do nothing to build a team concept of ministry. It can also foster a spirit in you that lacks the essential quality of godly humility.

As you probably know by now, when humility fades away, our perspectives about our ministry go through some damaging phases that cannot be healthy for you or your place of ministry. We must approach our ministry calling with a passion to preserve a humble heart before the Lord and in the presence of those he gives us to lead.

Personal Prerogatives

If we lose our balance and fall from humility into pride, we tend to give ourselves permission *not* to be humble by putting fences around categories of our lives to claim as personal prerogatives to be protected from the restrictions of a humble life. Biographies of great Christian leaders who chose to give up the luxuries of life, and in some cases what we would consider the rudiments of a normal life, intimidate us and put us on the defensive. Depriving themselves of every hint of a pampered life, many of God's most effective servants concluded that they did not need many things, nor would it benefit them to indulge themselves. Such examples provide a stark and unflattering contrast to the opulent lifestyles of "rich and famous" Christian leaders. Perhaps we need to realign ourselves with the spartan existence of saints who decide to forsake the pleasures of this world for the blessings of investing in the next.

The Right to "Live Large"

"Living large" comes with the territory for pastors who fulfill their calling in the wealthiest culture in the history of the world. The pull of materialism can be so strong that we allow the world around us to define what is essential. Pursuing simplicity in the way we live forces us to go against the grain of our culture.

Are you not refreshed and inspired by some of our colleagues in ministry who have chosen simplicity in the way they conduct their lives? At a recent three-day meeting, one of the pastors who spoke each day wore the same sports coat and tie at every session, while his counterparts followed the normal pattern and were "dressed for success" each time in a different suit. A friend attending the meeting returned more impressed by the example of humility in the one than the fashionable precision of the others.

In another case, a well-known Christian author, pastor, and leader demonstrated a humble lifestyle in his choice of housing, facing his retirement years in the close quarters of a small apartment that many would consider to be beneath one of his stature. However, his ego didn't need something bigger and better; he had nothing to prove, no statement he needed to make about his right to comfortable and easy living.

Considering the choices many pastors make today about where they will live and what they will drive, what clothes they will wear and what luxuries they will lavish upon themselves, one has to wonder where we will have to go to find models of humility of lifestyle for the coming generations. Even those who do not have the resources to provide a life of ease still long for it and secretly devise ways to attain it one day. If the truth were told, many who have personal ambitions tainted by thoughts of self-advancement have them not for the prestige of the position, but for the perks of the financial rewards they desire. God calls his shepherds to a life of service that does not necessarily imply deprivation and asceticism, but does call into question the presumption that we have a right to lay aside our responsibility to be practical models of humble living.

The Need to Be Held in High Esteem

Just as our lifestyle is not immune from the call to a humble life, neither is our notion that we have a right to be viewed as competent professionals (who happen also to be pastors). The insidious danger of this need to be held in high esteem becomes apparent when we see to what extremes many will go to establish and protect their status as peers with leaders in business, medicine, law, government, education, and so on. The latest trend among pastors is to return to school to work toward a professional degree of some sort. For some reason, pastors seem to enjoy being called "doctor," as if the title was able to give them value in the eyes of a culture impressed more with position than with character, more with formal training than with practical experience.

I have to agree with David Wells in his book *No Place for Truth* when he concludes that many schools are offering programs that are not as rigorous as doctoral programs used to be. He suggests this is evidence of a progressive shift toward "degree inflation."[3] Granted, there are many pastors who have a passion

---

3. David F. Wells, *No Place for Truth: Or Whatever Happened to Evangelical Theology?* (Grand Rapids: Eerdmans, 1993), 234–35, writes: "But why has professional status become so important in ministerial ranks? The answer is not hard to find. . . . In America, importance is conferred by professional standing. By the end of the 1960s and the early 1970s, ministerial standing in society was plainly in need of serious professional upgrading. . . . The response that was made across the board, under the

for more training and a desire to improve the gifts God has given them by sharpening them in a formal educational environment. However, I also suggest that there are many who've been led to believe that their value as a pastor depends on whether they've accumulated the credentials associated with success.

I do not mean to slight my dear, humble brothers and sisters in Christ who have excelled academically. If you are someone who has labored diligently to gain the ministry tools your advanced degree has provided, let me be up front: no, I have no doctoral degree and no plans to pursue one, but there may come a time when that is what I want to do. If that happens, I need to make sure that there is no hidden agenda in the back of my mind that suggests that my status will be enhanced and my ego fed by doing so.

We have to be careful not to rope off areas of our lives and put up No Trespassing signs when God brings a word for us that should be welcomed, not resisted. Ask him to show you your heart the way he sees it, then see if there are any remnants of pride, any shadows of ego, that need to be exposed and removed by the infusion of the wonderful humility of the Lord Jesus.

—— ∞ ——

Arthur Bennett, canon of Saint Albans Cathedral and Anglican rector in Hertfordshire for many years before his death in 1994, did the Christian world a tremendous service by publishing a book of prayers preserved from the Puritan era entitled *The Valley of Vision*. Consider this prayer:

Humility in Service

Mighty God,
I humble myself for faculties misused,
    opportunities neglected,
    words ill-advised,

---

careful direction of the Association of Theological Schools, was to upgrade degree nomenclature. What had been the B.D. became the M.Div. in the early 1970s, and for those seeking upward mobility, the D.Min. was shortly thereafter added to the arsenal of social tools. . . . Thus was the D.Min. born; in two decades, over ten thousand of these degrees have been issued."

I repent of my folly and inconsiderate ways,
      my broken resolutions, untrue service,
      my backsliding steps,
      my vain thoughts.
O bury my sins in the ocean of Jesus' blood
    and let no evil result from my fretful temper,
    unseemly behavior, provoking pettiness.
If by unkindness I have wounded or hurt another,
    do thou pour in the balm of heavenly consolation;
If I have turned coldly from need, misery, grief,
    do not in just anger forsake me;
If I have withheld relief from penury and pain,
    do not withhold thy gracious bounty from me.
If I have shunned those who have offended me,
    keep open the door of thy heart to my need.

Fill me with an overflowing ocean of compassion,
    the reign of love my motive,
    the law of love my rule.

O thou God of all grace, make me more thankful, more
    humble;
Inspire me with a deep sense of my unworthiness arising
    from
    the depravity of my nature, my omitted duties,
    my unimproved advantages, thy commands violated
    by me.
With all my calls to gratitude and joy may I remember
    that I have reason for sorrow and humiliation;
O give me repentance unto life;
Cement my oneness with my blessed Lord,
    that faith may adhere to him more immoveably,
    that love may entwine itself round him more tightly,
    that his spirit may pervade every fibre of my being.
Then send me out to make him known to my fellow-
    men.[4]

4. Arthur Bennett, ed., *The Valley of Vision* (Carlisle, PA: Banner of Truth Trust, 2003), 326. Permission to quote granted from the Banner of Truth Trust, PO Box 621, Carlisle, PA 17013, USA.

=9=

A Life Rooted in Humility

By their fruit you will know their roots (Matt. 7:16–17). If the fruit of humility does not appear on the branches of your life and ministry, you can accurately conclude that your root system is flawed and needs attention. You do what you do because you are what you are. Your essential nature will emerge in your actions, so as a pastor and as a follower of Christ, your life must be rooted in humility. You cannot hope to maintain balance in your ministry without nurturing a humble heart.

Attitudes are difficult to maintain without practical outlets for action. What measures can you take to act and think with humility? Sometimes I think I am too much of a pragmatist, but I need to know what to do next, once I am convinced of the rightness of an idea. If we are to maintain any biblical balance in our calling as pastors, we need to learn to make a habit of the practice of humble living. For the balance of this chapter and in conclusion of this section on humility, I offer twelve practical suggestions to cultivate a humble spirit that you can put into practice as soon as you put this book down.

1. Look for some way to serve each day.

Life offers a limitless variety of opportunities for serving others. Why not make it a point of special emphasis to find out how you can encourage humility in your own heart by taking it upon yourself to find needs and meet them? You can begin right at home. Imagine the surprise and delight of your family when they see you doing for others instead of demanding from others. Perhaps the best forms of service are those that go unnoticed and for which you get no credit anywhere but in heaven. If my wife makes the bed and does the dishes daily, I scarcely notice, nor does she call any attention to it. On those rare occasions when I do either job, I usually make sure that I make her aware of it! How childish and self-serving.

Once you leave your home, an entire world awaits a servant-minded individual who will care for the needs of others before his or her own. It may come out in how you treat the wait staff at a restaurant so they sense that, although they were paid to serve you, you did all that you could to make their load lighter. In your daily time in the car, the price you have to pay for simple courtesies is small. It only takes a brief moment to slow down for another car to merge. The small things matter to people. Bend down and pick up someone else's litter and throw it away so no one else will have to do it later. Bring someone a cup of coffee instead of having them get yours for you. Some Sunday when it is raining after church, grab an umbrella and walk someone to their car . . . even if you are the pastor (it will surprise them to see you practice what you preach!). I could go on, but you get the point. There is nothing difficult about it, but for some reason, primarily our pride and our preoccupation with what we want, we demonstrate very little humility in our attitudes toward serving others. Make it your commitment to do something every day to serve others.

2. Treat everyone with respect and without partiality.

Granted, there are some who make it very hard on you because that is just the way they are. It's natural to want to avoid such folks, but it indicates that we have a long way to go in nurturing a genuinely humble heart. Demanding people, complaining people, critical people, excessively needy people, you name it—churches are filled with them! Pastors interact with them all the time and, frankly, we can devise some creative ways to avoid them if we try. Can we really afford to do that while affirming our love for them and taking seriously the biblical charge to give an account for each of them before the Lord? It is fitting to show them respect, even honor, in the name of the one who places them in our care.

Likewise, we need to make sure that we do not show partiality to those with wealth or influence, as we already noted from James 2. God expects us to treat people with dignity and without prejudice. Each new day brings us new challenges in how we deal with others that are true tests of our humility.

3. Learn the art of asking questions and listening to the responses of others.

Having met many great people in my life, those with famous names and those with names only their family would recognize, I have concluded that one of the greatest marks of humility in a person is the ability to ask questions of others instead of doing all the talking. I love the challenge of meeting new people to find out if they are listeners or talkers. Once in a while, after an evening with friends, Cathy and I will reflect back on the time and realize that we monopolized the conversation and seldom gave the others a chance to say a word. What I really enjoy is asking questions that bring light into someone's eyes and gets them excited when they find out that I really do care about them and what is important to them. Drawing out the best in others requires that we sharpen our skills at asking good questions that come from our genuine interest in getting to know the other person, instead of making sure that they know and are impressed with us. Try asking questions the next time you are with a new acquaintance, and humble yourself by letting them do the talking for a change.

4. Boast of nothing but Christ and the cross.

Recently I had lunch with a friend who told me about a new friend he had made. What impressed him about his new friend was how thoroughly saturated his conversation was with Christ and how frequently he quoted first one and then another portion of Scripture in the normal course of conversation. I was convicted and then challenged by that thought. After all, I have no trouble talking about my family, my recreational activities, and my work at the church, so why shouldn't I become more consistent in bringing Christ into my conversations— taking me out of the spotlight for a change. Paul said he would never boast except in the cross of Christ (Gal. 6:14), while in Jeremiah, the Lord commends boasting only when a person boasts about knowing and understanding him (Jer. 9:23–24). When we determine that we are going to speak often of our first love, we need to make sure that we love Christ more than we do ourselves.

5. Never demand or even expect preferential treatment as a pastor.

A friend of mine owns a Christian bookstore. She once told me that her most difficult customers are pastors who come in demanding a discount because they are "clergy" and should get special consideration. At the time, her store was in the early years of building its business and reputation in the community, and a large percentage of her customers were pastors. "How can I afford to give discounts to the largest block of buyers? How would that be fair to my other customers?"

146

she asked. Pastors' presumptuous attitudes have done nothing good for our testimony in the community when people assume that we will come to them "hat in hand," expecting preferential treatment, presumably because of what we do and who we are.

I agree with a pastor who told me years ago that if he could help it, he never let people buy meals for him, because it communicated a message he didn't want out there. By putting our hands in our pockets when the check comes, we pour fuel on the fire that suggests that pastors believe everyone owes us something because we have made the great sacrifice to follow Christ in vocational ministry. It is time we get a grip! No one owes us anything that would show us preference over others who serve Christ in their own sphere. Some would argue that the Scripture teaches that those who "work hard at preaching and teaching" are "worthy of double honor" (1 Tim. 5:17). That is true, but do we have the audacity to think that Paul was suggesting clergy discounts and a place at the head table at the Rotary Club luncheon?

It all boils down to expectations. Do you expect to be shown partiality because you are a pastor? Then shock someone this week: take them to lunch and pick up the tab. Patronize a local Christian bookstore and tell them that you found a product in a discount book catalog but would like to invest in their business locally by paying the retail price because you support what they are doing. Granted, you probably cannot afford to buy all your books this way, but the very idea that you are willing to do so at all will be a humbling experience for you. Even as I write these words, I am sitting in the living room of a friend's beach house that he has made available to me free of charge. Out of gratitude, I must find a way to express my appreciation. I do not want to presume upon his kindness by taking advantage of such generosity as if it was due to me. The practical issue is this—find a way to combat the attitude that crosses the line and begins to expect, or even demand, special favors. There is a fine line between accepting such favors once in a while with grace and gratitude and being frustrated and disappointed when they do not come.

147

6. Take the initiative when meeting people to introduce yourself first so they do not have to feel awkward.

Never assume people know who you are. Years ago at a banquet in our church, we had a good friend come over to speak. One of our deacons was functioning as master of ceremonies and had the responsibility of introducing my friend before he spoke. As he was preparing for the introduction, the deacon pulled the speaker aside to get some information that would help in making the introduction. Trying to downplay the need for much comment, my friend said, "Oh, you don't have to say very much about me. I've spoken here many times, and they already know me." I thought his wife was going to double over with laughter when our deacon said, "Well, I've been around here for five years, and I have no idea who you are!" She told her husband, "That will teach you to be presumptuous!" Never assume people know who you are!

I find that it helps me and the other person if I assume nothing of them and take the responsibility to introduce myself first. That way, if they do know you, they can say so. But you get the added benefit of having them follow suit and give you their name in return (although sometimes they do not and you may have to humble yourself, admit that you do not know their name, and ask for it). This may seem like such a simple thing, but first impressions go a long way. I want to make sure that my actions convey humility even in this small way.

7. Believe the best of people and always give them the benefit of the doubt.

Humility will lead us to conclude that we are not always right and that we do not always command all the facts. Therefore, whenever possible, resist drawing conclusions until you have had a chance to give people the opportunity to tell their side of the story. When you do this, you are admitting that there is room for another perspective that may indeed be clearer and more accurate than your own.

When we hurry to rush to judgment, we feed our own ego needs: to stay on top of every situation, maintain control of the information flow, and remain in charge. Most of the time, though, if we will set aside our pride, we will do better by listening patiently and asking questions, admitting that we need help in sorting things out.

8. Learn how to accept praise and take compliments graciously.

This is tough. In our effort to practice humility, most pastors try to redirect compliments and praise to the Lord. That is as it should be, but how we do it matters. When someone compliments you on your sermon, you could say, "It was the Lord, not me." That sounds good on the surface, but it implies that the other person is less spiritually discerning than you and needs to be reminded that every good gift is from the Lord.

I heard about a young soprano soloist who sang just before a veteran preacher was to deliver his sermon. When she returned to her seat, the pastor told her, "That was really wonderful. You did very well." In a stab at humility, she replied, "Oh, it was not I . . . it was the Lord!" With a twinkle in his eye, he said, "Well, it wasn't *that* good!"

How hard can it be just to say, "Thank you! You are very gracious to say so." The person offering the compliment feels acknowledged, and then you can turn their praise immediately over to the Lord. An exceptional guitarist I once knew taught me a valuable lesson in this regard, one I have never forgotten. I asked how he handled the never-ending stream of praise he received from those who were amazed and blessed by the exercise of his gifts. He said, "I just see them as bouquets of roses instead of words. I receive them and thank the person, then I just turn around and lay them at the feet of Jesus." What a simple but elegant picture! No remedial lecture to the one bringing a word of praise but just a simple expression of thanks for their kindness and then an immediate transfer of the "bouquet" to the foot of the throne of Christ.

In the book of Proverbs, we read, "The crucible for silver and the furnace for gold, but man is tested by the praise he receives" (27:21 NIV). How we respond reflects what is in our hearts. Praise does not produce pride in us; it just brings to the surface what is already in our hearts. The old radio Bible teacher J. Vernon McGee wrote, "Flattery is like perfume. The idea is to smell it, not swallow it."[1] We do not have to swallow praise when someone feeds it to us. But we can smell the sweet aroma of it as we pass it along to the Lord.

9. Admit your mistakes quickly and seek forgiveness when your mistakes cause pain to others.

Making mistakes is not hard. If you are doing anything, you are going to make mistakes and fail occasionally. A humble person will be quick to admit those mistakes instead of insisting on defending himself and his intentions, justifying, rationalizing, trying somehow to make it work. I have wasted much time and effort trying to justify my mistakes, rather than admit my error and go humbly back to the place I took the wrong turn. The sooner you acknowledge your fallibility, the sooner you regain your credibility. For some reason, pastors have a hard time doing that . . . at least I do! Perhaps it can be traced to our sense that we have been called to shepherd the flock by God himself, and so we think that we should be capable of always getting it right. Well, the bad news is that we will not and cannot do that. Therefore, swallow your pride, take a deep breath, confess your mistake, and then take your medicine with humility, even if it comes as a dose of humiliation.

Admitting the mistake, however, is often just the first step. Frequently, the mistake has caused others to be hurt, or at least inconvenienced. Once you discover where your fault lies, go at once and ask for forgiveness for your part in their pain. Our

1. J. Vernon McGee, *Proverbs through Malachi*, vol. 3 of *Thru the Bible with J. Vernon McGee* (Nashville: Thomas Nelson, 1982), 92.

pride tells us not to take this step; humility requires us to do it. It is the only way to obedience to Christ.

10. Create situations that will remind you and others that you are not indispensable.

Pastors usually take on more than they should ever try to handle. I am not exactly sure what we are trying to prove other than that our pride tells us that we can handle anything. We make ourselves indispensable and then complain that we never get a break, never can leave for a moment without things falling apart. The more the ministry revolves around us, the more our egos get inflated, and our estimation of our importance to the grand enterprise called the church gets way out of line.

One of the best ways to combat this is to make sure that you are regularly delegating the things you normally do to others. This will serve three very useful purposes. First, it will give you a break now and then to catch your breath, get refreshed and revitalized so that you come back stronger. Second, it will allow others to exercise their spiritual gifts and multiply the ministry by developing leaders who can serve alongside you. But third, and the point I am making here, it will prove to you and to your congregation that you can be replaced and that the church of Jesus Christ will not fall apart if you are not running everything. That, my friend, is a good thing for you to know and a good thing for them to find out!

11. Honor others by recognizing their efforts, publicly and privately, by expressing thanks.

Once you have learned how wonderful it can be to get off the pedestal, you will want to do so more often. The efforts of many people make the load of the overall ministry much lighter for everybody, and it is important to look for ways to express thanks in ways that honor people.

151

12. Always look for ways to take the low place.

This last suggestion is really the foundation of all the others. If you can find a way to get to the low place, do it! There is always a backseat in a car when a group is going out together . . . take it. There is always a smaller piece of cake on the plate . . . take it. There is always a parking place farther away . . . take it. The point is to let someone else have the front seat, the larger piece of cake, the closer parking place. No one deserves the high place but Jesus, so let him be exalted and humble yourself before him and others. How much of your frustration on any given day can be traced to your sense that someone else got what you wanted or felt you deserved? If I am determined to take the low place, no one can take away from me what I have freely chosen to give them. Humility brings great freedom because it puts into practice the reality that I no longer live, but Christ lives in me. I have nothing to defend in myself since I have died. I have nothing to protect for the sake of my pride since it no longer lives.

Closing Thoughts on Humility

Humility takes a lifetime to cultivate but only a moment to plow under. A thoughtless comment, a brief indulgence, a selfish motivation that leads to a prideful action—in no time at all, the pure and simple life of humility we long for suffers a blow that knocks us off balance again. Diligence is the only solution. Again the Proverbs offer the best words of caution: "Watch over your heart with all diligence, for from it flow the springs of life" (Prov. 4:23).

My affirmation that Christ abides in me will be most evident when his humility prevails in me. Nothing stands in more direct contrast to the old nature with its selfish ambitions and its egocentric focus than a life that has been stripped of this and clothed with Christ. The only remarkable thing about me should be that I am like him, conformed to his image, dressed up in his righteousness, and clothed with his character. Every pastor should take to heart the simple chorus that says, "Let others see Jesus in you." No one can abide in Christ and continue to abound in pride. One will dispel the other. The fruit of your life will bear witness to the roots of your heart.

Last of all, our true character as a humble servant will be revealed when we are treated like one. How do we respond when we are treated in a manner consistent with what we say we are? O that God would cultivate a depth of humility in us as pastors not seen often enough in recent days! May God give us humble hearts that we might serve him alone.

"Not to us, O Lord, not to us but to your name be the glory, because of your love and faithfulness" (Ps. 115:1 NIV).

PART 5

LEARNING TO GROW THROUGH YOUR TROUBLES

=== 10 ===

OWNING MY MISTAKES

TROUBLE I BRING ON MYSELF

As I hung up the phone, I knew that the day I dreaded had come. The costs for the new building project had just come in and, as I'd expected, were well beyond the funds the church had available. Space needs were well past the critical stage. We had to do something, but we did not have the money in hand nor the prospect of gathering it in time to meet the need. How could we make up the difference? That was the question I had hoped I would never have to answer again.

Nearly six years before, through an enthusiastic error in judgment and a desire to prove that I trusted the Lord as much as any other pastor, I made one of the most costly mistakes in all my years of ministry. The issue at stake was not a grievous moral sin, nor was it inexcusable theological heresy. My mistake, one that nagged me for years, was how I had answered the question of whether a church should ever borrow money. Without considering the biblical evidence or the practical consequences, I'd taken a heroic public stand that proved to be ill-advised and probably rooted more in pride than in conviction. We would never borrow money in our church to do the work of the Lord, I had told the congregation. Armed with all the bulleted points from some popular national seminar leaders, I assured the church that we would make the sacrifices necessary to trust God, not some secular lender to raise all the funds we would ever need to pay for whatever he called us to do. Although I never called borrowing money a sin, the logical implications of the position I outlined led others to the conclusion that it could be nothing less.

Now six years had passed. My confident words that had resonated with such conviction now hung over my head as I was forced to admit to myself that I'd never been as sure of myself privately as I had communicated publicly. Did I dare reconsider what I'd already declared so unequivocally? Rethinking the issue of borrowing forced me to take a more comprehensive look at both the direct biblical teaching and the applicable principles. I carefully researched borrowing and lending practices and instructions in the Scriptures, consulted with other godly ministry leaders in churches around the country with a strong commitment to upholding the teaching of God's Word, and honestly evaluated the weaknesses of the case I'd made years before. I eventually was led to the humiliating conclusion that I had made a huge mistake. The unwarranted dogmatism with which I had stated my case now embarrassed me. This was no private, personal discreet matter. Church members have great memories when you don't want them to! I knew I could count on it—no one would have forgotten.

I soon found out how deeply some had embraced what I'd taught them. Many were not inclined in the least to yield what, for them, had become a firm conviction: churches should never borrow money! What was I to do? My previous understanding of what was biblical and true had now changed through an honest review of what the Bible taught about borrowing. Now I faced the distasteful duty of publicly owning my error and confessing my failure. I had to ask forgiveness from a congregation that had trusted me to teach the truth. I had unwisely led them astray by giving them far less than they deserved. In a perfect world, the church would have welcomed my admission of guilt, forgiven my failure, graciously accepted my apology, and moved on. Well, that is not exactly what happened.

For several weeks, we held public forums for listening to and answering questions, presenting opportunities for those who still held tenaciously to what I had once believed. Then the church voted by a very narrow margin to reverse the "no borrowing" policy of the past and move ahead with building plans for our much-needed additional space. The slim margin supporting the change of policy, along with the strength of the opposition to this move, led to a period of stormy weather in my life and in the life of the church.

Some seized the opportunity to accuse me of selling out my principles to support what they had decided were my personal ambitions to build a bigger building and have a more visible ministry. Others wondered aloud whether they could expect reversals in other areas of biblical teaching. After all, if we could present such a convincing case six years before and then come back with an equally convincing case supporting the opposite conclusion, just how firm were our convictions about absolute truth anyway? Was it going to follow that we would go the way of more liberal churches and accommodate our desires by adjusting the Scriptures to suit us?

Inevitably, some quietly found their way to other churches. (Ironically, some of them relocated to churches that borrowed money for their building projects also.) Others mysteriously decided to remain but with a strange resolve never to participate in a worship service under my leadership since I had proven in this situation to be totally unreliable. How that was possible I cannot fathom, but periodically I was reminded that there were still some of those folks out there—nameless people who had decided to take a stand in protest of what they considered an unforgivable failure, a mistake that was insurmountable for them.

Make no mistake about it. When you blow it as a pastor in a public matter, there will always be a great deal of pain, either by you upon others or by them upon you. However, there will always be an opportunity to learn and grow from it. If you haven't messed up as badly as I did in this case, may the Lord help you learn through a less difficult curriculum than the one I had to endure. Yet I would not trade the lessons I learned, because God has taught me that I can make it through the storms if I am walking with and abiding in him.

Taking the Initial Blow

Mistakes in our ministries hit us with the impact of a lance in a jousting tournament. If we are not prepared for the blow, we can get knocked off our horse and, frankly, may not be sure we want to get back on again. Therefore, it is necessary to prepare for the inevitable failures if we expect to spend our lives in balanced ministry, steady in the saddle, moving forward with a sense of stability.

The initial blow to your ego hits you hard as you are forced to acknowledge your own fallibility. The very fact that you are capable of a major error may come as such a shock to you that you might have a tendency to exaggerate the significance of what happened, to overreact and to magnify in your mind the impact of your mistake.

The good news is that most of our egos could take a few direct hits now and then. What we have to be careful of is not to let ourselves be thrown out of balance by plunging into a period of self-pity on the one hand or self-condemnation on the other. Neither choice is particularly useful in advancing the learning process and helping us grow from our mistakes. So fragile are our egos that we find ourselves scrambling to protect them. Instead of owning our mistakes and learning from them, we can suffer another lapse of judgment and start trying to cover up our failure in an effort to avoid the trouble we know we'll face if what we've done becomes known. We look for someone else to blame so we can find a way to save face and preserve the desired public persona, leading people to believe that we are indeed the master of all things ministerial.

But an honest admission of our fallibility can produce an environment for important periods of growth in our lives and

160

ministries. Making mistakes and experiencing personal failures does not mean that we have no more value or that we should step aside from a leadership role until we are perfect. Granted, some areas of moral failure do disqualify pastors from certain leadership roles, but God does not mark even those pastors as useless. God specializes in reclaiming broken people and restoring them to a right relationship with him.

There are benefits to admitting when we blow it. One of the greatest is that we find the freedom that comes from not having to be perfect all the time. You know you are not, but when you freely admit it, you are released to enter into honest relationships that no longer pretend to be something they are not. One of the most effective means of communicating honestly in preaching is to speak occasionally of your own struggles, failures, and inabilities. If you give the impression that you are above such things, people will have a hard time relating to you. Even more to the point at hand, they will be far less forgiving when you make mistakes.

Many pastors try to pull off the perfection masquerade and hold themselves up to a standard no one but Christ has attained. They then find themselves unnecessarily locked in by chains they have attached to themselves, chains of unrealistic expectations of infallible leadership skills and impeccable ministry instincts. Once you have failed a few times, you will find that admitting your fallibility gives you greater freedom than you could have imagined—not to perpetuate failure, grow careless, and increase your mistakes, but to live with less fear of having people discover what they should already know about you. You can and do make mistakes!

James writes, "Therefore, confess your sins to one another, and pray for one another so that you may be healed. The effective prayer of a righteous man can accomplish much" (5:16). If we try to keep our sin or our mistakes to ourselves, confessing them only to the Lord and hiding them from others, the value of our confession is diminished. Dietrich Bonhoeffer, in his book *Life Together*, advised the pastors in his small confessional community to be faithful in confessing their sins to one another:

A man who confesses his sins in the presence of a brother knows that he is no longer alone with himself; he experiences the presence of God in the reality of the other person. As long as I am by myself in the confessions of my sins everything remains in the dark, but in the presence of a brother the sin has to be brought into the light. But since the sin must come to light some time, it is better that it happens today between me and my brother, rather than on the last day in the piercing light of the final judgment. It is a mercy that we can confess our sins to a brother. Such grace spares us the terrors of the last judgment. . . . Confession in the presence of a brother is the profoundest kind of humiliation. . . . Does all this mean that confession to a brother is a divine law? No, confession is not a law, it is an offer of divine help for the sinner.[1]

Confession opens the door for the corrective work of the Lord in your life as he then begins his work to restore you. Correcting mistakes leads to growth, but they will not be so easily corrected if we insist that we have made none. The first step toward a deeper sense of Christ's presence in our lives is to accept his correction by admitting our failures and then experiencing his joy as we go on in obedience. How we take the initial blow of learning that we have erred will determine whether our mistakes lead to growth or paralysis.

Damage Assessment

The nature of your mistake often determines the degree to which you lose your balance, and for how long. If the mistake falls into the category of sin, the failure results in immediate consequences on your spiritual life and leadership. Moral failure, for example, lands a devastating and humiliating blow. Trivializing it by referring to it as "just a mistake" diminishes the way the Scriptures speak of the repugnance of sin to God. As we assess the damage moral failure causes, we are forced to take sin seriously and to be prepared for the fallout that comes

1. Dietrich Bonhoeffer, *Life Together* (San Francisco: Harper & Row, 1954), 116–17.

when we violate the sanctity of our moral purity. Whether we think it's fair or not, moral failure carries significant consequences, which nearly always awakens a survival instinct in us, an instinct usually born out of a powerful urge to cover up the truth in order to preserve a facade of propriety. We do this as a protection against the collapse of "life as it was" and the disintegration of the precarious balancing act that makes up the pastor's world.

Sins of self-indulgence can also be more mundane, like personal laziness, apathy, lack of self-control and discipline, unrestrained emotional outbursts, deeply buried resentment and bitterness. Yet all of these kinds of sin cause damage and cannot be ignored. When we choose to give free rein to selfish considerations and allow feelings to overcome our discernment, the result will frequently be hasty, ill-advised actions that get us into trouble. Sin has to be confessed and forsaken before we can regain our balance for ministry.

Not All Mistakes Are Sin

Not all mistakes can or should be categorized as sin. Some are just reasonable errors that can arise from many sources. They may be mental miscalculations when we underestimated the consequences of a decision or misread the impact a certain course of action or choice of words would have. Perhaps you honestly didn't know any better due to your inexperience, to some misinformation you had believed, or to a general lack of knowledge. Pretending to know what you do not know paints you into corners that practically guarantee failure. Admitting that you don't know something may be momentarily embarrassing, but it's certainly better than acting foolishly.

Another source of mistakes comes from nothing more than careless impetuosity. How often we jump to conclusions about what we should think, say, or do without giving proper consideration to the matter before us! Lack of thoroughness in our thinking and a tendency toward knee-jerk reactions will expose the truth that we failed to prepare properly. Such carelessness

163

will not continue very long before it produces the kind of calamity that cannot be hidden. You may get away with flying by the seat of your pants for a while, but eventually, it will catch up with you. Impulsive decisions and reactions lead us to act in haste and leave us to repent at leisure as we try to figure out how to remedy the mess we have made.

In the first few years of my ministry at Providence, I could get away with poor planning and communication because recovery time was usually short and the burden for my failure normally fell back on me. If I hadn't prepared properly in advance, I had to stay up late a few nights and work late a few days to catch up and no one was the wiser. As our church grew numerically, I found myself in a situation I did not like. My organizational skills and management practices had been sufficient for a small church and a limited staff, but they were inadequate for the next level of congregational growth. I soon realized that my failure to plan properly created a hardship on others. All the clichés applied to my work habits—shooting from the hip, flying by the seat of my pants, perpetual panic—you name it! After enough problems arose due to my growing number of failures, I finally learned that I had to grow up if I expected to continue to grow with the church.

One last cause of mistakes in ministry is the desire we have to avoid conflict whenever possible. As a pastor, you will be faced with conflict almost continuously. If you are not careful, your reluctance to address it will lead you to make mistakes of much greater gravity than any you could have made if you had dealt with the confrontation right away, regardless of how uncomfortable or even painful it might have been.

In many ways, the mistakes associated with avoiding conflict are much like those we make by not getting medical help when we first suspect we need it. By the time we finally get around to doing what we should have done immediately, the condition has gotten much worse, and the resolution more complicated than it ever needed to be. Although you are not wrong to dislike conflict, avoiding it when it should be addressed will often bring you into crisis situations.

Owning up to our mistakes puts us in a position God can use, because God will not waste any of our experiences. He is committed to shaping our lives so that Christ is formed in us as we are conformed to his image. Yet it is not just about you and me. Our mistakes impact others.

When Our Mistakes Impact Others

You never know what to expect from the members of your church. Sometimes they will surprise you with their favor; other times they will shock you with the vehemence of their reactions. Even some of your most ardent supporters may be disappointed in you, and that is hard to take. We hate to disappoint those we love, because their opinions matter to us.

When you own up to a mistake, the response will be mixed among those you have been called to shepherd. So what kind of response can we expect when we admit our mistakes and acknowledge our failures?

Critical People Will Condemn You

Unfortunately, there are people in every church who live to pounce on the problems of others, and their negative reactions will vary in intensity and form of expression. The oft-repeated expression that "some people just love a crisis" stands true in many churches. I will never understand why some people who profess faith in Christ can find so much joy in the troubles of others. We have all known folks who seem to come alive only when their sharklike senses smell "blood in the water" through others' failures or mistakes. They seem to find a perverse enjoyment in discovering, broadcasting, and gossiping about others' mistakes—and seem especially delighted when it involves their own pastor.

This activity can be cleverly disguised as a "prayer request" prefaced by pious-sounding explanations as to why the damaging words should be spoken. ("As a member of this church, I feel that you should know what the pastor did [or said, thought, or implied]. We really need to pray for him and for our church and . . .")

Of course, not everyone will talk about you behind your back—others will condemn you outright for making the mistake and refuse to listen to any explanation for what you did. These folks seem to have a very short supply of mercy and understanding, but they have an endless supply of condemnation that they heap on anyone who fails to measure up to their expectations.

Others consider themselves experts in discerning other people's motives and will often assign imaginary motives for why you did what you did. They will either assume, insinuate, or accuse you of acting on some sinister motive or design that they have "discerned." They take exceptional delight in "stirring the pot" by implying a plot or a scheme behind everything and refuse to accept the possibility that the mistake could actually have been completely unintentional. Unfortunately, Satan has always been able to count on such unwitting allies in his role as "accuser" of the brethren (Rev. 12:10).

Godly People Will Console You

No matter how long you have been in ministry, you have probably already witnessed scenarios like the ones above and many others. Do not be overly discouraged; God also sends folks who know how to come alongside you, console you, and restore your credibility as you correct your mistakes and allow the Lord to conform your character to his.

When God finds that you have a teachable heart and that you want to learn from, rather than hide your mistakes, he will bring men and women into your life who will minister to you with compassion, consolation, and mercy. They will affirm you without condoning or excusing your error or pretending that you are too perfect to have made it. They will extend to you the full measure of grace they have received themselves so that you can discover that failure does not have to be fatal. Instead of talking about you behind your back, they will talk to God about you in intercessory prayer. The Father longs to see you grow through this troublesome time in your life and ministry. Godly friends will stand by you, believe the best about you, and comfort you with their presence when others walk away.

God wants to surround us with people who can capture such teachable moments in our lives and lead us from the pit of humiliation to the heights of illumination as we learn valuable lessons impossible to learn in less desperate circumstances. As they share their wisdom and experience with us during our troubled days, God makes it possible for us to learn, grow, and mature through their pertinent insights. Eventually, as I have learned after I have failed, you will begin to appreciate the privilege of attending God's school of advanced learning. He will capitalize on those troublesome but teachable times to bring his unique light into what we thought was hopeless darkness.

Admitting you blew it is never easy, and the pain and grief of the public side of your failure cannot be discounted as irrelevant or minimized as trivial. But when you admit your mistakes and accept both the consequences and the opportunities they bring for you to grow, you will discover a new side of God's faithfulness that you could not learn any other way.

11

SEIZING TEACHABLE
MOMENTS

FAILURE CAN PRODUCE GROWTH

The trouble we can get into when we make mistakes and then refuse to learn from them cannot be exaggerated. What a different world it is when we seize those moments and decide that we are going to learn something for a change! God wants to take our failures and teach us not only how to correct them, but also how to avoid them the next time we face that situation.

One of the key verses of my life points out that God has provided a source for just such occasions: "All Scripture is inspired by God and profitable for teaching, for reproof, for correction, for training in righteousness; so that the man of God may be adequate, equipped for every good work" (2 Tim. 3:16–17). He has given us his Word to equip us for life in Christ by leading us to believe, think, and do what is right, and to avoid what is wrong. The Word of God heightens our awareness that we need to see our mistakes for what they are—departures from the path of godliness and wise living. We need to be reproved by the Scriptures, to be reprimanded when we take a course contrary to what is right.

According to 2 Timothy 3:16–17, seeing and understanding the error of our ways is a good thing, something that the Bible works to accomplish in us as it shows us our mistakes and reveals to us where we have failed to meet the standard God set for us. After pointing out our error by way of reproof, the Word of God then brings a word of correction so that we not only face up to our mistakes but are shown how to straighten things out again.

In other words, God offers us special encouragement in these verses. He will teach us through his Word, but he knows we won't get it right away and we will fail in our efforts. But when we admit we are not where we are supposed to be, he will provide the necessary instruction to help us return to his ways and learn to live righteous lives.

Do you see it? God has built into his Word a means of seizing the teachable moments brought on by our mistakes and failures so we may then be "adequate, equipped for every good work." With that in mind, how do we take hold of the teachable moments brought on by errors we make along the way?

Benefits to Be Gained

Life is richer because of what we learn through our troubles. There are many benefits to be gained after we fail when we open ourselves up to the things God wants to teach us when we are humble enough to listen and learn.

1. Failure destroys all our false notions of self-sufficiency, self-reliance, and self-righteousness.

All of us struggle with the idea that we should be able to handle life without any assistance from anyone, including God. While verbally affirming that we depend upon the Lord, we

169

often operate as if he has nothing to do with the daily affairs of our lives. Like little children, we stubbornly protest his offers to help and insist that we can do it ourselves. What a foolish error that is! Yet, as a pastor, have you not gone along doing the work of the ministry only to realize that you are not relying on the Lord for what you are doing now, and have not done so for some time? Failure forces you into a wall, arrests your forward motion, and curtails your aggressive pursuits—neither of which may have been following a direction given by God. Once you have had to deal with the consequences of a major error, you realize that apart from him, you really can do nothing of eternal value. Therefore, our mistakes and failures actually serve us well by compelling us to rely on the Lord.

2. Failure alerts you to weaknesses that need to be strengthened, directions that should be avoided, and mistakes that must not be repeated.

If you never realize that you have failed, you will never realize how far you are from all that God wants you to be. In your failures are the seeds of instruction you need in order to grow up to bear the fruit of the Spirit and to live out the life of Christ. Sometimes direct instruction from the Bible doesn't convince you as it should and the lessons you really need can only be communicated effectively after you've run headlong into the wall of your own inadequacies and weaknesses. Frankly, I hate to fail. More than that, I hate to have to admit that I am wrong or that my ideas failed. Yet without those admissions and without those failures, I would probably assume things about myself that are not true and see myself in a light that flatters me but unfortunately misrepresents me. If I labor under the delusion that I am incapable of errors in judgment, I become unteachable and my journey toward spiritual maturity and effective servant leadership comes to a dead end.

Many times I've been so convinced I was right that I built a protective wall around myself to prevent the intrusion of any ideas or suggestions that could have contributed to what I was thinking and actually improved it. I limited what the Lord wanted to teach me by closing my mind to the possibility that I could be wrong or that I could be missing some important details due to blind spots in my perspective. During those times, I earned a reputation among some for being unteachable, even stubborn—both of which were true! Eventually though, reality would set in and I would get my comeuppance, forcing me to admit either that what I'd been pushing wouldn't work or that it was underdeveloped due to my insistence on doing things my way. In those cases, failure became a vehicle to deliver God's mercy. Without falling flat on my face, I would have continued to deceive myself into thinking that I was above making mistakes and, moreover, was guaranteed success in every endeavor to which I put my hand.

A healthy dose of reality comes each time you stumble and reminds you that God still has much work to do in your life. One of his most effective teaching tools is your own fallibility, and he is not reluctant to use it whenever necessary to accomplish his purposes.

3. Failure demonstrates your need for growth and for greater depth to the roots of your faith.

When the high winds of the storms of failure blow up around you, you realize how important it is to sink your roots deep into the ground so you are not toppled by the adversities that come with failure. The absence of strong winds lulls us into thinking that surface living is all we need and that deep roots are a luxury we can live without. Only when the storms come do we realize that much growing still remains. Daily devotions and routines that help you stay in touch with the Lord become insufficient when you find yourself staring into the teeth of a massive storm generated by your own foolishness. You need to call upon the Lord from the deep places where he has anchored your soul with immoveable roots. Prayer that emerges from those "dark nights of the soul" tends to be weightier, more persistent, and much more honest than that which accompanies your scheduled devotional prayer times. When in agony the heart cries out to God from a feeling of desperate need, the roots of our faith reach deeper to attach themselves to the bedrock of his eternal steadfastness. Lives without the pain of failure and the embarrassment of foolish errors seldom sense the need to cling to the Lord. Therefore, we need failure and mistakes in our lives to keep us real but also to cause us to go deeper.

4. Failure builds endurance and the strength to stand firm.

Once the roots have reached sufficient depth, our mistakes and failures force us to flex with the wind—but in stretching we also become stronger. We need the depth of a solid foundation, but we also need the strength in the trunk and limbs above the surface. Enduring hard times and suffering from broken branches occasionally will prove to be an essential element for standing firm when the storms arise from forces beyond our control. By developing strength from our own struggles, we find that we have been conditioned to face the challenges brought on by other influences.

5. Failure promotes humility and persistence in prayer.

There are few things that drive us to our knees more directly than the realization that we did what we could and it was not enough. In those times we confront our humanity in a new light, the true light that reveals what God has said all along but which we could not appreciate. He wants us to know that apart from him we can do nothing. When we come face-to-face with our impotence, we resort to prayer as our last recourse in a desperate attempt to salvage some vestige of hope. Landing a blow to our egos is sometimes God's way of shaking us up and putting us in a position that makes his point through our trauma in a way that would never be learned if we continued to enjoy nothing but success.

Prayer is born out of necessity more often than any other motivation. Although it should be just as intense and focused when we are devoting ourselves to times of fellowship and worship, to praise and thanksgiving, even to general supplication and specific intercession, prayer that comes from the agony of our broken dreams and failed plans often carries a weightier character and a relentless passion. Charles Spurgeon said, "When things run counter to your wishes, expect that the Lord has provided some better thing for you. He is driving you away from the shallow waters and bringing you into deeper seas, where your nets shall bring you larger draughts."[1]

What we find out about prayer and even about God himself in the deeper seas would never be learned if we remained in control, always succeeding, always getting our way. Both our failures and the mistakes we so frequently make take us to places in prayer we would never have gone otherwise.

6. Failure develops a genuine appreciation of grace in our lives.

Can we continue to think we deserve all that God has freely given us when we see how easily we can mess things up? A humble assessment of our condition is all that is needed to open our eyes to the marvelous wonder of God's grace. In 1758, when Robert Robinson wrote the hymn "Come, Thou Fount of Every Blessing," he asked for God's help to guard against our inclination to wander away from him: "Prone to wander, Lord, I feel it; prone to leave the God I love; Here's my heart, Lord, take and seal it, seal it for Thy courts above!"[2] We can fully appreciate the depth of his grace and the fullness of his mercy only when we recognize how patient God is with us. Foolish errors and prayerless mistakes succeed in bringing proud hearts down so that we finally will look up and see what the goodness of God really means.

1. Charles Spurgeon, *Spurgeon's Expository Encyclopedia*, vol. 5 (Grand Rapids: Baker, 1978), 412.
2. Robert Robinson, "Come, Thou Fount of Every Blessing," 1758. Public domain.

7. Failure reinforces the value of character over reputation.

Who we are before God matters far more than what we want others to think of us. If we have to become people with no reputation in order to develop Christlike character, the cost seems too great for us under normal circumstances. But when we've fallen from pedestals where people once held us in high regard and have lost our good name, all that really is important to us then is to find favor with the Lord. When what pleases him matters more than what pleases people, the price we have to pay is worth it all. Failure and fallibility serve us well in removing the pride we had in our reputation so we can attend to the calling of Christ to be people of true character.

8. Failure opens our eyes and heart to empathize with others who have failed so that we will have compassion for them.

Harshness and judgmentalism fight a losing battle in a heart broken by its own mistakes and crushed by its own failures. In their place, tenderness and understanding win out and give us the ability not only to understand what it feels like to fail, but also to appreciate what is necessary to be restored. I feel sorry for people who will not extend a hand of mercy to those who have made mistakes, because those who've made mistakes need to know that the unconditional love of the Father is available in abundance through his people. Failure deepens our compassion and enlightens our minds so we truly understand.

9. Failure communicates your humanness, lets the people around you identify with you, and makes you real to those who look to you for leadership.

Perfect people are hard to identify with. Try as we might (we who know we're not perfect), their apparent perfection erects an impenetrable barrier between them and us. Of course they are not actually perfect, but if we never see them fail and make mistakes, we have a hard time relating to them.

You become very real and approachable to those in your circle of influence when you slip a notch or two in their estimation and they are allowed to see that you are just a sinner saved by grace like them. Let me hasten to add that this is not an appeal for you to do foolish things to gain favor with them. It is my way of urging you to be honest when you do not come out on top or when you are wrong. Let others see you as you really are and allow them to identify with your failures so they may then find hope and encouragement when you overcome through the power of Christ.

Capitalizing on Your Mistakes

What should you do when it becomes clear that you blew it? When you realize that God has offered a word of reproof to you, recognize the sound of his voice, because he will soon be bringing a word of correction to lead you back to what is right, to set things straight again.

1. As soon as you realize your error, give thanks to the Lord that he has given you yet another indication that he is still working on you.

It is erroneous to look at our troubles and think that God does not care about what happens to us, because if he did, he would protect us from harm, even from the kind we bring upon ourselves. In reality, the fact that he does care for us has been demonstrated in the way our struggles draw us closer to him. Paul said, "For I am confident of this very thing, that He who began a good work in you will perfect it until the day of Christ Jesus" (Phil. 1:6). One of the tools he has chosen to use is readily available—our failures! In a wedding prayer written by Louis Evans Jr., he prays for the newly married couple and asks the Lord to "give them enough tears to keep them tender . . . enough failure to keep their hands clinched tightly in Yours."[3] A sure sign of God's commitment to our growth is that he allows us to fall down so we can learn the pleasure of being picked up again, stronger and wiser than before because he teaches us as he reaches us.

2. If you are not sure where you went wrong, ask some trustworthy friends to help you assess the problem and give you a frank evaluation of what they see.

This can be a painful ordeal, because you are submitting to the scrutiny of those who love you enough to help you learn from your mistakes, but who understand that they cannot hold back anything that needs to be said. They may conclude that your mistake was due to a one-time error in judgment and help you find a way to avoid doing that again. Or they may identify a pattern they have observed for some time but never had the opportunity to address.

Knowing the truth, even if it hurts, allows you to find freedom from old ways of living and marks a starting point for genuine progress in your walk with Christ. One of the best ways to learn the truth, if you are willing to hear it, is to approach a small and select group and invite them to hold you accountable on an ongoing basis. Ask this group to tell you the truth in love so you might benefit from their wisdom and profit from their insights.

3. Find a way to summarize where you went astray and why, as well as what the right choice should have been.

Putting the thoughts down on paper sometimes helps to bring clarity to your considerations and organizes your thinking as you explore options that perhaps have not occurred to you. The mental discipline required to work through the issues will be good preparation and training for responding to similar

3. Louis H. Evans, *The Marriage Prayer*, http://www.wrvm.org/marriage_prayer.htm. Accessed on August 14, 2006.

situations in the future. Carelessness, impulsiveness, lack of thorough consideration, and many other such causes prove that sound thinking seldom precedes bad choices. Honestly critique what caused your failure so you can learn from your own experience. Following the same course of action over and over again and expecting to get different results is the height of foolishness. Therefore, find out what to do differently by applying yourself to a thorough review of how to avoid the same result next time.

As a part of your assessment and review, go ahead and take the next step, and propose a plan that will guide your actions in the future and outline legitimate options you can follow with confidence. Having said all this, I need to point out that you are still going to make mistakes. That goes with the territory of being a fallible human being in an imperfect world. The idea behind taking the time to process your mistakes is to learn all that you can so you do not have to go through the same situation again. God wants us to learn from failure so that we will grow up in Christ.

A Few Closing Observations

Repeating the same mistakes over and over again suggests either that you do not care or that you do not get it. If that has been your experience, welcome to the human race! However, we cannot excuse ourselves from God's call to spiritual maturity. If you do not care that you are repeating the same mistakes, then you have a bigger problem than just making repetitive errors. A heart that longs to grow in Christ cares about such things. But if you cannot figure out what you are doing wrong, then again, get some assistance from a group of discerning, wise consultants, counselors, mentors, or other friends. Let them hold you accountable until you reach some conclusions and demonstrate that you have a grasp of the problems and have some viable solutions.

I have watched with some sadness as pastors have bailed out of their place of ministry to save face rather than admit that they blew it. Instead of learning from their failures, they ran away from them and hoped no one would notice they weren't perfect! On the other hand, not every church is mature enough to cultivate an environment of grace where growth can take place among a group of fellow strugglers seeking to know Christ and become like him. Some pastors are forced out before they have a chance to learn from their mistakes. In those places, learning from mistakes gets buried under a load of condemnation; for both the pastor who failed and the church that would not help him, failure becomes very destructive.

What can I say? Life is not always fair, especially to those who accept the call of God to serve as shepherds of local congregations. You cannot control what others may do, but you can determine that, as far as it depends upon you, you will never allow your mistakes to be harmful. Choose to seize each one as a fresh new course in God's curriculum designed to grow you up as a balanced, godly pastor with a healthy understanding of his grace and your need for it.

If you choose to hide your mistakes and failures, you will not find any peace in doing so. Your paranoia will escalate and your insecurities will multiply with each day, because deep in your heart, you know that discovery is imminent. Covering up your mistake or hiding your failure gets in the way of restoration and impedes any progress God wants to work out in your life. If the failure is sinful, refusing to acknowledge it usually results in a hardened heart and the inability to hear from God or even to be heard by God: "If I regard wickedness in my heart, the Lord will not hear" (Ps. 66:18). If that happens, you may avoid losing your reputation, but you will eventually lose the privilege of keeping your ministry. Anyone who forfeits his place before the Father also gives up his right to lead the flock of God. On the other hand, when you develop an environment of grace by treating others around you with forgiveness and mercy, your flock will be trained through your example. Moreover, they will be more inclined to demonstrate mercy and grace toward you.

God wants you to learn that your mistakes and failures do not have to throw your entire ministry out of balance permanently.

Let him teach you, reprove you, correct you, and train you, even if the lessons come in the school of hard knocks. You are going to mess up, make mistakes, fall into disastrous errors of judgment, and even suffer devastating failures during the course of your ministry. As in the jousting tournament, the lance of your troubles can completely unseat you and dash you to the ground, or it can temporarily knock you out of balance and force you to scramble to recover a secure place in the saddle. When you bring trouble down on your own head by the choices you make, do not despair. Instead, turn them from tragedy to triumph by inviting the Lord to teach you valuable lessons that you would never learn apart from the unique character of your particular struggles.

═══ 12 ═══

WHEN YOUR CHARACTER IS UNDER FIRE

THE WITHERING EFFECT OF PERSONAL ATTACKS

The time for football practice to be over had come and gone. Already exhausted from the rigors of two-a-day practice sessions in the preseason, my team now labored to get through the repetitious drills of kickoff returns. Running the full length of the field over and over again tends to sap one's strength, and mine was gone.

Since each drill involved full contact, a moment's lapse of concentration could result in getting your bell rung by some teammate looking for an opportunity to make a good impression on the coaches. Well, you guessed it! I was working out with the kickoff unit, covering my assignment along the sideline to turn any player who came my way into the strength of the defense toward the middle of the field. The receiving team took the kick and came my way. To my amazement, no one seemed to notice that I had a clean line of attack on the ball carrier. Just as the adrenaline began to pump and I could visualize the play I was about to make, I got nailed from my blind side harder than I had ever been hit in my life. I literally saw stars, went numb for a split second, then felt the pain and panic of lying on my back with the breath knocked out of me. The guy who blocked me hit me after getting up a full head of steam. Much to my regret, I never saw him coming and could do nothing to protect myself.

The pastor's equivalent of the kickoff drill is the Sunday morning marathon, not exactly a day of rest for folks like us! Fighting fatigue after a day of fruitful labors, we finally set our sails toward home when, out of nowhere, someone nails our blind side and flips us over. The choice of timing for our critics always seems to catch us off guard. Sometimes it comes right as we are heading into the pulpit, sometimes by phone late Sunday evening, often on Mondays when the grievance still burns hotly, and once in a while it comes at us anonymously in a letter we start to read before we notice that it is unsigned.

Why every church attracts people like this remains a mystery to me. It seems that many professing followers of Christ feel responsible for making a pastor's job as difficult as possible. In a strange way, it seems they think it is right for them to keep their pastor under constant attack.

During the days of the first Gulf War, the most eminent danger posed by Iraq was to its neighboring nations that feared Saddam Hussein's ability to launch Scud missiles from mobile sites, making it almost impossible to anticipate when and from where the attacks would originate. The people of Israel were particularly vulnerable, since they were well within range of the missiles and also were Hussein's most hated enemy. Because the launches were from mobile units, the only defense available had to come after the missiles were in the air and were detected by monitoring devices. Patriot missiles and other defensive weapons succeeded in protecting Israel and Saudi Arabia from the majority of the attacks, but moving targets are difficult to hit.

Unfortunately, the attack methods of many within the church imitate modern warfare much too closely. Compounding the

181

problem is the fact that some of the attacks not only keep moving but remain hidden behind the scenes. They avoid detection, cloaked in secrecy and camouflaged behind smoke screens of verbal coverings that hide the origin of the attack. All of us have tried to trace the source of some of the attacks against us, only to reach this dead-end line: "Well, I was told this is true, but I cannot reveal who told me without breaking their confidence. You wouldn't want me to do that, would you?"

At other times, we know all too well the source from which we are being shelled. Marshall Shelley wrote a book called *Well-Intentioned Dragons* that examines the kinds of people who do such things and offers several helpful insights that both identify their methods and suggest possible reasons that might prompt them to behave the way they do.[1] If you've been a pastor any time at all, you will easily recognize them as Shelley describes them. You might have to resist the temptation to write names in the margin as you read along!

Troubles come in many forms for us pastors. Some of them we bring upon ourselves through our own failures and mistakes, as we discussed in the last two chapters. But as difficult as it is to learn from troubles that are our own fault, finding the lessons God wants us to learn in the middle of incoming, hostile fire seems to be even more difficult. When we are the cause of our own problems, we tend to be more lenient with the source, more forgiving and understanding toward ourselves. But when we see ourselves as the victims of unjust and undeserved attacks from others, it is easier to fuel our anger than to feed on God's wisdom.

How then do we prepare ourselves for the attacks on our character that seem to proliferate the longer we're in ministry? The role of pastoral leadership often functions as a lightning rod for the disgruntled people in the church, as if by assuming the title "pastor" we give them license to unload all their frustrations on us. I once heard Stuart Briscoe answer a question

1. Marshall Shelley, *Well-Intentioned Dragons* (Minneapolis: Bethany House, 1994). See chapter 2, "Identifying a Dragon." Shelley identifies twelve common tactics used by those who specialize in making life difficult for their pastors.

about the vulnerability of those in Christian leadership roles by inventing a new proverb that matches the experience of so many of us: "He that dareth to raise his head above the crowd inviteth the tomato." In other words, if you dare to assume the role of biblical leadership, especially as a pastor, some people think you are just asking for it—and they are glad to see that you get it! How do we learn to grow in the grace and knowledge of the Lord Jesus Christ in that kind of environment?

Different Kinds of Attacks

Why do we, as Christian leaders, have to prepare ourselves for attacks from those who are supposed to be colleagues in righteousness? Some of the most destructive attacks we face as pastors do not come from a pagan, unbelieving world (although some attacks still do arise from that quarter). The most frequent attacks come from within the ranks of those who profess to love Christ and those he has called to be his church. Just as there are new and different kinds of attacks emerging among the nations of the world today, different kinds of attacks are used to assault the character and ministry of those who have become pastors and other Christian leaders. Knowing as much as possible about these attacks can help us respond to them in a way that honors Christ and helps us trust him more.

As I have recalled my own experiences and reviewed those of others I know who are in ministry, the distinctive kinds of attacks on our character seem to fall into two basic categories: *intentional attacks* and *unintentional challenges*.

Intentional Attacks

Most of the attacks that target you as a pastor are deliberate, intentional, and have no redemptive purpose in the mind and heart of the one coming after you. The reasons behind such behavior are often not even clear to the one who aims at you but probably have very little to do with you personally. Of course, that doesn't make it less painful when they

183

score a direct hit on your heart! Saying "nothing personal" while they tear you apart seldom provides much relief from the suffering. Our consolation comes from knowing that God intends to mold us and shape our character through such experiences, so we can expect to learn lessons in godliness from our troubles.

Personal attacks. Personal attacks place us in the crucible where the fire becomes so intense that we wonder if we have what it takes to survive with the character of Christ intact. When someone comes after us personally, our first reaction is often to strike back and to defend ourselves. The best defense is a good offense, so it is arguably a good strategy to turn our guns on them before they can inflict any substantial damage on us. But wait. As a pastor you are not called to protect and defend yourself but to proclaim Christ. If you succeed in destroying your attacker, then you have failed to shepherd someone in your flock.

Attacks on your preaching style. As one who invests a lot of time, prayer, and energy into the preparation and preaching of sermons, you cannot be expected to remain objective about that part of your life. Consequently, when people criticize you for the way you preach, that kind of personal attack will generate a tremendous emotional reaction. I can still recall the sting of having a couple sit across from me and one of them offering this shocking comment: "I'm sorry, but I just don't see Christ in your preaching." After sticking that dagger in my heart, the follow-up comment was, "But don't take that personally." Oh, right! What do you say to that kind of "helpful comment"?

Attacks on your character. On another occasion, it was not my preaching that was under attack but my character. Integrity and honesty are fundamental to my understanding of what should characterize any person who follows Christ, even more so a pastor. Yet I found myself being questioned about my honesty, having to defend myself against an accusation that I had not spoken truthfully in a couple of incidents involving a painful personnel matter. In spite of having witnesses who verified my side of the story, I suffered deeply to think that people I knew and loved and trusted had been led to distrust me. The extremely

184

personal nature of that kind of attack strikes deep and inflicts much pain, and all the more because the assault upon my character was calculated and deliberate by one who knew the truth but dismissed it in an effort to damage my character.

A pastor is an easy target. Besides direct assaults on your character, there will be those who attack you simply because you are the pastor and your visibility makes you an easy target. Disgruntled people who have little or no joy in their lives cannot stand to see someone else doing well. As a result, they launch their attacks upon the nearest and safest target, and pastors usually fit the bill quite well. What they would not dare do at work or within their own family, they feel perfectly comfortable doing with you. Not only do disgruntled people do this, but also those who are themselves hurting. They are among the "walking wounded" who come to church looking for a way to relieve their pain. They come looking for a way to let someone else be the target for a while, and you look nice enough not to bite back.

In the case of disgruntled and hurting people, it really is important not to take it personally, because they could not care less about you. They are looking for a reason to vent their pent-up anger and frustration about life in general and a safe place to do it without serious repercussions in their own lives. And there you are, just a phone call away, or standing by the door as they leave the church building. The sheer convenience of it all is too much for them to pass up. Tag, you're it . . . you are their victim of the day! Depending on how well you know the person and how much their opinion of you matters, this kind of attack may or may not inflict much pain. Still, you wonder about a world in which those who claim to love Christ can be so insensitive and uncaring toward you.

A case of mistaken identity. As much as you try to distinguish yourself personally from the church you pastor, many will identify you with the church and the church with you. If they have a different idea of how the church should function, what its ministry philosophy should be, and where it should place its emphasis, guess what? They will come after you! Yet they seldom separate what the church is from who you are, so their assault on the church tends to be directed at you personally.

In all fairness, part of the identification of you personally with the church corporately can be traced back to the tendency most of us in ministry have to associate our sense of worth with the value we attach to what we do. If people love the church and its ministry, we feel affirmed and encouraged. If there are problems, we tend to take them to heart. Objectivity is hard to come by when pastors think and talk about the churches they pastor. They almost see the church as extensions of themselves. By the grace of God, that is not how he sees us, but as long as we struggle with that association we will feel defensive and wounded when people speak to us with a critical spirit about the church.

A Case of Faulty Information

Another segment of the church population that tends to want to storm the castle is the group that has received bad information and not bothered to check it out before assuming the worst. I cannot tell you how many times I have encountered irate church members who wanted to set me straight about something that turned out to be based on misinformation passed on to them by someone else. Most of the time the source of that misinformation is innocent and did not get all the facts before passing on a report that ended up generating more heat than light.

Occasionally though, information goes out that has intentionally been crafted to achieve a specific goal. I'll never forget a statement made by a city council member in our city years ago, after the council heard a report from a citizen who was determined to persist until his project was approved. One member of the council looked at the presenter as he left the podium and said, "On behalf of the council, I would like to thank Mr. Smith for his carefully managed presentation of the facts." Deception should never come into play among those who live for the truth. Yet when personal agendas get involved and the life of the Spirit gives way to the flesh, you will find that even in the body of Christ people will spread around "carefully managed presentations of the facts" in order to gain a more favorable hearing for their position.

When misinformation does make its way into the church family, you can rest assured that someone will approach you about it, and not always with a sweet and gentle spirit. What happens when such people find out that their reason for being upset is no longer valid? All the things they had rehearsed to say to you no longer apply, but attack mode is hard to withdraw from after the buttons have been pushed, so you may find it necessary to let them vent for a while, even after you've disarmed them with the facts.

A desire to gain control. People who like to control their world generally are not reluctant when it comes to trying to control you as their pastor. Those who wield power in their own world want to do the same in the world of the church. If they see you as the primary power figure in the church, they will not hesitate to try to overpower you. Sometimes their strategy will take the form of flattery and sometimes the subtle manipulation of personal favors to put you in their debt. If these don't work, and they have learned that many people in ministry wilt at the first sign of attack, they may eventually begin their assault on what they perceive to be the tower of power—the pastor's office (if they only knew how mistaken that perception is!)—to gain the upper hand in the affairs of the church.

Personal experience has shown me how unscrupulous and unprincipled people can become when they set out to have things their way. Manipulation, deception, and intimidation are only some of the means I have endured as I was attacked by those who tried to seize control of the direction of the ministry of the church—a direction that had been embraced and affirmed by the staff, elders, deacons, and congregation alike. All that mattered was that they wanted something different. They were used to getting their way, so any means was justified by the end they had in mind. What wretched times we sometimes endure at the hands of our friends within the church! Those attacks intentionally challenge you, press in upon you, drain you, and seek to wear you out—all for the sake of gaining control and wielding power on their own terms.

A desire to elevate themselves. Among the intentional attacks leveled at you will also be those that arise from insecure people who constantly tear others down in order to make themselves look better. Since they are not secure in themselves, they sense that their only way to elevate their own ego needs is to force other people into a defensive posture. They tend to be suspicious of anyone in authority. Whenever the opportunity arises, they will defiantly assert their voices in protest against you since you represent for them just another authority figure against whom they should rebel. When you realize that the church offers them the only safe place to rebel without immediate consequences, it helps you understand why they do what they do. Nonetheless, their barbed comments and sharp denunciations still cut deep.

Attacks from the adversary. One last source of intentional attacks upon you is not surprising at all—the concerted efforts of Satan to undo anything he sees God doing. His ability to find and to strike at your weakest and most vulnerable points has long been acknowledged in Scripture and in our own experience. The warning in 1 Peter 5:8 still applies as much today as when the words were first written: "Be of sober spirit, be on the alert. Your adversary, the devil, prowls around like a roaring lion, seeking someone to devour." Who better to devour than someone like you, who has been called and used by God to lead people into a relationship with Christ and equip them to walk with God?

Stories abound describing the diverse means employed by our enemy to bring down pastors and Christian leaders. By the grace of God, maintain the diligence that Peter advises so you do not become the subject of yet another anecdote of a pastor who was blindsided by the devil, whose ministry was not only thrown out of balance, but destroyed by the wicked schemes of the accuser of the brethren.

Unintentional Challenges

The second category of challenges we undergo as pastors comes from those who do not mean their words and actions to feel like an assault, but the net effect is still the same. Often

188

these troubles arise from thoughtless and careless words spoken with little regard for the weight of their impact.

Constant questioning. As I mentioned earlier, I once found myself constantly on the defensive with a couple of our church leaders. No matter what subject came up, I could count on hearing objections from both men as they raised question after question in what appeared to be a challenge to my leadership, concern for my common sense, and a subtle suggestion that I examine my motives for bringing forward any ideas that had to do with addressing our growing congregation's need for additional staff, space, expanded ministry opportunities . . . you name it!

They would become more determined to press their point in direct proportion to the strength of my objection to their objections. Eventually, I had to find out what was going on, because I had had it. After a meeting with some particular ill will, I called them both after I got home and asked if we could get together and work this thing out. We met that night, and I learned a valuable lesson from them, and I believe they learned some things as well.

When I told them how their constant undermining of my leadership had become a stumbling block in our relationship, they both looked shocked. Neither had any idea that their questions were perceived by me or anyone else as negative. In their minds, there was no intent to show either defiance or opposition. They honestly did not mean to come across in a way that put me on the defensive or challenged me. As we discussed the issues, I saw these men in a different light. They meant no harm by what they said and had no idea that I was feeling under the gun whenever they spoke up in meetings.

On the other hand, they realized they had to learn how to ask questions without any subtle insinuation that they were trying to uncover wrongdoing. Simply in the way they phrased their questions, the other people in the room sensed they were under attack. I know I certainly had felt that way! Out of our time together, we reached a comfortable agreement that I would be less sensitive in how I took their comments, and they would try to guard their words more carefully. We also agreed to extend a wide band of grace to each other when we fell back into old habits and refuse to allow ourselves to build any kind of barriers to our relationship. That night we reaffirmed trust. In spite of how they said what they said, I saw in each man a heart full of sincere interest in the things of Christ, and yes, even a deep interest in and care for me personally. Their manner and my oversensitivity had created an unintentionally adversarial relationship. I tell this story to encourage you to always try to talk out difficulties with the parties involved. You, too, may find that God leads the conversation in ways you didn't expect when you started, and you are able to strengthen the bonds of leadership in your church.

Differences of philosophy. On some occasions, people have tried to be "helpful" by coming up with ways for me to spend my time by recommending ministries that could have greater merit (at least in their opinion) than those currently occupying me. After a particularly exhausting discussion many years ago, the message was clear from a few of our leaders: the direction of our ministry was inconsistent with their perspective of what it means to be an effective church. Hours of deliberation had brought all of us to a conclusion. If the church had a chance of becoming what they wanted it to be, I was going to have to radically alter the way I did ministry—my priorities, my values, my ministry principles, my vision, all would have to change. Of course, they did not understand all the ramifications of what they were recommending, but we all grasped the essence of the issue. My approach to ministry would have to give way to something completely different.

Was I personally under attack? No, I realized that their concern was exclusively one of philosophy. For them, it was a simple shift of emphasis. For me, it was a drastic departure from all that I understood about what God wanted to do in my life and through the ministry he had given me. When we explored the implications of their plans and proposals, we soon realized that our visions were totally different and essentially incompatible.

Once we recognized the problem, we were able to address it without having to overcome any obstacles that would have been in the way if their challenges were intended to be a personal

WHEN YOUR CHARACTER IS UNDER FIRE

assault on me or my resistance to their ideas was a personal challenge to them. Unintentional attacks still carry a heaviness with them, but they are less threatening when you realize that there really is nothing personal involved.

Volunteers who want to "fix" your ministry. Then there are those who want you to measure up to a standard they assume is the only proper, spiritually sound, and appropriate way to handle whatever they have in mind at the moment. Frequently these matters are brought up by those who perceive themselves to be highly mature or well experienced in ministry, and all they want to do is help you catch up to their level of spirituality and church expertise.

People like these are not aware of how judgmental or condescending they sound when they come up to you and volunteer to "fix" your ministry. Somewhere in their background they have been exposed to a certain way of approaching a particular kind of ministry, and they want you to benefit from their experience. They have no real desire to suggest that what you are doing is inferior and ineffective—but the problem for you is that they seem to be suggesting just that!

Preceding their suggestions, they will usually include a foreword that details the basis upon which they are offering their expertise. Most of the time, they reference their previous church or ministry involvement (where everything was just wonderful!). Then they continue to explain why what you are doing is different—and consequently wrong. Beginning with the words, "In our last church, the pastor always . . ." they proceed to tell you how he or she did it right: the approach to the evangelism ministry, the emphasis on tithing during the annual stewardship series, the running of the staff, the kinds of music allowed in corporate worship, the organization of the churchwide prayer ministry, and so on.

They mean well, but they could hardly have realized that they were adding to the load of things we pastors already have to carry and deal with. Sometimes a good idea is suggested, so we cannot afford to dismiss suggestions, but when those offering the advice have not taken the time or trouble to learn what you actually do and why you do it, it is hard to

191

take such suggestions in the right spirit. But that is just the point. We must recognize that these unintentional intrusions are not intentional attacks, and we should not receive them with a wrong spirit.

Legitimate evaluation is needed. Another area of concern for pastors arises from legitimate evaluation and critique from those responsible for giving oversight and supervision to your ministry. All of us need to be accountable to someone. Every year, the pastors and elders meet together to evaluate the ministry at large. We review the past year and look for areas of unexpected success, ministries in need of improvement, and new focal points to emphasize. We evaluate the ministry so we as a church can continue to grow and learn how best to serve Christ together.

But I also need that kind of evaluation of my own ministry. The elders provide that for me and take great care annually to review how things have gone in my areas of responsibility in the previous year. Each elder offers insights and suggestions that are compiled into one evaluative document, which is then shared with me by a team of two or three. Although I usually have a good idea of where I have done well and where I need improvement, their perspective is always helpful. Without fail, there is always something in their evaluation that raises my awareness of issues I have overlooked. Human nature being what it is, regardless of how many kind and affirming words are in the evaluation, my eyes tend to zero in on the more negative points of critique. In order to avoid a defensive attitude, I always have to approach those times of evaluation with much prayer, asking the Lord to give me a heart willing to learn and a spirit open to change and growth.

Everyone has strengths, and everyone has weaknesses. Pastors need help in identifying both so we might excel still more in the area of our strengths and shore up the areas of weakness. Listen with a godly, humble heart so you do not miss this excellent resource for your own personal growth. Having leaders with discernment and wisdom who love you and embrace the same calling and vision for ministry allows you to place yourself in their hands, trusting them not to attack you by tearing you down, but to challenge you as they build you up. When we misread their intentions, we invite our own misery. When we truly believe that their intentions are wholesome and healthy, we can endure even those areas of critique that may not be expressed as sensitively or as helpfully as we would have wished. In Psalm 141:5 (NIV), David wrote, "Let a righteous man strike me—it is a kindness; let him rebuke me—it is oil on my head. My head will not refuse it."

Unintentional challenges and attacks consist largely of comments and behaviors that have nothing malicious about them. Prepare for the inevitability of having to deal with them by learning to assume the best and give the benefit of the doubt as long as possible. This skill will go a long way toward allowing you to keep things in perspective.

⸎

The way we handle attacks on our character and the character of our ministry calling demonstrates how much we are growing in the lifetime project of conforming to the image of Jesus Christ. Sometimes you will respond badly when the attacks seem unrelenting, merciless, and without justification. But getting knocked off balance, even thrown from your saddle, does not signify that you are doomed to repeat that mistake every time you come under fire. Unforeseen attacks can be so disheartening and discouraging that we sometimes question whether it is worth it to keep going. Who wants to put up with this abuse anyway? But that's not really the issue, is it? The bottom line is how we respond so that Christ is glorified and people are encouraged to see that it is possible to take direct hits—whether from enemy territory or from friendly fire—and still maintain a positive testimony for Christ. The way we respond speaks to the way we are growing up to maturity in Christ.

=13=

PREPARING A WISE RESPONSE

SEASONED MATURITY IN ACTION

Have you ever finished an argument and it wasn't until your antagonist walked away that you finally thought of just the right thing to say? If we could pull out just the right response in every situation, what a great advantage we would have! Preparing for ministry means more than just sermon preparation. Soul preparation matters as well, since we either authenticate our message with our lives or nullify it. Therefore, in this chapter, think with me about your response when people come after you in an aggressive and confrontational manner.

What Should You Do?

For anyone in ministry for more than a few years, responding to those who take issue with you is part of the routine. Seldom do we go very long without having an encounter with someone who is less than pleased with something about us or our ministry. The question then is not whether we should respond in a manner pleasing to Christ, but how we can do so consistently.

Any Kernel of Truth?

Before writing off the attack as the work of some accursed enemy, the first way to respond is to weigh the challenge carefully to see if it has any merit. Is there any validity to the charge or any substance to the accusation? Many extreme and bizarre challenges to you and your ministry may indeed contain a kernel of truth that needs to be received and processed properly. Even if you are above reproach in what has been brought to your attention, no harm is done in giving due thought to see if there is something either behind what they have brought up or a secret motive that their challenge brings to the surface.

Several years ago, I received a letter from a visitor accusing me of injecting too much of myself and too little of Christ in the sermon she heard. At first I was hurt that anyone would think such a thing, since it is my aim to keep every message as Christ-centered as possible. What had I said to give her the impression that the sermon was merely a vehicle for grabbing personal attention? Her comments forced me to examine myself. Had I gone overboard by using myself as an example? Her concerns didn't lead me to adopt a more clinical and impersonal approach to preaching, but they did make me stop and consider if I had become guilty of deviating too much from the primary point of the passage.

Take time to check out the validity of the accusation or attack before dismissing it as entirely without substance, until you are convinced that what you are doing is pleasing to the Lord.

A Call to Prayer

When a challenge arises, if you are not careful, your temper will too! A fundamental element in a godly response is to give the matter to the Lord in prayer. David was accused and attacked more viciously than most of us will ever be, yet he remained a man after God's own heart. Sometimes he invoked God's curses on his accusers and attackers, but ultimately, he would find his way back to a holy place and seek God's best: "Contend, O Lord, with those who contend with me; fight against those who fight against me. . . . In return for my love they act as my accusers; but I am in prayer" (Ps. 35:1; 109:4).

Ask the Lord to guide you through the flood of emotions you will experience so you can respond in a way that glorifies Christ. Until you have prayed, your perspective can be skewed and your attitude compromised. Only when we have taken our insecurities and hurts into the presence of the Lord can we expect to gain his point of view.

Praying before responding sometimes precludes the need to do anything. The Lord may direct you to wait or to pass on the concern to someone else to handle, or he might give you specific insight into the situation that only he can provide, which will dramatically alter what you end up doing.

Recently I received an unusually strident attack in the form of an email message. After attempting to answer the questions in a couple of replies, I suggested that we continue the discussion in person instead of in writing. As it turned out, that meeting could not take place for a couple of weeks. During that time I had the opportunity not only to pray myself, but also to invite the prayer support of a few other confidantes. By the time the meeting took place, God had given me a great calm and even some insight into the personal issues going on in the life of my accuser. God prevailed in response to prayer, and a peaceful resolution was reached without a volatile exchange. Make sure you allocate time to pray before you respond—even if it requires an on-the-spot plea for supernatural wisdom and self-control.

Quick to Hear, Slow to Speak

Another important aspect of a godly response is found in James 1:19–20: "But everyone must be quick to hear, slow to

196

speak and slow to anger; for the anger of man does not achieve the righteousness of God." Your first thought may not be your best thought when you think your character is being attacked. Give yourself some time to process what is really being said.

If you are not clear about the point being made, ask some clarification questions. Often they may be trying to say something entirely different and may be inadvertently insulting you without meaning to do so. If you take the time to repeat their accusation back to them and ask them if that is what they meant, you give them the benefit of the doubt and give yourself time to pray and collect yourself before you fire off a response you may regret. Who has not spoken first and thought second? There is great value in heeding the instruction of James.

Seek Godly Counsel

If the situation allows, seek the counsel of some godly friends and ministry colleagues. Granted, some of the most hostile attacks come without warning or a chance to regroup before you have to respond. But if the opportunity presents itself, postpone giving an answer until you've had a chance to ask for help from those who know you and, more important, who walk with humility and wisdom before the Lord. The insight of others can be a blessing in avoiding foolish and damaging engagements: "Where there is no guidance the people fall, but in abundance of counselors there is victory" (Prov. 11:14).

Be prepared for some surprises when you seek godly counsel. Your counselors may confirm what your accuser has said. At the end of a difficult encounter one evening, a church member made an observation about my leadership style that offended me. What bothered me was that he wasn't angry, not in an attack mode, but just made the comment in a matter-of-fact way that effectively ended our discussion. After telling him I did not agree with his assessment, I realized that what he had said had gotten under my skin.

The next day, I met a couple of friends for lunch and told them what the member had said to me, expecting them to come to my defense and offer me advice on how to refute him. Instead, they both stared into their plates, neither volunteering to speak next. Breaking the uncomfortable silence, I said, "Surely you don't agree with him, do you?" Well, don't ask for what you are not prepared to hear! These friends who loved me confirmed that they shared the same impression the other fellow had. Only in seeking the counsel of godly and wise friends did I discover a blind spot that I assumed was just a petty accusation but was in fact God's way of opening my eyes to an area of my life that needed correction.

Another time I found myself publicly challenged. An article appeared in the local newspaper that included false statements about our church. Incensed that such a thing had happened, I drafted a letter to the editor to set things straight. Before mailing it, I asked a couple of friends to read it and see whether it needed anything to strengthen the impact of my refutation. Each man, without consulting the other, complimented the letter's clarity and veracity—and then recommended that I throw it away without sending it! By following their advice, I avoided prolonging a public discussion of a subject that would certainly have been slanted to suit the editorial perspective of the paper. Their wise counsel protected me from my own impetuous nature and from making a serious error in judgment.

Arrange to Meet with Your Accusers

Make it your practice to arrange to face your accusers in a personal, private meeting whenever possible. This way you can hear their concerns firsthand and offer them a chance to express themselves directly to you. Not only is this somewhat disarming, since so many people avoid face-to-face confrontations of this nature, but it allows you to ask them questions and demonstrate genuine concern for them as individuals. For some, that is all that matters—they want to know that you care about them personally and are willing to listen.

However, in many cases you would be wise to have a third party present to make sure that the conversation remains civil.

If your conversation is later conveyed to others beyond the meeting, the presence of a third party can protect you from unfounded accusations about what you said and how you handled yourself. I failed to do that on one occasion and found myself accused of making all kinds of statements that were never said or even implied. But since it was my word against the word of my accuser, I couldn't prove that I was being falsely blamed for saying things I never said.

However, before you think that having a third party present guarantees your protection, let me tell you from experience—it doesn't! On at least two occasions I've had to deal with attacks on my integrity by people who swore I had made inflammatory statements to them in attempting to resolve areas of staff conflict. Even though a third party present in each of those meetings confirmed my version of the conversations, the aggrieved parties insisted that we were both wrong and their recollection was correct. With that said, it is still the best course to initiate a personal, private conversation as soon after you hear of any attacks against you.

Consider No One Your Enemy

Your role as a pastor is to lead the entire flock, not just those who agree with you. For the sake of your ministry for Jesus Christ, you cannot afford to have enemies. Although you cannot keep others from seeing you as their enemy, you can determine to never reciprocate and view them that way. If others hold grudges, develop roots of bitterness, and in other ways declare war against you, your responsibility in Christ is to rise above the fray and pursue peace with them. The writer to the Hebrews commands us to "pursue peace with all men, and the sanctification without which no one will see the Lord" (12:14).

Even when your hand gets slapped away in the process, hold out the olive branch to them and persistently treat them with respect. You can pray for their influence to be minimized as they seek allies to join their cause against you, all the while treating them with kindness in all your dealings with them. You want to let your godly character and demeanor bear witness to a genuinely humble spirit: your best defense against their attacks is a gracious, Christlike response.

Resist Taking It to the Pulpit

We have the responsibility of guarding the pulpit each week and ensuring that solid biblical food is prepared and presented to the flocks under our care. But we must also act with discretion and honor in how we treat that sacred platform when we are under attack. Making use of the pulpit to answer your critics may seem like a good idea if you want to provide a corrective word for the individual or group making things difficult for you. But everyone loves an underdog, and by bullying your accusers from the pulpit, you will quickly succeed in creating one. A small contingency of disgruntled and complaining people can become a majority in a hurry if other folks in the congregation get the impression that you are using the pulpit for your own agenda. Resist the impulse to address private attacks in a public forum unless it becomes so widespread that you have little choice. Even then, proceed with caution, and only after much prayer and godly counsel.

Don't Force People to Choose Sides

When a rift threatens the peace and unity of the body of Christ, your role as pastor is to take action as a peacemaker, not to muster support for your side. Those who have chosen to introduce the controversy and target you as the focus of their displeasure will in all likelihood do everything they can to divide the house and gather as many people who will agree with them as possible. They will have to answer to the Lord for sowing seeds of dissent in his church. God has no sympathy for those who are willing to destroy the unity of the Spirit among his people for their own agendas: "There are six things the LORD hates, seven that are detestable to him: haughty eyes, a lying

200

tongue, hands that shed innocent blood, a heart that devises wicked schemes, feet that are quick to rush into evil, a false witness who pours out lies and a man who stirs up dissension among brothers" (Prov. 6:16–19 NIV).

You cannot control what others do against you, but you can make sure that you do not contribute to the divisiveness by responding to their deeds with a "fight fire with fire" mentality. God has no patience with such things under any circumstances. As a shepherd of the flock you dare not be party to any tactic that would further divide his people. Therefore, do not allow yourself to encourage people to choose sides. Do not allow yourself to test their loyalty to see if they are with you. If your accusers do that, you must be determined to do everything in your power not to respond in kind.

Keep the Matter Confidential

Although some pastors are very discreet and keep matters to themselves, I have found that many are inclined to talk too much, too often, and to too many people. When I advised before to seek godly counsel, that counsel should be limited to a few trusted individuals who can be counted on to keep your confidence. The more widespread you make the attack known, the more work you make for yourself when the matter is resolved.

If knowledge of the attack becomes widespread, you will have at least three problems you may not be able to solve. First, the seeds of dissent you sowed may have taken deeper root than you intended in some of those who heard of your dilemma. It is natural to share such things with those who have a natural sympathy with you, or who have a similar problem with the person or persons challenging you. But for those folks, all you have done is add fuel to their fire, and you may not receive much objective or godly counsel.

Second, if you share the concern with someone who already has a history of difficulty with the person in question, you add fuel to their fire and give them even more reason to persist in the way they perceive the attacker. With such bias against the person, they will be unlikely to offer much objective or godly counsel to you.

Third, you will find that it is very difficult to track down all the places the reports of the attack have traveled. Someone once likened this to a stone thrown into the water, which sends ripples in every direction. With each person you tell, the risk of broken confidences increases. Eventually you may not know who else knows what has transpired—making it impossible to inform everyone of the way things got worked out (if and when they do!). You protect yourself and the reputation of the accuser by limiting the number of people you invite into the conflict.

When deciding who needs to know in order for you to receive the best counsel, consider the discretion and wisdom of each one, as well as their track record of keeping confidences. Among your trusted advisors there will be a few who stand out as those you can count on to give godly perspective and biblical balance. Some occasions may merit the involvement of a broader group, such as your elders or deacons, but in most cases, you will be better served to select two or three who are especially trustworthy.

Keep the Conflict in Perspective

Once in a while, when you get hit by a particularly unsettling attack, you will tend either to exaggerate in your own mind how widespread the perception is or to underestimate the legitimacy and breadth of the concern. Attacks can often begin with a statement like this: "I see this problem in you, and several other people I've talked to feel the same way." To the accuser, this gives credibility to their charge and greater aggressiveness to the way they can justify approaching you.

Early in my ministry, when people approached me this way, I believed that there must be several people who saw the same problem as my accuser and assumed that I had a huge problem on my hands. As the years went by, I learned to ask a few follow-up questions to see if I could assess the breadth of the problem. On several occasions, I asked for the names of others who agreed with the self-proclaimed spokesperson only to discover that "several other people" amounted to no more than a couple of others at best. Don't assume that you have a widespread insurrection on your hands just because someone says that "many others feel the same way." If they do, you need to find that out, but in all likelihood that is not the case at all.

On the other extreme, you may be inclined to dismiss all opposing points of view. That is as unhealthy as attaching too much importance to contrary voices. Granted, there will always be disgruntled people who are never happy anywhere about anything. These naysayers will never see anything good in what you do and will find ways to make their displeasure known. But before you write them off entirely, be careful not to ignore everything they have to say. They may happen upon some kernel of truth in their protests that you need to address.

As the negative comments persist, the tendency is to say, "Consider the source," and stop listening to their constant criticism. The concept has merit if you do in fact give thoughtful consideration to the source. In some cases, you can tell that no good will come from subjecting yourself to yet another attack on a matter you have addressed many times before. There are some people I can count on to send me emotionally charged, disagreeable notes about why they object to the way we do certain things in the church. Usually the objection is about the same subjects, and once they have stated their opposition, the notes that follow seldom introduce anything new to the discussion. So when I see that a note is from those individuals, I might want to ignore it since I have dealt with it numerous times before—and never to their satisfaction! But I must be careful not to apply a "consider the source" approach if that means I dismiss all communication from those people. In fact, some very helpful suggestions have come from the same sources that I would have missed had I made it a practice to turn a deaf ear to everything they have to say. I have had to learn to listen, even when the voices are less than gentle in how and what they have to say.

203

On yet another front, the criticism may come from trusted friends and allies in ministry. People in ministry cannot afford to surround themselves with "yes men" who tell them only what they want to hear. I have told our ministry team that I want people around me who put their love for Christ ahead of their love for me so that when they see something in me that needs confronting, they will be willing to speak up for the sake of Christ and for my good.

As painful as such times are, God can use them. Those occasions when I have sat around a table with men who loved me enough to confront me with an area of weakness, a problem with my attitude, or a question about my vision or direction have not been my favorite times as a pastor. But they have been some of the most important times.

Be Ready to Make Amends

Earlier we noted that there may be a kernel of truth in the attacks waged against you. If that element of truth includes a wrong you have done, be quick to admit it and seek forgiveness if the offense has been against a person. If the problem has to do with an error in judgment or a mistake in your understanding of the facts, do your best to take steps to correct the problem.

Some issues require a personal and private response—leaving your offering at the altar and going to the offended party to seek forgiveness and the restoration of a damaged relationship (Matt. 5:23–24). However, as a pastor, there may be times when your error makes it necessary to admit your mistake before the entire congregation. Having done this on a few occasions, let me tell you that it is no fun! But it is one of the most redemptively positive things you can do to build credibility in the trustworthiness of your own walk with Christ. People may not recall much else about your teaching and preaching ministry when all is said and done, but they will remember that you are a pastor with integrity if you are willing to humble yourself and admit when you are wrong.

Last year I stumbled into that situation while I was preaching. I made a sarcastic comment during my sermon about the young man operating the video equipment that projected the outline of the message onto the screens in the worship center. He hadn't been paying attention and had gotten behind in changing the slides. After several big hints to get his attention, he still wasn't responding, so I made a rather biting remark about what should already be on the screen if "someone" had been paying attention. As soon as the words left my lips, I knew that I had offended my brother, but worse—I knew I had quenched the Spirit!

Immediately, I started trying to figure out what to do to rectify the situation. Certainly I had to apologize, but could I get away with doing it after the service by going to him personally and privately? No, the Lord would not let me get away with that. My sin against the young man was public, before the entire congregation, and so my confession would need to be public as well. So before we came to the Lord's Supper table, right after the sermon concluded (which I finished with great consternation, knowing that the Lord was displeased with what I had done), I stopped before approaching the table and apologized, asking for the forgiveness of this poor young guy who had suffered unnecessarily because of my careless words.

Few people who were there that morning can tell you what I preached about that day, but God used the moment to humble me deeply and also to make it clear that pastors are fallible and need to admit it when they are wrong.

Intensify Your Time with the Lord

"There are no atheists in foxholes," someone once observed. Few things compel us to pray and seek the Lord more than coming under fire. When all is going well in your life and ministry, your prayer and devotional life is a pleasant source of spiritual nourishment and refreshment. But when the heat gets turned up and the fiery trials afflict you on every side, your need for times of refreshment become urgent and essential to your survival.

Without spending extra time with the Lord when the criticisms reach their peak, you will wither spiritually and begin to respond in ways that undermine your testimony. Your best witness is a life well lived in the power of the Holy Spirit where the fruit of the Spirit abounds because you abide in Christ. How many ministries have been cut short because a pastor neglected the most essential element for survival—his time alone with Christ?

In Psalm 73, David had a hard time understanding how the wicked could so easily prosper while treating him like dirt. We do not know if David spent a lot of time bemoaning what he perceived as the inexplicable unfairness of his situation by griping to his friends. What we do see is a man under attack, a man who was bewildered by the success of the unrighteous while he was being victimized by their mean-spirited behavior. But even as he registered his complaint with the Lord, he found what he needed because he took his concerns to the right place. Instead of turning away and blaming God for the rough treatment he was undergoing, David turned to him and went to the sanctuary to worship and come before God with his frustration. While in the Lord's presence, David made an astonishing discovery as the Lord revealed an important truth to him:

> When I pondered to understand this, it was troublesome in my sight until I came into the sanctuary of God; then I perceived their end. . . . My flesh and my heart may fail, but God is the strength of my heart and my portion forever. For, behold, those who are far from You will perish; You have destroyed all those who are unfaithful to You. But as for me, the nearness of God is my good; I have made the Lord GOD my refuge, that I may tell of all Your works.
>
> Psalm 73:16–17, 26–28

When you are in the crosshairs as the target of someone who has decided to launch an assault on you, discover what David meant when he declared, "The nearness of God is my good." Times of attack call for times of special pursuit of the nearness of God.

Set Your Mind on Things Above

When I was a child, a good friend of our family used to put things into perspective with an old saying she quoted regularly: "Child, a hundred years from now, who is going to know the difference?" There is great biblical truth in that homespun wisdom! Paul said, "If you have been raised up with Christ, keep seeking the things above, where Christ is, seated at the right hand of God. Set your mind on the things above, not on the things that are on earth" (Col. 3:1–2). In the Psalms, we find that David even welcomed affliction because he was enabled by the Lord to see through it to a higher end: "Before I was afflicted I went astray, but now I keep Your word. . . . The arrogant have forged a lie against me; with all my heart I will observe Your precepts. . . . It is good for me that I was afflicted, that I may learn Your statutes" (Ps. 119:67, 69, 71).

In the light of eternity, how big a deal is it that not everyone likes who you are and what you do? Sure there is affliction in the attacks upon our character, but when we learn to see them within the framework of "things above," or in the light of eternity, our newly elevated point of view allows us to see that, even in the midst of very trying times, God is still on his throne and has not forsaken us. Times of personal attack remind us to refocus on Christ and his calling to us, to forget what lies behind and press on toward those things that matter most to the Lord.

The Emotional Toll

Even when you do everything exactly right and respond perfectly when your character comes under attack, the experience can take its toll on you emotionally. You need to take this into account and give yourself time to recover your spiritual balance. Most likely, the experience will leave you drained and ill-prepared for the next wave of stresses and pressures unless you have had time to refill your reserves. Anger, frustration, fear, feelings of abandonment and loneliness, disappointment—these and many other reactions may follow an incident of personal attack on your character.

207

Most of the time we do not have the luxury of getting away somewhere to lick our wounds. We have to keep right on going because the demands of ministry give us little choice. However, if you make no provision for healing and recovery, you will be susceptible to more severe reactions the next time around, and it probably will not take as much to set you off.

Therefore, after a particularly draining season of attack on your personal character, make it your habit to abide in Christ. Invest more time in prayer so you can heed the counsel of his Word. Cast all your cares on him, for he cares for you (1 Peter 5:7). In the book of Hebrews, we are encouraged to admit our need and come to the Lord for help: "Let us then approach the throne of grace with confidence, so that we may receive mercy and find grace to help us in our time of need" (4:16 NIV). Even if you do not consider yourself to be an emotional person or a reactionary type of person, you still bear the wounds of the attack and need to allow the Lord to take you through the healing process.

I have even found that years later, an event long since forgotten will pop back up; if I let down my guard, it will occupy my thoughts, rekindle my anger or frustration, and push me in an unhealthy direction of thought about the individuals involved. I may have forgiven them, moved on, and considered it a closed case, but if I did not let my damaged emotions work through a healing process, the scars will make me vulnerable yet again to what I thought was past.

To recover fully, we need to take our emotional pain to Christ and leave it there. He will walk with us through the impact zone, heal each point of hurt, and remove the sting of each painful memory of what we endured.[1] Do not underestimate the emotional toll these attacks on your character can have on you. More important, do not neglect the provision God has made for you to recover and be stronger as a result.

1. A couple of books by David A. Seamands offer some interesting insights on this subject. See *Healing for Damaged Emotions* (Colorado Springs: Cook Communications Ministries, 1981) and *Redeeming the Past: Recovering from the Memories That Cause Our Pain* (Colorado Springs: Cook Communications, 1981, 2002). Seamands discusses how to yield the emotionally damaged areas of our lives to Christ and allow him to heal us from the long-term impact they would otherwise have on us.

208

Concluding Observations

More than likely, no one told you about this aspect of ministry before you became a pastor. And if they had, it would not have made any difference, since God called you and you would have answered the call anyway. Further, no one could have prepared you for how it feels to go through this kind of personal assault. As we conclude this topic, here are four observations that will hopefully help us recognize and deal with personal attacks in a way that will please the Lord and preserve our peace in him.

First, you will face these assaults and challenges throughout your ministry, often right on the heels of something great that the Lord has done in your life. God is aware of what is going to happen, and he assures you that he will make it possible for you to make it through. The enemy would love to use such encounters to knock you down and keep you there, but the Lord reaches out to lift you up and plant you firmly on solid ground when you turn to him.

Second, as much as we would like to think differently, many of the issues and relationships that threaten you during such attacks will never be resolved satisfactorily. Some of the parties involved will have no part in reaching a peaceful resolution. In an ideal world, they will wake up to the call of Christ and see the error of persisting in their attacks. But if you've been in ministry for very long, you know that there are some people who will not change. Most of the time, they do not go away and leave you alone, but insist on staying around to "help" you grow in grace and to protect the church from your failures—at least that's the way they see it. Your responsibility is to shepherd all the sheep, even the lambs that bite!

Third, although you are committed to the flock allotted to you, and you love them all, your primary calling is to serve Christ and enjoy his favor, not to serve in such a way that you curry the favor of the crowd. No one likes to do things that consistently upset people, but the bottom line is that we are not in ministry for the applause and approval of the people we serve. We are to be devoted to Christ first and foremost. It is for Christ that we do what we do, and it is ultimately to him that we will answer.

So if you know that you are doing what he wants, and as a result you stir up the ire of those around you, so be it. Basing your ministry on the eternal truth and unchanging principles of God's Word will seldom be without critics, or for that matter, seldom even be popular. But it is the Lord Jesus Christ whom we serve, and if he himself was hated, why should we be surprised when we run into opposition as well?

Fourth, as we follow Christ, we must remember that as he was wounded and suffered, so shall we. As the apostle Peter reminds us,

> Beloved, do not be surprised at the fiery ordeal among you, which comes upon you for your testing, as though some strange thing were happening to you; but to the degree that you share the sufferings of Christ, keep on rejoicing, so that also at the revelation of His glory you may rejoice with exultation. If you are reviled for the name of Christ, you are blessed, because the Spirit of glory and of God rests upon you. By no means let any of you suffer as a murderer, or thief, or evildoer, or a troublesome meddler; but if anyone suffers as a Christian, let him not feel ashamed, but in that name let him glorify God.
>
> 1 Peter 4:12–16

PART 6

FACING THE INEVITABILITY OF CHANGE

=14=

"SOMETHING HAS GOT TO CHANGE!"
KNOWING WHEN TRANSITIONS ARE RIGHT

Something has got to change!" How many times have you heard or said these words? Either you or other pastors you know have probably repeated those words often since following God's leading to become a pastor. I know from experience that lacking balance in either your personal life or your ministry results in frustration beyond words. Embedded somewhere deep in my brain is a warning light that begins to flash when my life and ministry tilt too far out of balance. Rather than live with the problem, I believe that when life gets out of balance, it can and should be corrected. In other words, something has *got* to change. The good news is that we *can* change.

Therefore, reason suggests that if we are to change, we should anticipate occasional times of transition as normal and inevitable if we expect to grow and mature in Christ. In fact, growth itself requires us to change, since all growth is a process of

213

change. Problems arise when the changes that are needed and the transitions involved threaten our sense of equilibrium, our delicate attempt to keep our lives in balance. Just when we adjust to our surroundings and become comfortable with the way we are or the way things are, without fail we will find ourselves confronting significant changes and have to go through the whole process again.

What pastor will admit that he or she does not want to grow? What church will suggest that no change is really needed? Although there are some notable exceptions in the anecdotal archives of my pastor friends, nearly all pastors and most churches will say that they are committed to growth. At the same time, vast numbers in both groups seem to invest inordinate amounts of time resisting even the slightest changes in their lives and ministries. Growth requires change, but people tend to dislike change because all change represents loss at some level or another.[1]

Understanding the Way Change Feels

Change does not feel the same way to everyone. Within each church, you will find advocates of two basic and contradictory points of view regarding the nature of ministry. One group asserts brazenly, "Some say you shouldn't change for the sake of change . . . I disagree! You should change things occasionally just to stir things up a little!" Another group states just as firmly, "Why do we have to change anything? Give me that old-time religion—it's good enough for me!" As a pastor, you must understand how change feels to different people within your flock, including yourself. Once you understand this, you must then be able to distinguish between what *must never* change (the eternal truths and principles of God's Word) and what *must* change for spiritual growth to take place.

1. Even when a change forces us to forsake something that is admittedly negative, it often seems like a loss. Some have said, "We would rather deal with the enemy at hand that we know than the one around the next corner that we do not know." There is a sense of loss when the familiar is taken away and the unfamiliar takes its place, good as the new might be.

214

Most of us fall into one of three categories: those who resist change, those who love change, and those who are willing to change. Obviously, there is some crossover between these categories. For example, I have noticed that I can be thoroughly excited about change in some areas and totally opposed to it in others. So we must acknowledge our own inconsistencies when we try to assess how change feels to others.

Those Who Resist Change

Within this category, there are a couple of ways people resist change. There are people who resist change at every point and whose response to any hint of change is "Never!" Of course, these are fun people to have in your church! Church business meetings usually bring them out in force. One church with which I am familiar has a nearly perfect record of never having a unanimous vote on any issue. A handful of dedicated change-resisters vote against every proposal brought forward, regardless of the subject. The only change acceptable to such a group would be a change in the bylaws to require that all votes be unanimous—thereby assuring that everything would remain the same since they intend to vote "no" on everything.

Then there are people who resist change by avoiding it as long as they possibly can. Eventually they can be swayed, but they will be the last hold-outs to go along with the change and the first to say "I told you so" if anything goes wrong. A subset of this group is the patience-trying enclave of those whose philosophy is to go along eventually, but to do so while making it as difficult on you, the pastor, as they possibly can.

You can take this resistance to change personally if you do not make an effort to understand how change feels to those who feel threatened by the insecurity and uncertainty of doing something different. Ask yourself these questions:

- What is at stake for them?
- What do they see as their greatest loss?
- Is their resistance based on *what* is to be changed or on *how* it is to be changed?

215

Whenever we can dig a little bit deeper and discover what makes people feel the way they do, we can then begin to understand what they, and we, are up against. Understanding them may not make any difference in their response, but it helps us relate to them and care for them as the changes take place.

Those Who Love Change

Some people love change and will persistently push to see it happen, which can be healthy and good if they love change for the right reasons. If they have a clear vision of what the Lord wants and are willing to press on with implementing that vision, this can be a very good thing. A hunger for doing what God wants generates a passionate love to see his people make forward progress in the kind of growth that brings glory to Christ. Among such people, a love for change can be a wonderful catalyst for growth in the body of Christ.

But for all of those who love change for the right reasons, there is an even greater group who love change for the wrong reasons. The impetuous love change—they are quick to start without counting the costs but are seldom around for the finish. A new idea, a novel approach, woos them, and without much careful thought, they are off and running, excited about life as it promises to be after the changes have taken place.

Then there are the malcontents who love change. For them, the grass is always greener over there somewhere, no matter where they happen to be. They are frequently not so interested in investing themselves in making the changes as they are in being the squeaky wheels that prompt them. They simply love to keep things stirred up and nothing does that better than constant change.

Last, there are the immature who love an adventure, a challenge, who find that change serves the same purpose for them as a thrill ride at the carnival. It takes them to the edge of possible danger and then catapults them without any particular purpose on a creative, wild, but nonproductive ride right back to where they (and we) started. They are willing to try almost

216

anything but rarely consider whether their new plans have any real value in advancing the cause of Christ.

Those who love change can be great allies for you if you want someone with enthusiasm to support you. However, they may not always be trustworthy when it comes to giving you a wise perspective on the change you intend to make. I hesitate to say it, but sometimes I must admit that I am a little suspicious of those who demonstrate a disproportional degree of enthusiasm when some kind of change is proposed. In that case, I prefer wisdom and discernment over the excitement and thrill of the chase after a change that may be nothing more than an ill-advised way of getting people worked up.

Those Who Are Willing to Change

The first two groups represent the extremes. This last group consists of people who are willing to change. They do not resist it at all costs, nor do they chase after it with no regard for the costs. These are the folks with whom you want to surround yourself in ministry.

The primary consideration of this group is not change itself, but the one from whom all appropriate change proceeds and to whom all change brings glory. Our chief concern must be what God wants. Once that is settled, the decision to change or not becomes a trivial matter in the eternal scheme of things. All that matters is what the Lord reveals to be his will.

Every believer should be willing to make any kind of change at any time when he or she is given the right circumstances, convinced by sound reasoning, confident of the anticipated benefits, and assured that it is consistent with the will of God. A willingness to change indicates that our hearts belong to the Lord, that our wills are controlled by the one who knows all things well and has determined what is best for us. Ministry among people who are more concerned with following Christ than with whether they need to change or not can be a joyful experience.

However, as pastors, we need to recognize what change means to all kinds of people and seek a greater understanding of how they feel, what they think, and where change fits into their worldview. This will make a significant impact on how you present new ideas and what steps you take to introduce changes in your ministry.

But first you need to understand which one of these groups best represents the way you personally deal with change. Do you respond differently when forced to change by others than you do when the idea originates with you? Are there areas in which change threatens you more than others? Try to get a handle on your own feelings about change in various areas. There is no doubt that God wants you to change. He himself wants to change you and keep changing you for the rest of your life until Christ is fully formed in you. You will not be very effective in leading others through the transitions needed to grow if you are not willing to change yourself. Therefore, to prepare for the inevitable, perhaps it would be helpful to explore the most likely areas of change you will confront as a pastor.

Preparing for the Most Probable Changes

To function effectively as an agent for change in your ministry, you need to know the landscape of pastoral ministry well and prepare for the times and places you are most likely to run into the need for change. From what I have experienced and observed, there are two major areas in which the need for change will arise: personal change (including change in ministry calling) and institutional change.[2]

Personal Change

We do what we do because we are who we are. When I acknowledge this, I realize that any talk about change must begin with who I am. I need to recognize what needs to change in me personally. Often, this is the last place we look when we think

2. By institutional change, I am referring to a change that will result in a significant change in direction or emphasis impacting the entire congregation. This will be discussed in the next chapter.

about the changes that need to take place. Limited self-awareness can dramatically impact our ability to grow and indirectly impact our ability to lead others into meaningful growth.

When Paul writes, "Do not think of yourself more highly than you ought, but rather think of yourself with sober judgment, in accordance with the measure of faith God has given you," he opens the door for us to consider accurately what we are like (Rom. 12:3 NIV). A "sober judgment" requires that we make the assessment neither too lofty and grand nor too low and awful. False humility is no more acceptable to God than selfish pride. Do you have a sane estimation of yourself? If you do, then you will never have any problem identifying areas of weakness that need to be addressed, even areas of strength that need to be improved. As a starting point, let me suggest three categories to consider: spiritual growth, mental stimulation, and interpersonal relationships.

Spiritual growth. No matter how long you have been a Christian or how long you have been in ministry, change needs to occur in order for your spiritual life to grow and move ahead toward maturity in Christ. The change may be practical, as in the structure of your devotional life or quiet time, or it may be more subjective and difficult to measure, as in the development of your character. Opportunities for spiritual growth await us every day for the rest of our lives. Each new day becomes an adventure to see if we can discover what the Lord wants to show us about himself, about ourselves, and about where he sees us in the journey toward maturity.

Mental stimulation. When you stop exercising your mind, it begins to decline. We need to stretch our minds so we can expand our ability to think clearly and logically. Sloppy and inconsistent thinking results from laziness and a lack of proper mental stimulation. If we aspire to be smarter, wiser, or sharper than we are right now, some things will have to change. Repeating the same thought patterns and never exploring new concepts, never considering new ideas, never grappling with new challenges to what we have always thought does not hone our mind skills. For personal growth to be complete, we cannot neglect the kind of mental stimulation that comes from pushing our minds to wrestle with grand ideas, lofty concepts, and provocative perspectives.

Do you think this is easy? Of course not! After a long day of putting out fires in the life of the congregation or struggling to make sense of a difficult sermon topic or biblical text for your next message, coming home to an evening of mind-numbing entertainment sounds very attractive. Reading a book on a closely reasoned argument for some fine point of theology scarcely appeals to most of us even during our best hours of the day. Diving into the depths of some noble theme offered by an ancient divine like John Owen (1616–1683) or Jonathan Edwards (1703–1758) may not be feasible when you are exhausted and have little energy left. But do you sense the need to test your mettle, to follow the example of Agatha Christie's fictional detective Hercule Poirot and "exercise the little grey cells"[3] by stimulating them with some worthy intellectual challenge?

I will be the first to admit my aversion to hard work in the classroom, as many teachers and professors from my academic career will attest. However, one of the ways I have changed over the years has been in the recognition of my need to read more broadly and to work my mind more diligently. Publishers have obviously noticed that I am not the only one who is likely to shy away from intimidating literature, even if it promises a great wealth of valuable information. Notice the design of modern publications compared with their older counterparts. For example, studying various commentaries on the Epistle to the Hebrews for a sermon series years ago, I was struck by the contrast in how the books were written and even in how they were printed. Nearly all of today's commentaries take great pains to use frequent divisions of the text with bold headings, wide margins, large print, and other publishing tools to make the page attractive and readable.

On the other extreme, John Owen's commentary on Hebrews[4] consists of seven volumes of sometimes tedious arguments

3. Agatha Christie (1890–1976), a British author, wrote nearly forty mysteries featuring her popular fictional detective Hercule Poirot.

4. John Owen (1616–1683), *An Exposition of the Epistle to the Hebrews*, 7 vols.; (repr., Carlisle, PA: Banner of Truth, 1991).

and minutely detailed reasons for his conclusions about the text. The page layout contains virtually no breaks, no headings, and very lengthy paragraphs, all printed in what appears to be six-point type. Most modern readers would take one look and then put it back on the shelf. And with it would go the opportunity to interact with one of the greatest minds in the history of Christendom.

Then again, I wouldn't go as far as one pastor suggested. He would purchase three books by non-Christian authors for every one book by a Christian in order to stay abreast of non-Christian thinking. As pastors, we also cannot invest the valuable time we have for ministry in the pursuit of the writings and ideas of every perverse or eccentric author out there.

Simply stated, if we are going to keep our edge in our personal growth toward maturity in Christ, we need to think well, and the only way to think well is to do it often and with care. To experience the personal change needed to grow, we need spiritual growth and mental stimulation.

Interpersonal relationships. Personal change cannot be said to be effective until it impacts our interpersonal relationships. The way we relate to others says more about the level of change we have undergone than we think. Love for others distinguishes us as those who have been with Jesus Christ. Paul mentions this specifically when he writes that we can be eloquent and well-versed in the mysteries and knowledge of God, demonstrate great faith, and live selflessly and sacrificially—but if we do not have love, none of this profits us at all, for apart from love we are nothing (1 Cor. 13:1–3). God wants to see us so deeply changed in the essence of our being that we excel in our relationships with one another because the love of Christ pours out through us.

How many marvelously gifted people do you know who have great spiritual depth, wonderful wisdom and insight into the mind of Christ, but have no ability to connect with others beyond the most fundamental levels of relationship? If you know someone like this, or if you consider yourself to be like this (with all due modesty, of course!), would you not agree that to be more like Christ, a change is needed? Not everyone

221

will be an extrovert or an aggressive, outgoing person, but we can all grow in the way we handle interpersonal relationships. The one change we all need is to model Christ in all of our relationships.

By nature, I am not a confrontational person. Rather than risk the controversy and the damage such a confrontation might bring, I sometimes avoid doing what is right and hesitate to speak the truth, even when I know that it would be done in love. This weakness must change if I am to become the kind of person people can trust. They need to know that I care enough about them to be direct when necessary. That character flaw in me has resulted in hurt feelings and confusion among folks I really cared about because I either waited too long to confront them or found indirect ways to bring the problem to their attention. As one of many interpersonal relational skills in which I know I am weak, this resistance to confrontation has had to change in order for me to make any progress.

What issues get in the way of your relationships? Are you afraid of the vulnerability of being known by others? Do you practice patterns of communication that allow you to hide what you really think or feel? Is your network of relationships composed only of those who will not disagree with you or who make you feel important? Have you transferred past experiences of bitterness and anger onto others with whom you currently have relationships to the extent that you cannot understand why you blow up at them with only the slightest provocation? Would your friends and family members consider you to be self-absorbed and insensitive to the needs of others?

Our interpersonal relationships need to be characterized by commitment both to intimacy and to integrity. Honesty, kindness, gentleness, submissiveness, servanthood, encouragement, and a host of other issues mark relationships that are valuable. Intimacy and integrity in interpersonal relationships must begin with our commitment to get better at how we interact with others and how we care about one another.

Change in Ministry Calling

For most pastors, a time arrives when it becomes necessary to evaluate their current situation in light of what God has called them to do. There are at least four possible scenarios in which change is mandated.

New vision, same location. First, a change in your ministry might be indicated if God has clearly called you to your present ministry location but has been working in your heart and mind to give you a new vision for what he wants you to do in that ministry location. This new vision may represent a radical redirection of what your calling is, or it may be an extension and expansion of what you have been called to do all along, but circumstances have prevented you from doing it. In either case, you know that you are compelled to change. You may have been a topical preacher and now sense that you are being called to learn to preach expositionally. You may have been more of an evangelist than a pastor, and the Lord is now calling you to spend more time equipping the saints. In any case, you welcome the new vision and can get excited about the prospects for a different kind of ministry among the same people in the same location.

Same vision, changed role, same location. Second, you might face a similar situation in which you still know that you are called to the same location and still have the same vision for your ministry, but you find that your role has changed—or needs to. You may have started as a great solo pastor in a small church, but now the church and its staff have grown, and the additional responsibilities are forcing you to change the way you spend your time. For the first nine years here at Providence, I was a solo pastor. My role then was very different than it is now that we have several other pastors on our team. I did not need to give up my vision for ministry, but my role changed. I have had to make significant adjustments to what I do in order to survive.

Therefore, if the fulfillment of my ministry vision allows me to stay in the same location but with a different role, I need to take the steps necessary to make that transition. For example, how can I be called to preach and teach the Bible and continue

223

to devote the time to that calling when there are increasing demands on my time? As the number of staff members, board members, and congregational leaders grow, I need to train them properly before I can delegate responsibility to them. That takes time and that time has to come from somewhere. With each addition to my responsibilities, I need to plan for a period of adjustment as old duties get assigned to others. I have been naive about this in the past and failed to allow for the season of double duties as I moved forward with plans to devote more time to preaching and teaching but at the same time had to include a training period for those who would assume responsibility for tasks which were formerly mine. If I understand the cost up front, I will not be as overwhelmed when the extra work piles up for a season. But if I plan well and make the move incrementally, it will only be a short season of transition with an end in sight. Then I can move ahead in my new role with confidence that I have delegated well and am free to engage fully in what lies ahead.

In such cases, our vision remains the same, the place remains the same, but our role has to change to accommodate the needs of the ministry and to fulfill this extension of God's call on our lives.

Same vision, same role, new location. Third, you may have a clear sense of your vision for ministry and a sane estimation of your role in ministry, but these two factors do not coincide with the church or ministry location in which you find yourself. This is the time to be ready for a transition to a new location to pursue your ministry calling more effectively. To be honest, some church situations do not work out and mesh with what God has called and equipped you to do. These mismatches may not be apparent at first, but as the church grows in one direction and the pastor goes through growth and changes in another, a change of location is inevitable. If it doesn't happen, eventually everyone will detect that something is amiss; then the change may not come in the positive, fruitful, and affirming way it once could have.

God has a place of ministry for you where your vision for what you are called to do and the role you play in filling leadership responsibilities will line up. A word of caution to those inclined to pull up stakes too quickly—make sure that the Lord is not trying to stretch you where you are before you take off for pastures where the grass looks much greener.

New vision, new location. Last, some pastors will find that God has brought them to a place of radical transition. If you are in this position, you will find that your vision for ministry has changed so radically that you have no choice but to begin anew in a different location. You need to move on if the Lord has reworked your vision for ministry during your time with your current congregation but has not indicated that he intends for that vision to be implemented there.

I have watched pastors try to impose a new vision on churches that could not respond to the kinds of changes required to make the vision work. Many of you may have witnessed the demise of congregations that once thrived because their pastor forced them into a mold unsuited to their unique character and calling. Integrity requires us to allow our vision to grow and develop in a way that is separate from the vision of the place we currently serve so we do not force the congregation to change when, all along, God intended us to be the ones who changed. A new vision for ministry may indeed require a relocation to a new place.

Within these four possible scenarios are an incalculable variety of extenuating circumstances and adjustment factors. But this fact doesn't change: we need to face the inevitability of change in our ministry lives with an open mind to what God may be doing to lead us into new fields of effective service.

Personal change starts when we admit that change is necessary and that we are not all that we hope or pretend to be. We need to change in so many ways that we only need to ask the Lord occasionally for more fuel to keep the fires of change burning on and on. He will show us all kinds of areas that need to change and ways we need to grow if we are to be examples of godliness worthy of his name.

=== 15 ===

LEADING THE CHARGE FOR CHANGE

YOUR ROLE IN MAKING IT HAPPEN

Something happens when we undergo changes that result in personal spiritual growth. The more we grow, the more we see how much more we need to grow. Our eyes are opened to areas of need previously undetected. As that happens, we also become aware of the need for change in the church or ministry we serve. Learning to change personally paves the way for us to lead the way for positive change institutionally.

Signs That Change Is Needed

How can you distinguish between a genuine need for change and an unhealthy desire to escape from your current situation? Unfortunately, there is no objective formula. However, the Lord has ways to communicate his will, especially if we long to know what it is and he can trust us to do what he tells us. Rather than trying to hide what he wants, we know that, according to Psalm 25:14 (NIV), "The LORD confides in those who fear him; he makes his covenant known to them." When the time comes for you to make the changes the Lord wants in your life or ministry, he will show you. As a starting point for your thinking, let me suggest three signs to consider.

A Growing Sense of Discontentment

Once in a while, most of us find ourselves struggling with a lack of contentment. Knowing that we can be content in Christ, we have to be careful that the source of our discontentment is not a lack of trust in him. I am not referring to a shallow dissatisfaction, but to the awakening of a deep longing for more. When I am hungry, I am not content to remain so, but that does not imply that I somehow have lost confidence in the Lord's ability to provide. My hunger creates a longing to find and consume food. In much the same way, when I sense a longing to reach out for more of God's plan for my life, my discontentment with my situation does not arise from a lack of faith, but from a hunger for a deeper faith and a more significant ministry.

To avoid succumbing to urges that do not come from the Lord, we need to have the discernment to recognize the shallows of personal immaturity and the wisdom to recognize the stirrings of God. Maturity in Christ brings wisdom and discernment, both of which are necessary to measure the true motives of our hearts when the time comes to consider making changes. If you find yourself dealing with a discontented heart, ask the Lord to show you the source of your dissatisfaction before you impulsively do the first thing that comes along that promises contentment. We need to be able to know the voice of the Shepherd if we expect to walk with him as the sheep of his flock.[1] Having cultivated a depth of spiritual understanding

1. "When he puts forth all his own, he goes before them, and the sheep follow him because they know his voice" (John 10:4).

227

and discernment to recognize the voice of the Lord, you can ask him to show you whether your discontentment is from self-absorption or from the Holy Spirit.

Another possible source of discontentment could be an awareness that your current situation has become a bad fit for your calling, gifts, and strengths. Either the people or the circumstances have made your ministry unnecessarily difficult, and you find yourself swimming against the current over and over again. Of course, this may not be their fault or yours but just the way the Lord has chosen to cause you to be more attentive to the need for a change of ministry location.

Sometimes the Lord has to blast us out of our complacency to get us to listen to what he wants to say. If we remain comfortable and settled, we may not be willing to uproot our family and our security in a place of ministry we know for one that is unknown. Consequently, we may find that he stirs our hearts to lose our sense of contentment in one place to prepare us for his plans to move us to another location. At any rate, whenever you find that you are becoming discontent in your ministry, you need to pay attention and not brush it aside as inconsequential.

If your discontent is the result of dissatisfaction with what Christ has called you to endure to fulfill your ministry where you are, then that must be addressed. You must come to terms with him. However, if the source of the discontentment is a longing and a hunger for more of his fullness in ministry, then stay tuned for what he will yet reveal.

A Fresh Clarity of Insight

Another means that God may use to instigate a change in your life or ministry is the introduction of new insights to your heart and mind. Through a variety of means, God can bring you to a new level of expectation and a new aspiration for your ministry or your life. He may use someone else's teaching or writing to awaken a fresh passion for a ministry area that you had never known before. Or he could take a series of unrelated events in which different speakers addressing different topics hit on a common theme, which causes you to reconsider what you are doing. This could then be confirmed by your own reading and studying over a period of time. You may conclude that this new insight from the Lord was not just for the sake of giving you new information, but for planting a new desire within you. Your prayer life may also be the platform the Lord uses. Who knows which form or from which direction the insight might come? But before you are ready to change course, you will need clear insight from the Lord that the transition you are about to make is his idea and not yours.

A Providential Opportunity

When the Lord wants you to change, he could show you by dropping the opportunity to do something about it in your lap. Through absolutely no initiative on your part, a possibility to make a change may appear. In itself, that does not mean that you must make that change. But it does force you to review your calling, your vision for ministry, and your current circumstances. Many factors could combine with the new opportunity to cause you to conclude that the Lord is leading you toward some kind of change.

Does that mean you should never take the initiative to pursue a change? Of course not! There will be times when you must do so as a part of following the steps for change the Lord has been showing you.

Whether through a growing sense of discontentment, a fresh clarity of insight, or a providential opportunity, God wants us to be ready to recognize the signs of transition and be attentive to them when he is ready for us to make a change in our lives or when he wants us to lead the way to change at an institutional level.

We explored several dynamics involved in personal change in the last chapter. How do they relate to institutional change? Should the Lord lead you to stay where you are and lead the way for change, what factors should shape the process so the transition can be healthy and effective?

Institutional Change

Beyond the need for personal and ministry change, every pastor has to prepare for the inevitability of institutional change. Personal change can be threatening, but in the final analysis, only you and the Lord really know what has truly taken place. Unfortunately, institutional change is very public. It makes you very vulnerable because the people who do not like change are seldom reticent to let you know it. And it makes your church vulnerable because how you handle the change as a body is on display for the world to see.

Occasionally, when I read accounts of the lives of pastors in other eras, I am almost envious. For generations, pastoring a local congregation differed only slightly from one decade to the next. Until the latter part of the twentieth century, what a pastor was expected to do was pretty much the same in 1720, 1820, and 1920. Churches as institutions did not vary much in what they did and how they did it.

With the introduction of better means of transportation and communication, people became more mobile, and their exposure to a variety of ministry possibilities grew dramatically. The local small town Methodist church no longer was compared with the local Presbyterian and Baptist churches, but was compared with churches in the big cities with their smorgasbord of programs and wide range of ministry offerings. Then came radio, and later television, with their respective polished preachers and sophisticated worship services. Soon the comfortable, homey atmosphere of the local congregation was considered old-fashioned. It no longer satisfied the growing consumer approach of those shopping for a church home that would "meet their needs." Pressure grew for pastors and churches to keep up with the times. Today the movement toward institutional change continues to shake up most churches as we all find ourselves dealing with a culture that bears little resemblance to the one pastored by our predecessors of only a few generations ago.

Granted, this is not all bad. The body of Christ needs to maintain that fine balance of keeping in step with the times in which we live while keeping in step with the Spirit as we walk daily in his eternal truth. Tucked away in the middle of a list of David's troops in 1 Chronicles 12, there is an intriguing comment about the men of Issachar. The text states that they were men "who understood the times and knew what Israel should do" (12:32 NIV). We live in a day that demands leadership from those who understand our times and know what needs to be done to fulfill our calling to declare the matchless glory of Jesus Christ.

If we rightly understand our times, we cannot help but see that the church needs to change the way it goes about its ministries. For much of the last twenty years of the twentieth century, evangelical Christians worked hard to recapture a more biblical foundation for ministry. After nearly a century of theological drifting, some churches and institutions have been successful in restoring a scriptural perspective to their ministries. Although the struggle to regain a first-century theology succeeded in some ways, many of the same institutions that gained theological victories seemed determined to hold on to eighteenth-century methodologies.

What is involved in bringing about institutional change? I don't pretend to have the definitive answer to that question. However, I have found that certain steps can be taken to minimize the trauma of change while smoothing the ruffled feathers of the foes of change. As pastors, it is both our privilege and our peril to take the leadership in initiating change in the body of Christ. What can we do that will make the inevitable transitions less stressful for us and for the people we serve?

1. Teach the Biblical Principles

When you think about it, why should anyone change just because you say they should? Why should a church go through the aggravation of giving up its familiar traditions and comfortable routines? Well, I promise you it will seldom be because of the power of your personality. People need to know that what they are doing is not only reasonable, but well-rooted in the timeless truths of God's Word. They may argue with you and

231

match opinions with you all day long, but when people are serious about the authority of the Scriptures, they will listen and seek to understand if you will take the time to teach them the biblical principles involved in the areas you wish to change.

Principle-based ministry always begins by looking to the Bible to find out what the Lord has said about the issue at hand. Practically speaking, we should never dream of offering any idea for serious consideration that has not first answered the question, "What does the Bible say about that?" Since the church is God's idea and not ours, it only stands to reason that he has much to say about how it should fulfill its ministry calling. Where God speaks directly, we obey him. Where he does not speak directly, we have to observe what he has said, figure out what he meant by it, and discover how we can apply the truth we have learned. In other words, God has revealed the essential principles upon which the ministry of the church must be built. Our task is to identify them and then teach them.

Any change you initiate that begins before you have taught the biblical principles underlying that change will face major obstacles along the way. Without understanding the "why," people may go along for a while, but eventually they will need more than your word to go on. You can count on many long hours of agonizing debate over the questions of style, structure, focus, vision, and so on if you haven't laid a careful foundation of the biblical principles upon which such factors can be grounded. Even if members of your church have questions about the biblical principles you teach them, they can at least see that you are not attempting to make arbitrary changes just for the sake of doing something differently. Instead, you are working toward the application of what you see to be in line with God's will for the church.

Therefore, find a way to summarize the biblical principles by which you are functioning, and make the time to present them to the congregation. Depending upon the magnitude of the change, this process may be a major thrust of your ministry for several months, or it may become an integral part of the training of new members so that everyone understands both the "what" and the "why" of your ministry's unique calling.

2. Bank Some Credibility

One of your top priorities as you move into a new position of leadership is to build trust. You need credibility in order to be trusted. Some of that comes during the trial/probation period just after you arrive in your new congregation, a time often called your "honeymoon" days. People will cut you a lot of slack initially as they see how you handle yourself and how reliable you are in the way you get things done and in the decisions you make. They want to see if you have discernment and good judgment.

With that in mind, an old adage among leaders in new situations is that you need to bank some credibility, to do things that will let people know that you can be trusted. A great way to do that, of course, is to take what has been done and do it better. A common mistake among pastors in transition is to try to make wholesale changes during the honeymoon period. Moving too fast into too many new areas inevitably results in occasional failures or in offending someone whose cherished tradition is sacked for the "new preacher's pet project."

By taking time to understand the culture of your new environment, you will find that "improvement" sounds much better to people than change. I know, it is actually the same thing, but it does not sound so radical. In fact, improvement feels less threatening because it affirms what is already in place and merely suggests that, with a few adjustments, the good will be even better. Therefore, taking what has been done and doing it better gives you the credibility you must have before engaging in more dramatic changes at an institutional level. Wise leaders who understand this principle will exercise patience and bank the credibility that long-term change requires.

3. Prepare the Leaders

Since team ministry plays such an important part in maintaining a balanced life for a pastor, trying to implement change without a solid base of support from your team leaders would be foolish. To prepare your leaders for change, you must teach

233

them the basic biblical principles of ministry in the local church. Otherwise, you do not stand much of a chance.

Working with the leaders before broadcasting the plans you have for change works to your advantage in several ways. First of all, it allows you to test your ideas in an environment that offers you the opportunity to learn without losing credibility. If the leaders realize that you are sincerely soliciting their feedback, they will respect your openness and teachable spirit. They need to know that you do not pretend to have all the answers, but that you are willing to learn from their thoughts, suggestions, and perspectives on the ministry principles you would like to teach. Pastors who are unwilling to listen to those called to serve with them will not only miss gaining valuable insight from other godly leaders, but they will enjoy only limited receptivity to their ideas.

The thrill of discovery leads many pastors to run ahead of their leaders and go straight to the congregation with their freshly articulated principles for ministry. Only later do they find out that by skipping this step, they have risked alienating and marginalizing those who could have been key supporters had they been included early enough to help clarify points that seemed vague, unsubstantiated, or controversial. Let your leaders share the joy of moving ahead by including them in the refining process. That way, when you go forward, your leadership team will be solidly behind you. Even those who disagree will be able to say that their concerns were considered and their questions answered.

Another benefit of preparing the leaders is that they can share the responsibility for taking the principles to the people. Some great ideas and wonderful principles have been unfairly buried before they saw the light of day simply because an excited pastor didn't wait for the other congregational leaders to embrace the ministry principles themselves. The burden for presenting the ministry principles fell upon one rather than many. When this happens, teaching the principles becomes confused with "selling an idea." Instead of having many voices expressing a coherent statement of accepted principles, you become a lonely voice that is vulnerable to the charge that you are overly ambitious and too eager to make a name for yourself. I realize how unjust that can be. Nonetheless, going off on your own before preparing, teaching, and equipping your leaders with sufficient resources from God's Word will leave you vulnerable and exposed.

What should you do? Well, as someone who has sometimes led very badly, I can attest to the problem of running ahead of the leaders. On the other hand, I have observed the value of taking a few leaders into your confidence early on, as soon as you realize that change is going to be needed to be faithful to your ministry principles. In some cases that may be your entire board, but in others it will probably be shared with a few leaders close enough to you who can be counted on to share your enthusiasm for the possibilities, but also to tell you the truth if they think you are off base. As these few take ownership of the principles and the need for change, let them help shoulder the burden of carrying it to the next level of leaders who should share in this time of instruction and consensus building. Along the way, you will run into those who disagree with you, those who oppose you, and even those who will become angry over the changes you are proposing. Still, that is better managed among the network of relationships of key leaders than by throwing the matter before the entire congregation. Once the leaders have been prepared for the institutional changes indicated by the principles you have taught them, you will be on your way to a less stressful transition.

One more point on preparing the leaders needs to be noted. I am sure you are aware that not all of your leaders are in official positions or offices in the church. Include those who have impressed you as leaders, not by election, but by the way they influence others. Frequently, the official leadership structure of a church and the "behind-the-scenes" leadership are composed of different people. Failure to take that into account when you are preparing the leaders for change can make your life more difficult than it needs to be. Ask yourself who needs to be informed, instructed, and included when you see that change is on the horizon, and then draw them into the process.

4. Describe Your Vision

Vision is an elusive concept. Trying to define it can prove to be exasperating, since so many different ideas of what constitutes a vision have been batted around in leadership and management books and seminars for years. When I speak of outlining your vision, I am referring to a description of the way things will be one day if all goes the way you would like.[2]

The value of drawing out the implications of where you believe the church needs to be becomes apparent as people catch on and can imagine what the difference will be. I learned this lesson the hard way. After years of teaching biblical principles, preparing not only the leaders but the congregation, a regular refrain hit me from many quarters: "We don't know where we are going. You may understand where all this is leading, but we are clueless." Hearing this from some of the very leaders with whom I had spent years communicating why we were doing what we were doing, why the changes we were making were consistent with the direction set by our ministry principles, I couldn't figure out where the breakdown was coming from. Complicating matters was the fact that, among our board members, the variety of definitions of what a vision was made it extremely difficult to offer a satisfactory answer. The answer that satisfied one seemed to cloud the issue for another. We tried mission statements, purpose statements, goals and objectives statements, core value statements, and extensive explanations of ministry principles, and still there seemed to be no common understanding about our vision.

Finally, it dawned on us that all we really wanted to define was what we expected the church to look like when our ministry principles were fully operational in the power of the Spirit. That prompted a year and a half of working through a description of what could happen if we followed the Lord in the direction we believed he was leading. What kinds of

2. For a broader understanding of what I mean by "vision," refer back to section 2: "Sharpening the Focus of Your Vision."

ministries would we offer? How many people would we anticipate being involved? What staff and facilities would be necessary to be effective in serving that many people? Who would we expect to reach through evangelism, edification, and worship? As we began to answer these questions and a host of others, the vision of our future began to emerge with more clarity than ever. We had been faithful to the principles and had been making good decisions based on those principles, but now we could help people grasp the changes that would come if we stayed on the course we had been following for so many years.

Some questions about the vision cannot be answered fully since we are not able to see into the future. But when we take what we do know and imagine its possible implications for the future, it can make a tremendous difference in our understanding of the days ahead. Then when changes in institution occur, they do not appear as isolated and random suggestions with no context. They instead follow as the next logical steps in the process of making the transitions from where you are to where the Lord wants you to be. Describing the vision provides the much-needed context for change.

5. Present Your Plan

So how do you get there? Knowing where you want to go is no guarantee that you have a way to get there. A vision that has been described with clarity needs to be supported with practicality. You need a plan.

Breaking down the vision into manageable intermediate steps can be done in a variety of ways. One way is to set measurable goals with clear objectives and a recognizable connection to the overall purpose and vision you are pursuing. Another approach is to work on the plan from the perspective of a problem-solver. You assess the situation in terms of what obstacles stand between you and the fulfillment of the vision; then you figure out how to remove those hurdles. Whether you function better as a goal-setter or as a problem-solver will determine the approach you choose, but understanding that distinction can save you much frustration.[3]

In concert with your leadership team, prepare for the changes by putting a plan together with both short-term and long-term elements. By working together, you can capitalize on the strengths and gifts of the various team members, and the design of the plan will be more likely to include areas that would otherwise have been neglected. Once the leaders agree on the plan, you can present it to the congregation.

Hosting a series of small group presentations before the plan goes to the entire congregation will allow you to correct any oversights, identify any issues that arise as common themes in the questions being asked, and build a broader base of people who understand and support the plan before going public. Of course, the opposite can be true as well. You also give any opponents the opportunity to rally support against what you are proposing, but the benefits of open discussion and communication usually overshadow the negatives. Whether the plan you are presenting is your annual ministry plan or a major directional shift, I have found this process to bear much fruit in helping people feel both informed and involved in the decision making that affects the direction of their church family.

6. Acknowledge the Resistance

In most cases, you can count on a certain amount of resistance to nearly every step in the change process. Some will disagree with the principles themselves. Others will not like the fact that the leadership team gets to be in on the early stages of shaping the direction of the change and will complain about being marginalized and excluded. Presented with a sound basis for the changes coming, some will recognize the futility of arguing the merits of their case and resort to attacks on the credibility of the pastor and other leaders. For a variety of reasons, objections will be raised about the nature of the vision

3. For a full discussion of this topic, I highly recommend Bobb Biehl, *Stop Setting Goals: If You Would Rather Solve Problems* (Nashville: Random House, 1995).

and the assumptions behind the vision will be challenged. The mere presentation of any plan invites resistance because there are, admittedly, "many ways to skin a cat." Those who object to the proposal can always find other means that, in their minds, accomplish the same end but in a better way.

Resistance will always confront any attempt to initiate change, so do not be surprised when it comes. There are three dangers you need to avoid. One danger is not to listen. When people get the impression that you have no interest in what they think or say, they, understandably, can get a little testy. Provide opportunity for listening in the small group sessions in which you present your plans. You may be pleasantly surprised to receive insights that could result in vast improvements to the plan.

The second danger is to take the opposition personally. Even if it becomes personal on the part of those who openly disagree and resist the recommended changes, you cannot respond in kind. Admittedly, you are the most public representative of the change, so attacks on the change may feel like attacks on you. But don't let yourself stand alone as the target. If you have done your job as far as basing the changes on sound biblical principles, preparing the leaders, and communicating openly and clearly to the congregation, you will be standing shoulder to shoulder with many who agree with you, which will go far in helping you deal with those who resist the change.

The last danger is to act condescendingly toward those who disagree with you, to act as if they have no reason or right to meddle in matters best left to the experts (presuming that means you!). By acknowledging that there is resistance and affirming the dignity and integrity of those who hold a different point of view, you provide a model of grace at work. Disagreeing is never the problem. Being disagreeable is.

As pastor, you can elevate the deliberations by responding with love and affirming those who take issue with the changes. Or you can descend into a "win-at-any-cost" mentality and do positive harm to your prospects for credible spiritual leadership in the future. Therefore, treat resistance with care and respect those whose preferences follow different paths than yours.

7. Cultivate Supportive Unity

Institutional change works best when those within the institution, in this case the church, are united in their support and
enthusiasm for what is to come. Find ways to keep the vision
before the leaders and the congregation, faithfully reminding
everyone that it is the Lord Christ whom you serve. If you do
not have firm convictions that the way you are moving is God's
way, then by all means abort the mission! But if you do sense
the moving of the hand of God in directing your steps, then
let the folks know this. Help them cultivate the excitement
that comes when God's people find themselves laboring and
sacrificing and serving together with people they love for a
Savior they adore.

Once the decisions have been made, make every effort to build
bridges for those who might feel estranged by the outcome. Invite
their participation and include them in celebrating the victories
along the way. Strive for unity of heart and purpose even when
there cannot be perfect agreement about the fine points of what
you are doing. Surely there is room for all to come together when
the course you follow has been directed by the Lord.

8. Move Ahead

Finally, take action and move ahead. Getting ready to change
can be such a monumental task that when the time comes to
go we find ourselves stranded at the starting gate. In the book
of Proverbs, we find a word of exhortation in a simple observation: "All hard work brings a profit, but mere talk leads only to
poverty" (Prov. 14:23 NIV). Sometimes we talk about change
and its impact for so long that we become entangled in minutiae instead of taking off with joyful anticipation to see what
God is going to do.

These eight steps will not ensure success as you launch into
the stormy waters of institutional change, but they can make
a difference in the toll the transition takes on you and your
congregation. Obviously, there are many ways to generate institutional change, and I make no claim for either originality

or for having the final word.[4] I do claim that it makes sense to make institutional changes in a good and reasonable way if we want to continue to grow and improve the ministry of our churches.

A Few Closing Observations about Change

Change is a necessary part of the Christian life. Unfortunately, when it comes around, it throws many of us out of balance. Instead of being excited by the growth possibilities, we become exasperated at the losses the change represents to us. All growth requires change, but change always brings loss. We may lose something we despise, but at least it's familiar to us and we've learned how to cope with it. Change threatens to usher in a whole new realm of unsettling issues we do not know how to handle. This, in turn, forces us to walk by faith and to learn to trust the Lord in a new set of circumstances—therein lies the growth!

If you like change too much, you might have a tendency to become fickle and foolhardy. To avoid having convictions that are constantly shifting, you must be sure that the times of transition in your life and ministry are always rooted in a thorough study and application of sound doctrine and biblical principles and are bathed in concentrated prayer. On the other hand, if you resist change too strongly, you will become hardened and inflexible to the point of becoming unusable for any purpose God has in mind for your life or ministry. Find the balance between jumping at every new change and digging in your heels with stubborn resistance at any new change.

Change may be as simple as arising tomorrow morning with a determination to love your wife more practically and sensitively, or as complicated as resigning from a place of many years of ministry with no clear sense of what the Lord wants next. But in either case, the key is to know the answer to the

4. John P. Kotter, *Leading Change* (Boston: Harvard Business School Press, 1996), 21. Although many books have been published on effective leadership through the change process, I have found Kotter's "Eight-Stage Process of Creating Major Change" most helpful in taking a step-by-step approach through this complex maze.

question, "Is this what the Lord wants me to do?" If it is, then he will fill in the blanks by writing them on a heart that is willing to do his will.

When you find yourself crying out to the Lord, "Something has got to change!" rest assured that the Lord was well aware of that long before it occurred to you. As you have teetered on the brink, dangerously close to losing your balance and falling off the edge, the Lord has prepared a way for you to take your stand upon a rock that will not shift. But you have to step away from the edge, change what you are doing, and follow the Lord to the place he has prepared.

What kinds of changes do you need these days? Are you ready and willing to follow the Lord as he shows you how and what to change to get your life and ministry back in balance? It may not be easy, and the road may get rougher before it gets smoother. But when the changes stem from your determination to walk with Christ in the power of his Spirit, even what appears risky could not be more certain and secure.

PART 7

COMBATING
SPIRITUAL DRYNESS

= 16 =

RECOGNIZING THE
SYMPTOMS OF SPIRITUAL
DRYNESS

The attic was hot and dusty, the old card table was shaky, but I finally had a place. With young children in the house and all other rooms accounted for, there was nowhere else to go. Our young congregation had finally moved into a nice but small building that provided an office for me but not much by way of quietness or privacy so I could get away for study and solitude. For many months I had struggled to find that special place I needed to be alone with the Lord. But now I was there in my own "upper room," ready to see if I could find my way back from the spiritual drought I had endured for too long. A spiritual desert had been my home for a while and I knew that, as a pastor, I was not supposed to go through dry spells, right? At least that was what I assumed to be true. Although my mind was still engaged and my thirst for knowledge as keen as ever, my heart was parched, as dry and empty as that attic.

245

How many mornings I'd been going to my appointed time and place, I cannot remember, but as clearly as if it were yesterday, I remember when the clouds broke and God poured out rain from heaven on my heart! For some reason, I had bought a little book I had run across in a Christian bookstore with perhaps the worst, most uninviting title I have ever seen—*Lectures on Levitical Offerings* by Harry Ironside.[1] On that particular morning, after reading the Scripture portions scheduled for that day, I picked up Ironside's book, and within a few minutes, tears were forming in my eyes, then flowing down my cheeks, the overflow of a heart flooded with a fresh vision of my Savior. The remedy for my spiritual drought was simply a vivid picture of God's love for me in the redeeming grace of his Son. As each of the Levitical offerings revealed, the provisions the Lord made for me in Christ were perfect in every way.

A quiet joy and a gentle peace returned to me that morning, all because the Father redirected my gaze and focused my eyes on his Son. Leviticus would not have been my top choice of books in the Bible to bring someone out of a bout with spiritual dryness![2] But with the sacrifice of Christ unveiled in those offerings, the living water of the Spirit streamed through me again.

Was that the last time I struggled in the desert? Hardly! Many times since I have experienced varying degrees of spiritual dryness, episodes of spiritual dehydration complete with the same kinds of symptoms of physical dehydration . . . among them a general disorientation and a loss of equilibrium and overall balance. As we pursue the course of our ministry, we

1. Henry Allan Ironside, *Lectures on the Levitical Offerings* (Neptune, NJ: Loizeaux Brothers, 1929).

2. Several years later, I did a sermon series entitled "Portraits of Christ in the Levitical Offerings" and once again savored the insights God had prepared in that often neglected Old Testament book. Of course, not everyone found as much delight in the study as I did! A few years after the study, one of our senior high girls reminded me that she had first started attending our church while I was preaching that series. She asked, "Do you remember that when I came you were preaching about Leviticus?" Her follow-up question still makes me chuckle every time I remember it. Thinking she was going to say how much the study had meant to her, I was understandably knocked off my pedestal when she said, "Yeah, Leviticus . . . can I ask you . . . what were you *thinking*? Did you actually think anybody was interested in that?" Oh well, God makes sure that we remain humble!

will inevitably travel through some arid wastelands. But we do not always have to suffer from dehydration and spiritual dryness when we run into those days in the desert.

Christ promised that through my innermost being would flow rivers of living water (John 7:37–38). He fully intends to keep that promise and to restore my soul by making me lie down in green pastures and leading me beside still waters, refreshing me from a well that never runs dry as often as I thirst! Since that is true, I need to be able to recognize the symptoms of spiritual dryness when they first appear so that I might quickly rise up and return to the water Christ offers to satisfy my thirst.

Symptoms of Spiritual Dryness

What signs can we look for along the way to warn us of an approaching desert? Is there any way to avoid the dehydrating impact of dry times and maintain our spiritual equilibrium? I have identified the following symptoms we can recognize in time to take appropriate steps to avoid severe spiritual drought.

1. We have lost the real sense of his presence in our lives.

Your faith is not compromised and what you believe has not changed, but perhaps your sense of the nearness of God has diminished. Your prayer life is consistent but lacking genuine affection and personal communion with the Lord. Your time in the Word has remained faithful, yet the freshness and vitality of meaningful meditation and reflection escape you as you try to connect and hear his voice. How can we explain it? Once there was the thrill of discovering new and wonderful insights into the heart of the Lord. But somehow, almost imperceptibly, your relationship with him became routine. He is still there, but for you, his voice is silent and the sound of many waters has become an occasional trickle. Losing that real sense of his abiding presence can be a clear indication that you are either in or approaching a period of spiritual dryness.

247

2. We experience great weakness and feel powerless, impotent to face the daily routines and challenges of walking with Christ (much less leading a congregation).

Every believer knows what it is like to feel powerless before the awesome responsibility of living for Christ with consistency and courage. Otherwise we would be tempted to rely on our own strength, becoming overconfident in our own ability instead of trusting in and depending on him. But the impotence of which I speak is the kind that plagues the heart and troubles the mind with doubts and insecurities. We question whether the direction we are heading is the right one, the means we are using appropriate, the resources we are gathering sufficient, and frankly if we are the leaders God wants to use to move his people where they need to go. A new task presents itself, or a new challenge crops up in our ministry, and we can only think of why we cannot take on one more thing, cannot possibly meet one more expectation.

Adding to our helplessness is the host of ministry leaders we often hear stories about. Their resounding successes keep ringing in our ears, while we sit back and wonder why the Lord seems to have reserved his best work for them. Why are we so often left behind, feeling overwhelmed, when others seem to have it all together? What you and I do not know is where the journey has taken them before we got to see the success . . . where the road diverted into a desert, a strength-draining wasteland where their souls began to dry up and their spiritual batteries lost their charge. When you feel powerless and drained of spiritual strength, you know that you are approaching a dry spell and need a time of refreshment with the Lord.

3. Our perspective on life leaves out God's point of view and forgets his sovereign design.

When we begin to adopt a way of thinking that does not take into consideration that our God is a sovereign Lord, cynicism and skepticism overcome our hope and confidence. Instead of seeing life with a positive frame of reference, we dwell on all that is wrong; rather than rejoice and give thanks in all things as we are instructed in God's Word, we resent all that we are missing and all that is being asked of us. I have observed this pattern in myself and others as our attitude begs the question, "How can you trust the Lord and have such a lousy attitude?" If God is in control, then how can we dismiss that major factor when we choose to descend into a dour view of life? Those who trust and follow Christ are not expected to be naive optimists, but neither are we intended to be fatalistic pessimists. This symptom of the approaching desert often shows up when our perspective on life effectively dismisses any significant role of a sovereign God.

4. We become cynical, moody, critical, condescending toward others, demanding, even hardened in temperament.

Once we leave God out of our perspective, the next step toward the spiritual wastelands moves us away from a life under the control of the Holy Spirit and toward a life with no effort to temper our attitudes. Rather than putting a check on our hearts and disciplining our demeanor, we begin to demonstrate decidedly unspiritual thought processes. Eventually we may even act out our attitudes with words and actions unworthy of those who have been transformed by Christ. Listen to yourself. Monitor your attitudes. Check your spirit. If you find that you have more of your old nature showing and less of your new nature in Christ, you may be well on your way to a drought of the soul.

5. We lose God's peace and contentment and become anxious and restless more readily.

If you find that the peace of God no longer rules over your heart, the problem may be that you have been uprooted from your place by the rising rivers of life (Isa. 43:2). Prayer and supplication with thanksgiving have been overtaken by anxiety, contentment has been abandoned, and an undefined, nameless sense of unrest keeps you unsettled. Although you cannot put your finger on it, you have a feeling that all is not well and wonder if the peace of God you once knew can ever be yours again.

Paul addressed this malaise by offering a solution: "Be anxious for nothing, but in everything by prayer and supplication with thanksgiving let your requests be made known to God. And the peace of God, which surpasses all comprehension, will guard your hearts and your minds in Christ Jesus" (Phil. 4:6–7). Yet when we enter the desert of spiritual dryness, we tend to neglect the answers, bypass the ways of escape, and trudge ahead in our sullen and discontented state. Even knowing the answer, we refuse to appropriate it, preferring instead to stew over our problems and indulge ourselves in the self-absorbed pit of anxiety and worry. Those who try to encourage and console you with assurances from God's Word annoy more than help. You already know every verse they quote to you and every truth they speak to remind you of God's goodness and faithfulness. You just want to be left alone so you can savor whatever perverse satisfaction comes from worry instead of prayer, anxiety instead of trust. When this symptom shows up, welcome to the desert!

6. We neglect or reduce our time with God.

When we become spiritually dehydrated, we often do the opposite of what we should. Convinced that our time with the Lord is not working, not providing what we need, not satisfying our thirst, instead of going deeper to draw from his well, we pull up our buckets and give up. For a while, we make token efforts to let the bucket down again so if anyone is watching they will think all is well. But the truth is, we expect nothing. Consequently, after an extended dry spell, we find no value in continuing the masquerade and eventually either cut back on the time we spend by the well or just stop going.

Have you ever felt like that? Your devotional life lost its vitality and you could not connect with God, so you backed off instead of pressing on. In the presence of an oasis, you felt as if you were perishing but could not muster the determination or the will to remain steadfast in seeking him. You gradually slipped away from your commitment to spend time with the Lord, and now the dryness parches you. And you are not sure you can gather the strength to draw and drink from the only water that can satisfy your deepest thirst.

7. *Our thinking becomes muddled, our priorities confused, and our values inverted.*

The disorientation of spiritual dehydration mirrors that of physical dehydration. The dryness in our souls impacts the ability of our minds to process information, reach sound conclusions, and take decisive action. When we lose the flow of living water through us, we find ourselves laboring to know what to do, so we frequently do nothing, paralyzed by our inability to think with clarity. Mundane and insignificant matters become just as puzzling to us as complex and critical ones. We agonize over every decision and cannot distinguish between what could not matter less and what will determine the future of our ministry—we are equally indecisive in either area because the balance of our thinking has been thrown off by the parched condition of our hearts. If any of this sounds familiar and describes your situation, you are not just approaching the desert, you are in it.

The danger of this condition is that you just want someone else to decide for you so you will not have to do it yourself. This isn't a problem when the decision is where to go for lunch. But when you yield your leadership on issues of vision, direction, doctrine, and the like, you abdicate your place as shepherd of the flock for which God holds you accountable. Parched hearts adversely affect clear thinking. A muddled mind does not function as the mind of Christ, but signals that you may be suffering from a severe case of spiritual dryness.

251

8. We have no room left in our lives, because we are using up every available moment and have drained every possible resource, leaving ourselves with no margins to absorb the unexpected.

Life without margins may sound like a very efficient way to live, but in fact, the absence of any margin for error or miscalculation adds a level of stress that few can bear for very long. It's like ignoring the fuel gauge on your car as long as you possibly can before stopping to refill your tank. You may make great time for a while, but you do so at the risk of running out of gas at any moment!

Evidence that this problem has become more pronounced in recent years can be noted in the positive reception to books such as Grant Howard's *Balancing Life's Demands*,[3] Henry Cloud and John Townsend's *Boundaries*,[4] and Richard Swensen's *Margin*.[5] Each author traces the dangers associated with living with no boundaries and making no provision for the inevitable interruptions life brings our way. We leave no flexibility in our overloaded schedules, and we falsely assume we will be able to adjust when the time and circumstances demand. But adjust how and rearrange where? If there is no "wiggle room," we have taxed ourselves with a no-win approach to life that cannot help but drain any reservoir of strength and vitality we may have once kept in reserve.

God created the world with intentional margins to allow his creation to be restored. Just observe the division of the day into night and day, the need of the body for physical rest and spiritual replenishing through nightly sleep and weekly sabbaths, and even the seasons of the year. All speak to God's design for there to be margins of flexibility interwoven into the fabric of our being. The Lord has provided perfectly for all he called

3. J. Grant Howard, *Balancing Life's Demands: A New Perspective on Priorities* (Portland: Multnomah, 1983).

4. Henry Cloud and John Townsend, *Boundaries: When to Say Yes, How to Say No to Take Control of Your Life* (Grand Rapids: Zondervan, 1992).

5. Richard A. Swensen, *Margin: Restoring Emotional, Physical, Financial, and Time Reserves to Overloaded Lives* (Colorado Springs: NavPress, 1992).

you to do. In Christ he has "granted to us everything pertaining to life and godliness, through the true knowledge of Him who called us by His own glory and excellence" (2 Peter 1:3). And he has done so with perfect sufficiency, as Christ says, "I came that they may have life, and have it abundantly" (John 10:10). God created margins in our lives that we might enjoy that abundance and not exhaust it by saturating every moment of our lives with an ill-advised and frenetic[6] pace.

Our obsession with maximizing our efficiency has resulted in disastrous inefficiency as we waste our lives in "marginless" desperation. We dread hearing the phone ring because we have no capacity left to respond if there is an emergency. We dutifully check our messages and mail hoping that no one else demands any more of our time or energy, because we know we cannot take one more straw on the camel's back we call our life! How did we come to accept the myth that has deceived us into thinking that this unbalanced, depleted existence is what it means to be totally devoted to Christ? There will never be any commendation from Christ for such an abuse of the life he has given us. You can search all you want and you will not find a beatitude that says, "Blessed are the marginless, for theirs is a desperate life with no room to enjoy all of my fullness!"

Unless we are willing to take steps to streamline every area of our lives around godly priorities[7] and biblical principles, our reserves will be drained and the well will dry up. We will be left with nothing but dryness instead of the fullness of God's design.

---

6. The definition in Noah Webster's *American Dictionary of the English Language*, 1828 edition, captures the essence of what I mean by *frenetic*: "phrenetic—subject to strong or violent sallies of imagination or excitement, which in some measure pervert the judgment and cause the person to act in a manner different from the more rational part of mankind; wild and erratic; partially mad."

7. J. Grant Howard gives a very helpful insight into the matter of godly priorities in *Balancing Life's Demands*. Richard Swenson credits him for that insight when he wrote, "We cannot achieve balance by stacking our priorities one on top of another, even though this is a common practice. As Dr. Howard goes on to advise, it fits better to think of God as central to everything and then build outward from that point. We do not love God, then spouse, then children, then self, then church. We love God, spouse, children, self and church all at the same time. Similarly, we do not love God 100 percent, spouse 95 percent, children 90 percent, church 80 percent. God's standard requires that we love all of them all of the time." Swenson, *Margin*, 220.

253

When the margins of our lives disappear, we ought to recognize that we have just developed one of the classic indicators that we are prime candidates for a spiritual drought.

9. We fall prey to sin and temptation more easily than normal and find ourselves vulnerable to enticements that otherwise would have no appeal.

As we hear the steady stream of reports of our colleagues in ministry who have made devastating choices that effectively ended their ministries, we are inclined to wonder what could have prompted them to make such catastrophic decisions. However, if our thinking becomes muddled and clarity of mind gets buried in the arid sands of a spiritual desert, each of us can become susceptible to the most foolish and egregious sins and temptations. Impaired judgment combined with a heart naturally predisposed toward sin creates a dangerous situation for anyone. Spiritually dry hearts entertain the prospects of thirst-quenching alternatives more readily than hearts that draw daily nourishment from the fountain of everlasting life. A sponge already saturated with water has no room to soak up anything else; neither does a heart saturated with Christ. But when dryness sets in, we are particularly vulnerable to other offers that promise to satisfy our thirst.

Interviews and conversations with those who have fallen victim to their own sinful choices agree that their impaired judgment resulted from walking through a spiritual desert and looking in the wrong place for relief. David's relief came when he sought help from the Lord: "O God, You are my God; I shall seek You earnestly; my soul thirsts for You, my flesh yearns for You, in a dry and weary land where there is no water" (Ps. 63:1). We need to take note if arid lands surround us and dust is blowing across the landscape of our hearts—we may be particularly vulnerable to sin.

These nine symptoms of spiritual dryness do not necessarily show up all at once. But when they do appear in your spiritual

254

life, they serve as a warning that drought is imminent and measures must be taken to return and be refreshed. The normal Christian life consists of being like a "tree firmly planted by streams of water, which yields its fruit in its season and its leaf does not wither, and in whatever he does, he prospers" (Ps. 1:3). As Jesus described it, "If anyone is thirsty, let him come to Me and drink. He who believes in Me, as the Scripture said, 'From his innermost being will flow rivers of living water'" (John 7:37–38).

The conclusion? If you are like most people in ministry, you will find yourself like a deer panting for water at some time in your life, your soul thirsting for God (Ps. 42:1–2). When the symptoms begin to appear, be ready to come to him and drink!

=== 17 ===

HOW DID I GET HERE?

FACTORS CONTRIBUTING
TO SPIRITUAL DRYNESS

After several bouts with skin cancer, I have become an avid student of the symptoms that indicate that another problem is beginning to develop. No longer am I content to "wait and see" if anything more serious develops. After having three surgeries in an eighteen-month period, I finally understand that although early detection is important, prevention is much better!

In the same way, we pastors must do more than recognize our symptoms of spiritual dryness (as discussed in the previous chapter). We must learn to identify factors that cause spiritual dryness and take preventive measures to avoid them.

1. Someone or something "turned up the heat."

The old saying is that the same fire that melts wax hardens clay. When fiery trials come your way, they will tend to do one or the other. Either they will melt your heart, making you more pliable in God's hand, or they will harden your heart, making you turn away from him. In ministry you know how easy it is to come under fire from people in your congregation (as we saw in chapter 14).

There have been a few times in my years as a pastor when I found myself inches away from the glaring eyes and snarling lips of a member who was not shy about communicating my shortcomings. Even now, as my mind rewinds and plays those scenarios back, I can still feel the heat generated by the exchange. Frankly, I did not handle all of those situations graciously. Typically, I became defensive and responded in kind, not a very helpful thing to do! On other occasions, I internalized the emotions of the moment and got hotter about it when I had time to be alone and process how unfair and mean-spirited and wrong their comments had been. I let those fires dry up my soul.

Anger and frustration drain the waters of spiritual vitality quickly, opening the way for the piercing heat of bitterness and unforgiveness to dry up the surface and leave a parched gully where once a stream of water had flowed. Because you know you have not responded well, you feel guilty, causing the little remaining moisture to evaporate, turning the dry, cracked surface to dust. You get the idea. People can generate a lot of heat in the way they treat you. If you lose control, you can subject yourself to the wilting power of fiery words spoken against you.

The source of heat could also be a tough situation. Churches face problems all the time and, as a pastor, a lot of the pressure falls on you to solve them. Problems can arise from personnel issues, financial woes, declining attendance, doctrinal disagreements, power plays, crisis counseling, scheduling conflicts, or building programs. When these and other issues stack up around you, they become like kindling, just waiting for the right circumstances to ignite into a soul-searing conflagration. You've been warned at some point in your life that "if you can't take the heat, stay out of the kitchen." God called you to this "kitchen," yet the heat becomes so unbearable at times that you can hardly breathe!

During my middle and high school years, my father ran a laundry and dry cleaning plant where I was employed on weekends and over several summers. You've probably never experienced the kind of heat that comes from working around steaming pipes and boiling water in a flat-roofed building with no air-conditioning during a hot, humid North Carolina summer. To avoid cramps and other consequences of dehydration, we had to drink plenty of liquids and replenish the minerals we lost through perspiration with vitamins and salt tablets. When friends would ask why I didn't just work somewhere else, I had to explain that this was a family business and my father counted on all of us to do our part—regardless of how hot, parched, and weary we became.

As a pastor, you are engaged in the family business with your heavenly Father. When the heat becomes more than you think you can stand, whether the fires come from people or circumstances, you can count on one of two possible outcomes. Either your heart will soften and you will come to Christ to be rejuvenated or your heart will harden as you turn away from Christ and perhaps even blame him for not keeping you from the heat.

You know heat is coming, so prepare for it. Get ready so you do not let it parch your soul and drag you into a spiritually dry desert. Peter reminds us that trials like these are not out of the ordinary.

> Beloved, do not be surprised at the fiery ordeal among you, which comes upon you for your testing, as though some strange thing were happening to you; but to the degree that you share the sufferings of Christ, keep on rejoicing, so that also at the revelation of His glory you may rejoice with exultation. If you are reviled for the name of Christ, you are blessed, because the Spirit of glory and of God rests on you. . . . Therefore, those also who suffer according to the will of God shall entrust their souls to a faithful Creator in doing what is right.
>
> 1 Peter 4:12–14, 19

Fires will come. But they do not have to result in spiritual dryness if you can anticipate the heat and get even more firmly planted by the water.

258

2. The purity and holiness of your walk with Christ has been stained by sin.

The presence of unconfessed sin in your life makes you particularly susceptible to periods of spiritual dryness. When you allow a barrier to build up between you and the Lord, there is nothing to protect you from the harsh, searing winds of a guilty conscience. If sin remains unconfessed and you are also unwilling to turn away from it, you cut yourself off from his forgiveness and isolate yourself from his mercy. Prayer can no longer be your place of consolation, and the lack of prayer accentuates the problem. Sin has broken your fellowship with the Lord and severed the flow of his grace into your life.

In two passages, sin and broken relationships are described as the reasons for restricted access to the wellspring of a life in Christ. The first is from the Psalms: "If I regard wickedness in my heart, the Lord will not hear" (66:18). Holding on to sin and refusing to relinquish or turn away from it drives a wedge between you and the Lord. As a result, he will not hear, or even listen, until the matter is resolved—that is, the sin is forgiven and your heart once again purified and cleansed of unrighteousness.

All of this you know. But even knowing these basics, how often have we all allowed a distance to develop, separating us from the channels of mercy and blocking the streams of his love? When we cut ourselves off from the only source of life-giving water, dryness in our spiritual lives is inevitable.

The second passage specifically addresses another blockage that restricts our access to Christ in prayer. Peter makes it perfectly clear that we risk hindering our prayer life when we do anything to dishonor our wives. "You husbands in the same way, live with your wives in an understanding way, as with someone weaker, since she is a woman; and show her honor as a fellow heir of the grace of life, so that your prayers will not be hindered" (1 Peter 3:7). When we find our hearts all dried up before the Lord and cannot figure out what is going on, Peter reminds us to consider how we have been treating our wives. That might hold the answer. Although I have no personal experience with

259

this and the Scriptures do not address it directly, I imagine the same would also hold true for women in various places of ministry who dishonor their husbands. Hard as it is to admit, if we dishonor the person God gave us to work with side-by-side for the glory of his kingdom, God himself warns us that our prayer lives will be hindered. Consequently, we will have limited access to the water of life that would otherwise prevent a long spiritual dry spell (Rev. 21:6).

Sin can and will dry us up spiritually. By keeping short accounts with the Lord regarding our sin, we can find a way to avoid the searing influence it can have on our relationship with Christ.

3. You have placed a limit on your willingness to serve and established a plateau on your growth in your relationship with Christ.

Have you settled in? Are you content to pursue no more of the Lord than you are presently experiencing? If you make a choice to go no further in your walk with him, your spiritual life will reach "status quo." In reality, there is no such thing. You either are moving forward toward a dynamic, spiritual maturity or sliding back into a dusty, spiritual desert. The decision to limit where and how you will serve Christ or where and how you will seek him is usually not a conscious choice, but more than likely just a series of seemingly insignificant decisions. If you resist his will often enough, you eventually close the door to forward progress and begin to move backward.

Sometimes you reach a plateau in your spiritual growth because you are concerned with how others will view you. You may have an ideal of how a pastor should live and behave, and anything that goes beyond that ideal strikes you as being somewhat fanatical.

For example, the worship habits of the tradition you grew up in can govern how you expect a "good pastor" to behave. I grew up in the revivalist tradition of the fundamentalist movement. My early worship experiences were punctuated by shouts of

"Amen!" and "Glory!" and other exuberant responses from the congregation. The sermon was always preached in a manner that could easily be described as vigorous shouting by a passionate pastor (who was always referred to as "preacher"). For those who did not grow up in a church like that, such "enthusiastic" worship experiences could prove to be quite disconcerting! For me, that was just the way it was done. Yet as I myself became a pastor, my approach to preaching and to worship have been very different . . . not necessarily better, just different.

Other worship traditions have their own distinctives as well. The problem we usually run into is not with the theological content but with the stylistic character of what we observe in those not like us. The informal and exuberant pastor may look down on the formal and reserved pastor as spiritually dead, just as the latter views the former as fanatically challenged! In areas of ministry that are more a matter of style than theology, we need to be careful not to show disrespect for traditions just because they differ from our own or because they do not align with our preferences.

Beyond worship distinctions, denominational issues and church polity issues can place arbitrary barriers to where we put our limits. I have heard folks say unequivocally that they could never be a part of a church that is not governed the right way, that does not have their preferred children's or missions or women's program, that allows the church to incur indebtedness to build facilities, that does not offer preaching that adheres to their particular formula and structure. Where people define their limits tells you more about their temperament and biases than it does about their longing to live a life totally sold out for Jesus Christ.

But what if you have drawn the boundaries around yourself too closely? What if you have told the Lord and anyone else who would listen what you would and would not ever do? Yet what if there is no biblical basis for your declaration? If I have decided that I will never raise my hands in worship, what do I do in the midst of corporate worship if the Lord prompts me to do so and I cannot pretend I did not hear or understand? If I have brazenly determined that my preaching style will only be verse

261

by verse exposition, what do I do when God puts a message on my heart that is topical? How do I handle my bold pronouncements on any subject that cannot be supported biblically when the Lord leads me in a different direction? If I am determined and resolved to hold fast to my limits, my stubbornness can restrict the flow of living water in my direction and usher in a period of dryness. Since the Lord will not find a willing heart regarding what he desires for me on one matter, why should he be willing to trust me in another?

We are often quick to speak of how much we want to grow to maturity in Christ, but what we really do has been limited and restricted by our own estimations of how far is far enough. Therefore, when Christ calls us to go beyond our comfort zones and follow him to new areas of trust in our walk of faith, we are reluctant to do so. As dry spells then come upon us, we cry out passionately to know and understand more of his will, but we cannot hear his voice. Eventually it dawns on us that he has already spoken, but we did not want to hear. He has already shown us his will, but we were determined not to obey. We then stand our ground stubbornly while simultaneously demanding that God open the floodgates of heaven and pour out his blessings upon us. We complain about our dry spell and protest that, in spite of our diligence and persistence in seeking him, he will not break the silence.

How foolish we must appear to the Lord! The rivers of his delight are actually right behind us in the place where we have refused to go (Ps. 36:8).

Let me give you a practical picture of this. When I was coming to the end of my last year in seminary, I, like most others preparing to graduate, was praying that the Lord would show me where he wanted me to serve him. The catch was that I had already explained to him what I was *not* interested in doing and therefore turned a deaf ear whenever that kind of ministry opportunity presented itself. I had been involved in student ministries for six years, and now I considered myself ready to take on the responsibilities of pastoring a church.

Yet no matter what I did, how hard I prayed, how many résumés I sent out, all I heard about were youth ministry positions.

Dry times accompanied my pursuit of God's will because I had shut myself off from the very direction he wanted to take me. I could not understand why he would allow me to suffer through such a spiritual drought when I really needed to hear from him more than any other time in my life. Finally, after five independent referrals to one particular youth position, it occurred to me that perhaps he was already speaking, but in a way I did not want to hear. God knew what I needed, but I had decided that I knew better. I couldn't see the river behind me for the desert in front of me—until I turned around and realized it was there all along. I nearly missed his plan for me.

The same thing can happen when we decide that we need to pray in one direction for our spiritual growth when the Lord wants to work on another area entirely. We cannot limit what he can do or place restrictions on how far he can take us as we grow in Christ. When we presume to do that, dry and dusty days are ahead!

4. Preparation for public ministry serves as a substitute for personal spiritual growth.

One of the occupational hazards of leaders in ministry is that we can allow our familiarity with sacred things to make them commonplace for us. The responsibility we have for preparing sound biblical teaching week in and week out forces us to spend time studying, and hopefully praying, to get ready. After all, if Sunday morning and the other preaching times arrive and you have not invested the time, you will be embarrassed and the people will not be patient with your negligence for very long. The external-discipline factor, and yes, the fear factor, keep our preaching and teaching preparation time high on our priority list each week. Early in my ministry, I determined that I would never step into the pulpit without adequate preparation time, even if that meant pulling all-nighters, to make sure I was fulfilling my calling to equip the saints for ministry through faithful instruction in the Word of God.

Although I have struggled with what "adequate" means throughout my years as a pastor, to date I have never gone into the pulpit with anything less than a completely prepared set of sermon notes. But there was one harrowing experience, just a couple of years into my ministry, when the Lord spoke to me while I was showering on a Sunday morning that what I had prepared was not what he wanted preached that day—that made for an exciting morning of scrambling and praying and trusting! Each week I know what it takes to get ready and schedule that time as best I can, knowing that it always takes longer than I think!

But beyond my responsibilities as a pastor, I am a child of God, a redeemed and adopted son of the Father. Therefore, I am called to invest time each day in nurturing that relationship as an order of first priority in my life. If for some reason I were no longer a pastor, I would still belong to Christ, and I'd still need to pour myself into a growing fellowship and relationship with him in a personal, intimate way. Even before I became a pastor I realized that I couldn't allow my vocational calling to shepherd a flock to interfere with my eternal calling to know and love the Shepherd. Paul spoke of the "surpassing value of knowing Christ Jesus my Lord" (Phil. 3:8) and the infinite wisdom of recognizing that "whatever things were gain to me, those things I have counted as loss for the sake of Christ" (Phil. 3:7). These verses helped me make a pivotal decision—I cannot allow even the privilege of pastoring to obscure the value of knowing Christ Jesus.

This conclusion led me to keep my personal time with the Lord separate from my teaching and preaching preparation. That is hardly an absolute, of course, since there are many things I learn in each area that inform and enrich the other, but as a practice, I have chosen not to allow my sermon work to be a substitute for my devotional life. Nothing will dry up the soul like not hearing a personal word from the Lord on a daily basis. When I have failed to keep this commitment, I have realized how easy it is to allow the words of conviction and instruction intended for my own heart and soul to be redirected and applied only in the context of the congregation to whom I would be preaching.

Granted, I would be hearing my own sermon as I preached it to others, but that is not the same as listening for the voice of the Lord in the stillness of a daily time in his presence that is designated for that purpose alone. Reading and studying God's Word for my own spiritual nourishment prepares my soul so that when I later come to the sermon, I am better equipped to hear what God would have me offer to others.

These same concerns apply in the area of prayer. If I allow myself, I can justify a reduction in private prayer because of the frequency of my times in prayer with others and before the congregation. A ministry colleague once told me that he seldom prayed much privately. Instead, he arranged his schedule so that he would meet with others regularly for prayer. He felt that that practice fulfilled what he saw as his prayer needs. Very efficient . . . but is that sufficient to satisfy the heart's desire for intimacy with the Lord? No. There is something distinctively valuable about being alone with the Lord in prayer, a practice commended in Scripture both by example and instruction (Mark 1:35; Matt. 6:5–6).

Another concern that can only be addressed in private is the place of meditation and reflection as a means of sealing God's truths in our hearts and anchoring them in the development of Christlike character. In the preface to his book *Solitude Improved by Divine Meditation*, Puritan pastor and writer Nathanael Ranew wrote these insightful words.

A pious heart hath three happy ways of self-entertainment in solitary; three rare ways of being least alone, when most alone.

The first way of self-entertainment, is the ordinance and searching the Holy Scriptures, the pure, perfect, and infallible word and will of Christ concerning us. . . .

The second way of self-entertainment, is divine meditation, by either pondering of spiritual things, for improving knowledge, and exciting practice; or by a weighing all other things whatever, for reducing them to a spiritual end and use.

The third way of self-entertainment, is private praying, such as is both founded on and bounded by Christ's will in His word; such as is both prepared and assisted, made wise and warm by serious meditation.

265

Meditation stands between the two ordinances of reading and praying, as the grand improver of the former, and the high quickener of the latter, to furnish the mind with choice materials for prayer, and to fill the heart with holy fervency in it.[1]

How can our hearts be filled with holy fervency without time solely devoted to personal time alone with the Lord? Being alone with the Lord is as vital to our heart preparation as time for Bible study is essential for sermon preparation. They are not the same, nor are they intended to be.

Without a clear delineation between our public ministry and our private devotion and spiritual nurture, pastors can drift toward the desert and find themselves choking on dust instead of being refreshed by the water.

5. Sound doctrine and orthodox biblical theology have satisfied the appetite of your mind but never penetrated the hunger in your heart to know, love, and serve God.

Believing the right things anchors our faith in eternal truth. Without a foundation in what is true and a proper basis for sound thinking, we build our faith on the sandy ground of vain imagination and speculation. Christian faith takes its stand on the rock of revealed truth. Yet that truth must do more than find a home in our minds. It must invade our hearts!

While I was in seminary, I first learned the phrase "dead orthodoxy" and understood what it meant in theory. One Sunday, while attending a church noted for its meticulously precise theology, I came face-to-face with the reality. Reciting all the right words in the right combinations and citing the right biblical references, the worship service unfolded sound doctrine like a theology text book. But what was missing was life, spiritual vitality . . . a sense that what they were professing was actually a radical and life-changing truth. From an objective standard,

1. Nathanael Ranew, *Solitude Improved by Divine Meditation* (1839; repr., Morgan, PA: Soli Deo Gloria Publications, 1995), vii–viii.

266

nothing was amiss. But from a subjective perspective, the experience gave every appearance of death, not life.

Believing correctly does not guarantee freedom from a dry and dull formality of religion that holds "to a form of godliness, although they have denied its power" (2 Tim. 3:5). True belief not only embraces the facts, but also demonstrates the transforming reality of new life through the resurrection power of Jesus Christ. Adherents to various orthodox belief systems invest untold hours defending the minutiae of their individual points of doctrine, but often do so without regard for the prevailing purpose of God in delivering the truth undiluted to his people. Yes, we are to "contend earnestly for the faith which was once for all handed down to the saints" (Jude 3) and to "always be ready to make a defense to everyone who asks you to give an account for the hope that is in you" (1 Peter 3:15). But we are to do so out of the overflow of the dynamic reality of a renewed and a transformed mind[2] as we live out the genuine life of those who are daily being conformed to the likeness of his image.[3] "Right believing" without righteous living produces desert conditions that dry up our souls.

No one professing biblically orthodox and theologically sound beliefs would ever consciously choose to be spiritually dead. But if you are not careful to "pay close attention to yourself and to your teaching" (1 Tim. 4:16), your natural tendency will be to gravitate toward the easier choice. Teaching what is right is far easier than living right and working it out in practice.

6. A broken relationship has not been reconciled, and the weeds of bitterness and unforgiveness have choked out your spiritual vitality.

We have already addressed the deadening and drying impact of sin, so I will only briefly speak to this issue. It's almost a guarantee that every pastor will have to face the problem

2. Romans 12:2.
3. Romans 8:29.

of dealing with hurtful behavior of and disagreements with members of the congregation.

You will not always have control over how your actions impact others. Some people who are part of your ministry will never understand or appreciate you. In fact, they will be easily offended and constantly disappointed that you have never lived up to their expectations for what a pastor should be. Within the first year after our church started, a small group from the original twelve families decided to leave because the ministry of the church had not turned out as they'd hoped; specifically, my ministry as a pastor did not meet their ideas of what I should be doing. The pain of those departures remains vivid. Even though it was difficult for me, I sat down in a living room with some of the couples who were leaving and sought to make sure that we were parting on good terms. It was a painful but necessary part of growing up in Christ, making sure that there was no animosity, no negative emotional baggage to be lugged around, and no ill will on my part, and if I could help it, on theirs.

Biblical instruction and basic civility make it my responsibility to be at peace with others, even when they do not embrace the olive branch I offer. Paul wrote, "If possible, so far as it depends on you, be at peace with all men. . . . So then we pursue the things which make for peace and the building up of one another" (Rom. 12:18; 14:19). When someone's peace is disturbed by something I did, I know that I must seek forgiveness. Even if the slight was unintentional, if the inconsiderate deed was done out of ignorance, or if the loss that was suffered could be justified on principle, if a relationship with a brother or sister is damaged, I need to go and make amends.

Broken relationships loom like heavy, dark clouds over your ministry. Many times, as I have stood to preach, I have almost been able to see the darkness settled over a brooding individual in the crowd who I knew had unreconciled differences with someone else present in worship—on occasion that someone was me! If I choose to ignore the signs of the coming storm and decide to pretend nothing is wrong, I invite a time of parched ministry upon myself and those who are at odds with me. Nothing dries the soul more quickly than the searing glare of an enemy who once was your partner in ministry. David mourned at this scenario in his own life when he wrote, "Even my close friend, whom I trusted, he who shared my bread, has lifted up his heel against me. . . . Yet when they were ill, I put on sackcloth and humbled myself with fasting. . . . But when I stumbled, they gathered in glee; attackers gathered against me when I was unaware" (Pss. 41:9; 35:13, 15 NIV).

When those circumstances arise, there is but one acceptable course if you intend to abide in the presence of the fountain of living water: Christ leaves no room for misunderstanding when he commands us to give first priority to being reconciled with those who have something against us. "Therefore if you are presenting your offering at the altar, and there remember that your brother has something against you, leave your offering there before the altar and go; first be reconciled to your brother, and then come and present your offering" (Matt. 5:23–24).

You may need to go more than once, and if my experience is representative, probably several times to the same people through the course of your ministry. Their response depends upon how receptive they are to the work of the Holy Spirit in their lives. You cannot do his work, but you can do what he calls you to do in order to make sure that no obstructions block the channels of mercy he wants to flow through you. Failure to go to the offended party or refusal to forgive will stop up the pipes that irrigate your soul. Harboring any bitterness or ill will toward those who have wounded you will often be of little or no consequence to those who make it a habit to inflict pain on others, but it can be devastating to your own spiritual health.

How often must you forgive? Well, Peter asked the same thing. The answer was anything but encouraging for those who want a quick fix. By saying we must forgive seventy times seven times, Jesus removes the statute of limitations on forgiving others. Every time you realize that you are still carrying a grudge, holding on to a root of bitterness, or bristling at the mention of a name, you can count on feeling the nudging of the Spirit to reappropriate and reapply the forgiveness you once gave—as often as you need to do it until all malice and every broken part of the relationship has been removed from your heart. Then you will enjoy the unimpeded flood of the rivers of delight from the Lord (Ps. 36:8). If you hold on to your right not to forgive, you can count on seasons of drought. Unforgiveness will drain you of your spiritual vitality and cause you to wilt just as surely as if you had been cut off from the vine.

———⚬∞⚬———

Desert experiences can be thoroughly disconcerting and leave you completely off balance. Identifying the symptoms and causes of the dryness does not mean that we have resolved the problem and regained level ground. Reeling from our condition and left staggering from the effect of the spiritual dehydration forces us to find a remedy as soon as possible. We need to get out of the desert!

=18=

COMING OUT
OF THE DESERT

HE RESTORES MY SOUL!

The thirst that takes over when spiritual dryness sets in can make us desperate enough to drink from any source, but we all know that this is unwise and could lead to even greater problems than thirst. If the source is contaminated, or even worse, poisoned, we can do more harm than good.

On a mission trip to Haiti, a few of us decided to hike over the mountain at the edge of the plains where we were working to see the ocean and enjoy both the view and the breezes coming off the water. Our guide assured us it was not too far, so off we went with limited provisions—only one canteen of water for the four of us to share.

We decided to wait until we'd reached the top of the mountain to have a drink, in spite of the scorching sun and baked sand under our feet. Imagine our dismay when we reached the top and discovered that this was only the first mountain between us and the sea!

Our guide again assured us that the sea was not far, so we took a drink and started our descent so we could ascend what we assumed would be that last mountain. A couple of hours

271

later, we realized the futility of this venture. No matter how far we managed to go, there was always another mountain. By this time we realized that we would have to ration our water if we were going to make it back without someone passing out.

We did make it back with no serious incidents, but we were absolutely worn-out and felt completely dehydrated by the time we completed our adventure. We rushed to the nearest source of liquid refreshment—a small stand selling Cokes and Fantas. They could have charged us anything they wanted, and we would have paid. We needed a remedy for a thirst that was as great as any I have ever known. I bought two Cokes and guzzled the first one in one big gulp. The second one I savored, because it was not only wet, but cold! Then something unexpected happened. Although there was immediate relief, the high sugar content of the soft drinks made me thirstier in a very short time. The satisfaction I needed could only come from a pure source of water, which I eventually found and which was a welcome relief.

I tell you all of this to make this point: when you need refreshment due to spiritual dryness, you need to make sure that your remedy is one that really satisfies. Many people in ministry find that times of dryness push them to find solutions that further exaggerate their problem. Some will immerse themselves more deeply in the very same circumstances that got them into that condition. Others will try inappropriate solutions that appear to offer help but soon prove to be inadequate and even harmful. The only way to find a satisfying remedy is to follow a course that leads you back into the fullness of the presence of the Lord.

1. When you recognize the symptoms of spiritual dryness, do not postpone treatment, but begin immediately to develop a plan of action.

In our episode on the mountain in Haiti, we thought we'd made adequate preparations for the challenge before us. After all, we had a canteen we could share filled with clean water sufficient for a short hike to the top of a mountain and back. Little did we know that the journey was farther than we imagined, harder than we anticipated, and hotter than we could stand! Operating with insufficient data ("not too far" was not too accurate), we had too little provision for too much need.

Looking back now, after climbing the first mountain, we should have made the wise decision to turn around and head back. Our thirst at that point should have been enough to convince us that we couldn't postpone finding a solution to our problem. Instead, we chose to press on and make do with what we had, insufficient as it was.

How many times have you found yourself thirsting from an arid period in your ministry, but instead of wisely seeking an immediate source of relief, you convinced yourself that the mountain ahead could not be that hard to climb, so you just kept going? Hindsight is always easier than foresight, but after a few such experiences in ministry, should we not learn to recognize the symptoms and causes as they are drying us out? When we see them coming and we feel their effect, that is the time to take action and find a way to refill a dry and empty vessel. Postponing treatment will only complicate the problem and increase the amount of replenishing that must be done.

The decision to keep pressing forward when your soul is perishing from lack of spiritual vitality suggests that you think that it is acceptable to operate without the fullness of the Spirit. In other words, you are willing to attempt ministry without the benefit of the only power that can make ministry effective. Using brute force to push a car that is out of gas is never a long-term solution. When spiritual dryness hits, we should not delay in developing a plan of action to be replenished with the living water of Christ.

2. Dangerous circumstances call for drastic measures. Your plan of action needs to include a break from the routine.

Designate extra time and attention to restore what has been lost. Life carries on whether we are in the midst of a crisis or not. After a particularly difficult death in our congregation, many of us were grieving with the family and friends, trying to manage the deep wounds inflicted by the painful and tragic

273

loss of life. While we were sitting in that family's home, I happened to glance out the window and noticed that the community around us had not slowed down, altered its course, or in any way adjusted to accommodate what we were experiencing. One day the deceased had been with us, now he was gone, and next week we would all be moving on with a new version of normal, one that would compensate for the one who had died.

This sounds so clinical and detached, but that is the way life and its hard times seem to work. Others will not rearrange their lives for very long, if at all, when you are going through a crisis. Therefore, it is up to you to make sure that you meet the crisis of spiritual dryness head on. Make the time to deal with it adequately. The symptoms serve as a warning to take the necessary measures to do what must be done to be refreshed and restored.

If I am satisfied that my spiritual dryness is a passing blue period that will soon disappear, I will usually not take extraordinary measures to seek relief. But if I am suffering from the incapacitating imbalance that serious spiritual dryness produces, I will be more inclined to alter my normal routines and reconnect to the water supply Christ promises to those who thirst after more of him.

In my own case, that might mean taking a personal day to get away and sort the whole thing out in a time of special reflection, study, and prayer. It might mean a brief change of pace in which I adjust my schedule to allow for more time for physical exercise. Whatever specific activity I choose, I make sure that I set aside some of the draining duties pastors face to take time to reconsider my priorities in light of God's promises and provisions. You cannot continue to drift along with the flow of life's routines when you are parched. Even if others can go along as if nothing has changed, you know better, so you need to make the arrangements required to take care of the problem.

3. Refocus your time on reading and studying God's Word.

This is no time to be stingy in the amount of time given to listening for the counsel and encouragement of the Lord. If ever you needed to hear his voice, it is during prolonged periods of thirst. Therefore, extend your time to include a greater margin for meditation and reflection out of which will flow more concentrated times of prayer. In Psalm 119:18, David wrote, "Open my eyes, that I may behold wonderful things from Your law." As you approach the Scriptures, ask the Lord to show you where to read, how to stay focused, and what he wants you to know from him.

Find the method that works for you. Some find great comfort and nourishment by immersing themselves in Scripture, reading large portions and losing themselves in the vast terrain of the biblical landscape. This helps them regain their perspective and realize that God can be trusted to work out his will and accomplish his purposes. Such a "big picture" method serves to soak the soul in a greater awareness of both the immensity of the Lord and his active engagement in all aspects of our lives.

On the other hand, some find it too overwhelming to cover large volumes of information when their tanks are dry. They need a more intense exploration of a smaller portion of God's Word to allow them to concentrate on a few ideas and truths. Personally, I find meditation and reflection on a few verses or a couple of paragraphs at a time most helpful. Only you can decide which works better for you—taking in more with less intense meditation and reflection, or taking in less with more intense efforts to dig deeper. Get into the Word and give God a chance to speak to your heart and refresh your soul.

4. Any one of the factors contributing to your spiritual dryness will need its own remedy, so respond appropriately as you recognize how each parching element influences your life.

As the Lord reveals what the problem is, deal with it in an appropriate manner. If you have committed a sin that has cut you off from fellowship with the Lord, you already know the remedy because he has shown it to you over and over again in his Word—confess your sin and turn away from it. I am amazed at my own reluctance to accept this simple resolution. How much of my spiritual dryness comes from my resistance to act on what I already know . . . that Jesus stands ready to forgive and restore when I am willing to confess and repent.

If the source of my problem is relational, again God tells me what to do—reconcile with my brother or sister. For each broken relationship, we can offer hundreds of reasons why reconciliation will not work, so we avoid doing anything that would bring about a confrontation. Yet the emotional and mental drain of strained relationships takes its toll on us. The only way to refill what has been drained is to take the necessary steps to restore the relationship. Until we do that, the reservoir of spiritual vitality we need to walk in the fullness of Christ will empty faster than we can plug the leaks. Throughout the Scriptures, God places the responsibility for reconciliation squarely on us. We cannot take responsibility for how the offended party will react to our overtures to be reconciled, but our course is clear: "If possible, so far as it depends on you, be at peace with all men" (Rom. 12:18).

If your dry spell has resulted from neglect of your time alone with the Lord, simply make it a matter of conviction and discipline to resume your time with the Lord. Set up a plan and schedule your day accordingly so you do not ignore the only lasting source of refreshment.

Perhaps you attribute your dryness to the burdens of ministry, family problems, financial setbacks, health issues, or any of a thousand things that weigh you down with anxiety. You know what you should do—stop worrying about them! Try making a list of all that is worrying you and drying you out. This is one of the most invigorating exercises I have ever practiced. Begin by memorizing or meditating on Philippians 4:6–7: "Be anxious for nothing, but in everything by prayer and supplication with thanksgiving let your requests be made known to God.[1] And the peace of God, which surpasses all comprehension, will guard your hearts and your minds in Christ Jesus." Once you have identified the key concerns and weighty cares that are draining

---

1. "Don't worry about anything; instead, pray about everything. Tell God what you need, and thank him for all he has done" (Phil. 4:6–7 NLT).

you, follow Peter's instructions, "casting all your anxiety on Him, because He cares for you" (1 Peter 5:7). Why should we sit back and run on empty when God invites us, even commands us, to throw off all those concerns and worries that drain our reserves? His counsel is simple yet profoundly effective: give it to the Lord and leave it there.

Another reason we may be spiritually dry is that God has shown us what he wants us to do and we have not obeyed him. We keep asking for the Lord to show us his will, but, in fact, he already has. We did not really want to do what he wanted and chose another way instead. Can we really expect the Lord to fill us back up so we can persist in heading in the wrong direction, pouring all our energies into an endeavor that is keeping us from obedience to his will? You may be able to trace your spiritual dryness to a fork in the road where you chose your own way instead of the Lord's. Turn around and go back to his plan and see the floods of his fullness restore you.

5. Read or reread a favorite author who has stirred your heart in the past and prompted you to long for more of Christ.

Normally, I have a hard enough time reading a book all the way through once—it is rare for me to reread a book. But when the need demands it, the only intelligent thing to do is respond. There are a few books that have served me well over my years of ministry. I find that they are like old friends who have an incredible ability to encourage and challenge me. Their value may be in the reminders of truths once learned and recently forgotten, or in a return to the familiar, friendly voices of more profitable and less stressful times. Find your way back to some of those treasures and ask the Lord to rekindle your passions and fill up your heart so the desert within awakens to new life.[2]

2. Among my favorite "old friends," these works have been particularly helpful over the years: A. W. Tozer, *The Knowledge of the Holy* (San Francisco: HarperOne, 1978); E. M. Bounds, *The Complete Works of E. M. Bounds on Prayer* (Grand Rapids: Baker, 1990); Henry Scougal, *The Life of God in the Soul of Man* (Fearn, Rosshire, Scotland:

6. Revise or reinstate the way you spend time alone with the Lord.

What has worked best for you over the years? Is this a good time to resume that approach? If I am not careful, I can fall into a rut and go for long periods without realizing that I am going through the motions without engaging my affections or my mind. Consequently, as a creature who needs diversity and change, I have to mix things up occasionally to stay connected.

When life is dry, I have sometimes found myself carefully keeping the ritual and order of my spiritual disciplines but not experiencing the benefits of them. At those times, I catch myself at the end of my devotions without remembering one thing I read or recalling one thing I have sought or learned from the Lord in prayer. When we can perform all the right duties without investing our hearts and minds, if we are not dry yet, we soon will be! Shifting things around and breaking out into new territory will help us overcome the tendency to be lulled into a sense of complacency.

Periodically, I believe it is helpful to stir things up a bit and rearrange the way I spend my quiet times with the Lord. Shifting my Scripture reading patterns around, alternating between praying first and then reading, or reading first and then praying, even changing locations once in a while, all help keep me from falling into a rut and allowing the familiarity of sacred routines to lull me into a spiritual stupor. Sometimes I have found that I can take a passage of Scripture that addresses categories of spiritual maturity and do a self-evaluation by rating myself and seeing where I need the most work. For example, I might take the nine characteristics of the fruit of the Spirit from Galatians 5:22–23 and rank them according to my greatest strengths and weaknesses. Then I can see quite clearly where the Lord still has much to do in my heart

Christian Focus Publications, 1996); John Piper, *The Pleasures of God* (Scotland: Christian Focus, 2002); J. C. Ryle, *Holiness* (1877; repr., Peabody, MA: Hendrickson, 2007); J. I. Packer, *Knowing God* (Downers Grove, IL: InterVarsity, 1993); Arthur Bennett, ed., *The Valley of Vision* (Carlisle, PA: Banner of Truth Trust, 2003).

to conform me to the image of Christ! Discipline can lead to drudgery if we are not willing to institute some change even in our devotional lives.

7. Share your struggle with someone who will pray for you and hold you accountable to see you through to the fountain again.

Don't get isolated! If at all possible, set up a way to get together with others who can walk with you through the dry spell. Admitting to yourself that you need the help of others is a big step. Admitting it to others is a bigger one. Over the years, I have been blessed with several people who were willing to listen and offer support and encouragement when I was down—and who I trust to do so again when I call on them. The first source of help for me is my wife. She knows me better than anyone else and has a vested interest in seeing me do well spiritually. Because she has a keen insight into spiritual truths, she not only offers me personal support, but can also guide me to helpful resources and ideas that benefit me greatly. Many Christian leaders bemoan the absence of anyone around them to provide supportive counsel and encouragement, but they never even consider the primary one God has given them.

In addition to your spouse, seek the counsel of godly, mature men and women whose consistent and steadfast walk with Christ serves as a model of what you would like your walk to become. There is special value in having a standing group of accountability partners with whom you can share your life. If they are at all perceptive, they will be likely to spot the trends affecting you adversely before you identify them yourself. Open yourself up to the possibility that the Lord has a small group of people who are exactly what you need to help bring you out of your desert. Ask him to show you trustworthy and discreet friends who love Christ and love you enough to come alongside you until your spiritual vitality is flowing again.

8. Remember that as you seek Christ, he has promised and assured you that he is seeking you!

The Lord opened my eyes to an interesting insight a few years ago that has been a great encouragement to me. When I struggle in my pursuit of him and flounder around trying to make sure that I stay connected in meaningful relationship with him, he assures me that the pursuit is not one-sided. He is pursuing me!

This first hit home for me while reading Psalm 119. At the very beginning of this psalm, David speaks to our pursuit of the Lord: "How blessed are those who observe His testimonies, who seek Him with all their heart" (v. 2). Just as parched people passionately seek the water that satisfies their thirst, so a person suffering from spiritual dryness will seek passionately after the Lord. But notice that David ends the psalm with this appeal: "I have gone astray like a lost sheep; seek Your servant, for I do not forget Your commandments" (v. 176). The psalm begins with us seeking the Lord and ends with the Lord seeking us.

When I am seeking the Lord, my inability to find and understand him is immediately overcome by his perfect ability to find me and make me understand all that he wants me to know. I sometimes forget that and act as if it all depends upon me. God reminds me that he has pursued me all along and will never give up. In the desperation my dryness produces, I am more inclined than ever to forget about every other pursuit but the one that matters most. I need to come to Christ—the Living Water, the Fountain of Life eternal—and find the perfect refreshment that has been missing in my life, making it "a dry and weary land where there is no water" (Ps. 63:1).

So the need is real and the solution is sure. Draw near to the Lord, the one who gives the kind of water that satisfies so that we thirst no more!

> But whoever drinks the water I give him will never thirst. Indeed, the water I give him will become in him a spring of water welling up to eternal life. . . . As the deer pants for streams of water, so

my soul pants for you, O God. My soul thirsts for God, for the living God. When can I go and meet with God?

John 4:14; Psalm 42:1–2 NIV

Sitting alone feeling sorry for yourself in the desert when God himself has directed a river of living water toward you just does not make sense. No one actually intends or even wants to do that, but sometimes you become so disoriented, confused, and unbalanced in your thinking that the sensible thing to do escapes you completely. The way out of the desert has been graciously offered to each of us through Christ. For those who have been called to be filled with the Spirit, living with emptiness and dryness can never be an acceptable condition. God does not want that for you and me. During those times when you find the arid wastelands surrounding you and no water appears to be available, lift up your eyes. God has promised that you will find streams of living water ready to refresh your soul once more!

=19=

CONCLUDING THOUGHTS

Hopefully you have found help here in identifying some common threats to your balance. And I hope you realize that you are not alone in your struggle.

When Jesus Christ placed his call on your life, he never intended for you to get so focused on some areas of your life that you neglected others. He does not want you to walk by the Spirit in one area and continue to depend on your natural abilities in another. Facing each area of life and ministry with equal confidence begins with the assurance that Christ is sufficient. He will enable you to stand firm no matter what comes your way. The goal, of course, is to be like him, mature in all things, complete in every way.

By facing the balance issues we have addressed in this book, the Lord can prepare you to stand firm in every way—your calling, your vision, your shared ministry, your humility, your troubles, your transitions, and your spiritually dry periods. Any one of those can become a problem that threatens to throw you out of balance if you are not aware of the dangers and are not expecting how hard the blows can hit you. Whether the source is spiritual warfare, human enemies, personal issues, or general circumstances, we can stand firm. We can live lives of balance when we appropriate the resources God has provided. Paul counsels that the best way to be equipped for every good work God calls you to do, and every challenge you are forced to endure, is to "take up the full armor of God, so that you will be able to resist in the evil day, and having done everything, to stand firm" (Eph. 6:13).

By the power of the Spirit and the Word, may we stand firm together and maintain our biblical balance as we pursue the special calling the Lord has set before us. May the glory of Christ be seen through you as you present a balanced and vibrant testimony through a life well lived for his praise!

= APPENDIX =

THE WEIGHTS AND COUNTERWEIGHTS OF YOUR CALLING

Using the following chart, fill in the competing concerns or demands of your unique calling to ministry. In doing so you will be able to see the areas that need to be kept in proper balance for you to maintain your equilibrium.

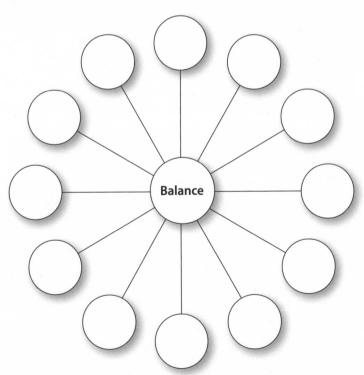

David Horner is the executive director of Equipped for Life where he equips leaders for the work of the kingdom. He holds an MDiv from Gordon-Conwell Theological Seminary and a PhD from Southeastern Baptist Theological Seminary.